MARRYING
— the —
BOOGEYMAN

THE HIDDEN EVILS OF
DOMESTIC ABUSE

JEANELLE MARAID

BALBOA.PRESS
A DIVISION OF HAY HOUSE

Balboa Press books may be ordered through booksellers or by contacting:

Balboa Press
A Division of Hay House
1663 Liberty Drive
Bloomington, IN 47403
www.balboapress.com
844-682-1282

Print information available on the last page.

ISBN: 979-8-7652-4764-8 (sc)
ISBN: 979-8-7652-4765-5 (hc)
ISBN: 979-8-7652-4763-1 (e)

Library of Congress Control Number: 2023922400

Balboa Press rev. date: 03/19/2024

CONTENTS

MONSTERS ARE REAL

THEIR DARKNESS ROAMS FREELY AMONG US EVERY DAY

WHAT DO YOU PICTURE IN YOUR MIND WHEN YOU THINK OF A MONSTER? We all have our version of what it would look like. It could have come from a movie we watched, a book we read, a nightmare, or several other reasons. The Oxford Dictionary defines a monster as "an imaginary creature that is typically large, ugly, and frightening." So, as adults, we understand that monsters aren't real and don't exist. They are fictional characters or beings. If they existed, we would naturally be afraid of them, like when we were children and thought they were real. I used to have nightmares about monsters when I was a little girl that lived in my closet and under my bed and came out when it was dark at night. I was afraid to go to sleep and would cover my head with blankets so the monsters couldn't see me. I thought they couldn't get me if I could hide from them.

If I told you that monsters were real, you wouldn't believe me and think I was crazy or on drugs. We just established that monsters were imaginary, but I'm here to tell you that monsters exist and walk among us daily. For many people, monsters don't just live under our beds; they are in bed, lying beside us. Now, you may be thinking that I'm over-exaggerating or being dehumanizing. Well, my response is that I'm completely serious, and any abuse is not only dehumanizing, it's also inhumane, evil, and therefore monstrous. So, if someone is fully aware and deliberately abuses any living creature or another human being, they should be considered a monster. Abuse is real, larger than life, ugly, frightening, and is a choice. When I say the word abuse, does your mind automatically think about violence by an angry individual? Violence is only a small part of abuse. All abuse is about power, control, dominance, and breaking down boundaries. Abuse is how it's obtained and maintained. Abuse can be violent or nonviolent and is carried out in many ways. It can occur through relationships, parenting, the workplace, or from strangers, and can occur towards people, pets, or any other living creature.

Abuse is an act of hate and evil, and abusers are out to hunt and destroy their prey. I thought my reference to monsters not being under the bed but lying next to us was clever when I wrote it and was also original, but then I read almost the exact words in many Instagram and Facebook posts. So, that should be even more convincing that monsters are real. I was abused and couldn't pull the blankets over my head to hide from my monster. He was my living nightmare in the horror movie that wouldn't end.

"The Real Monsters

Our mothers tell us that there are no monsters under our beds, or hidden inside our closets but they don't warn us that sometimes monsters come dressed as people that claim to love you more than the sun loves the moon."

Nikita Gill

Are you afraid yet? Now I think you are ready for my story.

I still have a hard time believing what happened. My journey through nonviolent domestic abuse started 25 years ago in 1998, not even knowing what that meant, and I have so many mixed feelings. On the one hand, I wish the night we first saw each other had never happened. On the other, I have the most precious daughter in the world. She is the greatest gift I will ever receive. Looking back, I had no comprehension of what lay ahead through my marriage, parenthood, friendships, good and bad experiences, abuse, escaping, healing, divorce, the aftermath, advocacy, and the valuable wisdom I now have to share. So, I find myself looking back with such sadness amid the joys. This story is triggering for those who are in or have been in a similarly abusive relationship. Still, one of my goals is to help victims and survivors put words, meanings, and feelings into their experiences, which I didn't have during my relationship. Knowledge is taking back power, and I want to give power to the powerless like I used to be. For the general public, my goal is to bring awareness, education, and understanding to what a victim/survivor goes through in abusive experiences, as well as emotionally and mentally. There will be no changes in this world until everyone knows of the hidden evils of abuse. I want to open every door and every window in every house.

I'm still in the process of starting my life over again. It's like I was a puzzle, and I'm fitting all the pieces back together, one by one. At the very least, I hope that what happened will be able to help others. Knowing what I now know, I wouldn't want anyone to experience what I experienced both as a spouse and mother and feel the pain and fear of being unable to keep yourself and your child in a safe environment. I'm writing my story with as much detail as possible so anyone in a similar situation can pick up on things that are going on in their lives and relationships. My story is also imperfectly written by me. I could have chosen to use an editor but decided it was more critical for authenticity than better writing skills or grammar. Any of the experiences in this book could significantly impact someone in what they are going through themselves or know someone who is going through something similar. This is not the story about me, my abuser, and my daughter; it's about what happened and how it can be used to bring awareness, education, understanding, and change, and represents everyone who has ever gone through abuse, those going through it now, and for the future. To have acknowledged the red flags could have saved me, but I may not have my precious girl.

I didn't understand anything about nonviolent domestic abuse during most of my relationship. Most people aren't aware of it and can't even comprehend what it is. They think it may be yelling, cursing, name-calling, or being angry and lashing out. Most of that is technically just arguing and can be typical in a relationship and healthy if it's safe and leads to conflict resolution. We all lash out in anger as a reaction. Nonviolent abuse is premeditative, calculating, strategic, hateful, and a CHOICE. It's a hidden evil unlike no other. My abuser didn't need to raise his voice during verbal attacks because if his voice were raised, it would prove he was attacking and abusive. Speaking in a lower voice was to fool me into believing it was a conversation, but I always felt his evil. He would only raise his voice if he thought it was necessary for theatrics or if I tried to defend myself. I used to describe what he was doing as mean, judgmental, self-righteous, threatening, and controlling, not knowing it was abuse. It starts so subtly that you have no idea what's happening. You fall in love with someone and believe they are who they say they are and their actions and what they say are genuine. This is not the case with domestic abusers or commonly called narcissistic abusers. They wear masks to the outside world and aren't the person you fell in love with. It was an elaborate lie to fool you, and their actions and words are manipulations to confuse you later into believing in them and not yourself.

This story needs to be told. I can't just let it go, heal, and move on. If I did that, it would be as much of a tragedy as the acts themselves. My silence would be protecting the lies and abuse, enabling everyone else who is abusing, and not helping those abused. I understand there are both vocal and private survivors. I am vocal, but my daughter is private, so I will try my best to respect her as much as possible while telling my story. My education and advocacy are for her. I didn't have the knowledge I have now, and since I couldn't help us, I can at least help others. Especially as a mother, I felt helpless and afraid I couldn't protect us. Now that I know, I couldn't live with myself if I knew my speaking up could help battle this evil and didn't do it. There may even be people who won't believe a word of this, and with most people, their brains can't comprehend such evilness. I know some of those people, and yes, it is hard to believe any human being can do things to purposefully hurt those who love them with such calculation and hatred. That's why I call them monsters, and their actions are evil, like they sold their souls to the devil, because any normal, flawed person would never do such vile actions against anyone.

2

MY EDUCATION

What I learned after escaping the relationship - I went to "school" to find out as much as possible

I AM PLACING MOST OF WHAT I LEARNED AT THE BEGINNING OF THE BOOK because I had none of this information until after my escape. There is a lot to understand and comprehend, and it could be skimmed or skipped over if that's your preference, but it is here to refer back to when you need it. In this book, I'm explaining abuse mostly through my perspective on what I have experienced and learned, but abuse can happen to anyone in many different situations. As I said and will continue saying throughout this book, the goal of abuse is for power, control, dominance, and breaking down boundaries. The actual abuse is secondary and is the tactics, strategies, and actions carried out to achieve the goal. Every bit of it is done on purpose and is a choice. I feel it is extremely important to first go over types of abuse, tactics, terms, and other valuable information that will help educate and relate to my story. Many tactics abusers use toward their victim include, but are not limited to:

- Belittles, criticizes, insults, puts you down
- Blames/accuses you for things you have no idea about
- Blames/accuses you for things they are doing, projection
- Shames you for your past
- Severely judgmental towards you and your children
- Pathological lying about you to others and you about anything
- Playing you and your children against one another
- Yelling, name-calling, calling you a victim

5

- Verbally attacks your character, self-worth, feelings, and dreams
- Jealous or possessive
- Treats you like you're a servant, child, or possession
- Humiliates or embarrasses you in front of others
- Controls your emotions and mental state
- Controls your friendships, isolates you in any way
- Controls where you go and what you do, including your career
- Stalks your social media, phone, or emails
- Constantly checks up on you
- Refuses to be pleased
- Gives you the silent treatment, pouts, sulks, and sighs
- Manipulates, intimidates
- Shows entitlement, but you aren't allowed to do the same things
- Pressures you to do something you don't want to, coercion
- Makes you feel guilt for things you shouldn't feel guilt over
- Makes you feel like you're being punished
- Makes you apologize for things you didn't do or for things unnecessary to apologize for
- Makes you feel like your memory is slipping, gaslighting
- Twists your conversation to use against you
- Threatens you in any way, including financially, taking the children away, violence, hurting pets
- Displays any type of weapon
- Destroys or disposes of belongings

What if you were in a relationship where almost everything on this list was done to you? Would you think you were with a monster? What does this abusive behavior do to victims?

- Destroys self-worth
- Leads to anxiety and depression
- Leads to lost sleep and other physical symptoms, including panic attacks, PTSD, rashes, gastrointestinal issues, eating disorders, or substance abuse
- Makes you feel helpless, terrified, alone, and withdrawn
- Makes you feel like you are crazy and to blame

- Makes you feel emotionally numb
- Confuses reality, cognitive dissonance

Since most of my focus is on nonviolence, let me start by bringing attention to the eight main types of nonviolent abuse:

Nonviolent Physical Abuse:

Physical abuse is not only violent. Nonviolent physical abuse escalates through time and may eventually lead to physical violence. Here are several examples, but are not limited to:

- Intimidation – standing over you or getting right into your face, refusing to back off, throwing things or punching/hitting walls, slamming doors, etc., baiting you to hit them.
- Isolation – limiting the ability to walk away or leave, driving recklessly or leaving you stranded, preventing medical treatment or help, destroying personal items.
- Restraint – holding you back, blocking a doorway, locking doors, imprisonment of any kind, threatening if you walk away from them.
- Destroying objects or other property.
- Threats to physically harm anyone or anything, including suicide.

Take any of these things, including the threats, as it will happen. Do not believe if they say it was a joke or that they didn't mean it.

Nonviolent Sexual Abuse:

Sexual abuse – I believe we can all agree that when we think of sexual abuse, the first thing that comes to mind is rape. Other ways to sexually abuse include, and are not limited to:

- Treating you in a sexually demeaning manner, such as an object or possession they can grab or touch sexually, makes you feel violated or uncomfortable, harassed, intimidated, coerced, guilted, or threatened.

- Persuading, threatening, manipulating, and coercing you into doing anything sexually that you usually wouldn't have participated in or feel uncomfortable with, such as adding another partner, sexting, picture taking, video-taping, porn of any kind, or using objects.
- Persuading, threatening, manipulating, and coercing you into doing anything sexually that you wouldn't have participated in to prove your love.
- Threatening or participating in acts of infidelity, withdrawal of sex, accusations of cheating, and other threats if you don't comply.
- Refusal to use birth control or have safe sex or forced pregnancy.
- Requires you to meet their sexual needs.

These examples, and anything else to take advantage of you to possess and break down boundaries and to possibly use the sexual activity against you later to cause humiliation and embarrassment, as well as blame, threaten, and coerce, is considered sexual abuse.

Verbal Abuse:

"Sticks and stones may break my bones, but words can never harm me."

That statement should never be said EVER again. Words may not hurt the flesh, but they hurt the mind, heart, spirit, and soul.

Part of verbal abuse is what they say and how they say it to confuse you into believing what they are saying, even if it's a blatant lie. Verbal assaults are to convince you of their superiority and dominance over you. This is usually through verbal attacks that attack your character while building up theirs. These attacks also catch you off guard and put you in a defensive position, giving them an edge to get you to submit.

- Varying tones of voice intimidate and confuse you into not even realizing it's an attack. They will say it's just a discussion or conversation, even though it's completely one-sided and is to belittle, criticize, blame, and accuse you of whatever they see fit. These attacks are intended to manipulate, threaten, cause fear, and for you to believe you are the one who is responsible for everything wrong with the relationship, finances, or children.

- Blocking your remarks and putting you down further if you try to defend yourself or your children. They will accuse you of playing the victim, as they want you on the defensive, but at the same time, you are not to argue back. They will invalidate and judge your opinions for you to adopt theirs.

- Shaming you for anything you have ever done, continually bringing it up to prove to you they are better and you are the problem. They will tell you about all the people in your life that don't like you. They will say anything to make you feel defeated and to get a negative reaction.

- They will further confuse you by blaming you for the entire attack, making you accountable and responsible by saying you were cruel to them, and for you to apologize for the entire thing. As soon as you apologize or take the blame, their demeanor can change instantly. They hug, kiss, and tell you they love you and that no one would ever put up with what you do; they are there for you and want to help you grow, mature, and become a better person.

All of this is calculated and premeditated. These attacks can last for as little or as long as they feel necessary and could be as little as 15 minutes or over an entire weekend. When they attack, it is also very strategic, and most likely, when you least expect it to catch you off guard.

Emotional Abuse

Emotional abuse is how an abuser controls your emotions or uses them against you. This is to manipulate and control you into doing something or to be molded into the person they want you to be.

- They will blame or accuse you of something to shock you and get a reaction and then use your reaction against you.
- They will control your feelings by putting down your emotions or invalidating them. You are not allowed to have a bad day or be in a bad mood. You need to be happy when they want you to be happy and grateful when they want you to build up their ego.
- Your accomplishments or aspirations are belittled or ridiculed, or you will be put down to make you feel inferior. They will minimize your emotions as being too sensitive and invalidate whatever is important to you. They will make you feel insecure about yourself.
- They will tell you that people don't like you and that you need to change. They will ruin your friendships to isolate you, as they don't want you caring about others and others caring about you. They will limit your communications and stalk your social media.
- They will say or do something to put you in a quiet or bad mood when you are going out with others to make them look good and for you to look bad. They want to have a good time but don't want you to. They will also embarrass, shame, or humiliate you in front of others.
- They will guilt you when you do something for yourself, making you feel ungrateful and selfish.
- They will treat you like a child, leading you to believe they should make all decisions.
- They treat you as an extension of themselves. They tell you how you should think and twist your or their words to sabotage you. They will question your every decision and every move. They will hold out love or intimacy, blame it on you, or threaten to leave unless you meet their demands.
- They will shame you by reminding you of your shortcomings or lead you to believe you are treating them poorly while they are treating you wonderfully. They will make you feel unappreciative if you don't react in a way that satisfies them.
- They will control your sleep by waking you up in the middle of the night so you are exhausted or frustrated.

These examples lead you to feelings of depression, anxiety, and lack of self-worth. It makes you feel helpless, angry, terrified, emotionally numb, alone, and withdrawn. It leads to lost sleep/exhaustion and other physical symptoms.

Mental abuse:

Mental abuse controls and affects your mental state, opinions, and beliefs and modifies your behavior and the way you think for their benefit or agenda. Tactics are calculated and premeditated to manipulate your mind intentionally and are essentially psychological torture.

- They confuse you by mixing insults with compliments, truth in between lies, and talking in circles.
- They will try to catch you off guard with anger out of nowhere or overreaction for no logical reason.
- They will gaslight you into believing you are losing your memory and make you feel like you are going crazy.
- They will play mind games by giving you the silent treatment, ignoring, pouting, sighing, and intensely staring to intimidate and instill fear or to make you feel like you did something wrong and need to apologize or do something for them.
- They will project and falsely blame you for things they are doing and twist the truth to make you feel like you are doing something you really aren't, to deflect responsibility and accountability.
- They will coerce and manipulate you to instill fear by telling you that you've done something wrong and that your relationship is over if you don't change.
- They will play the victim and at the same time tell you that you are playing the victim to gain sympathy, control your behavior, make you believe you are the abuser, put you on the defensive, or so you comply.
- They will want you to believe you are the narcissist, the sociopath, or the psychopath to make you feel like you have

a personality disorder, while they are really the ones with the disorder.

- They may even threaten suicide if they think you want to leave them or if they feel unwanted.

These examples can lead you to believe you are crazy or losing your mind and memory, cognitive dissonance, PTSD/Complex PTSD, panic attacks, eating disorders, substance abuse, and possible thoughts of self-harm.

Financial Abuse:

An abuser will try to control you financially to keep you dependent on them and for you to rely on them for all your financial needs. They will use money, your career, and assets to control and have power and dominance over you. This strategy is to make you financially helpless and fear leaving.

- When they use assets to control you financially, they will strategically ensure little or no assets are in your name and always in theirs. If you question their motives, they will say they are protecting you, and you will be accused of not trusting them or dismissed. They will make sure the house, the cars, and any other assets are in their name and not jointly or in yours, so they can threaten that if you ever leave them everything is theirs, nothing is yours, and you will have to leave with nothing.
- They will give you gifts, but their motives are for you to submit to them or to look good. If you don't comply with their demands, they will threaten to take it away because it really isn't yours; it's theirs. They are entitled to what is yours, but you are not entitled to theirs. It is also a strategy for others to think they are a great partner and will flaunt their generosity.
- If you have anything of value before the relationship, they will want you to get rid of it, make it a joint asset, or have you put it in their name for your protection. If you have previous personal wealth, they will view it as though it's theirs.

- They will ensure that all savings, retirement accounts, and investments are in their names. Assets will be in their name, and bills will be in yours. There will always be excuses for why they want it that way. Your access to credit will be limited as much as possible.
- If a family business is involved, they will ensure the business is in their name only, as well as any business assets such as buildings or equipment. You will be guilted or required to work with them and will make sure you don't earn income or retirement in your name.
- As far as your career, they will limit it as much as possible. They don't want you to be able to support yourself. If you have an outside career, they will try to control your income and distract you while working with texts, calls, or showing up at your workplace. Your career or job will be belittled, and you could even be accused of infidelity with your boss or coworker. If you want to further your career or change careers to something that interests you, they will try and prevent it. If you do happen to have a thriving career, they will try to control your income or use it for their own spending.
- Besides assets and career, abusers will limit your access to money by controlling the amount in bank accounts and won't want you to have separate accounts. If you buy something for yourself, they will question your needs. Your budget will be restricted, and you will be accused of poor budgeting or spending while their spending habits are superior. Another tactic is for the abuser to hide money. They may have a stash or other secret accounts for various reasons or strategies.
- Abusers have no problem using children for financial abuse. They will threaten or extort anything in your children's lives to scare you or to get you to comply. They will threaten if you leave that you won't get much in child support or alimony to instill fear.

These are some of the financial strategies that are not only to control you but also to deceive and prevent you from leaving.

Spiritual Abuse:

Spiritual abuse can take place in any religion or belief.

- Abusers use religion against you by expecting certain spiritual expectations. They will tell you that people won't accept you unless you act a certain way and use religion to bring shame, comparison, or inadequacy.
- They will require you to agree with their beliefs and belittle others as incorrect so they look right and others look wrong. You must adopt the abuser's beliefs, or you will also be put down.
- They will lead you to believe their way of worship is superior, and they will require submission, or you will be verbally or spiritually convicted. If you are in a religious or church group, others will share their struggles, but you are not allowed to share the truth and must represent that your family has no struggles and everything is perfect. You must look and act a certain way to make the abuser look good. They will require the appearance of perfection or an image to the public, even though that isn't an accurate picture. They will use church lessons against you to belittle, shame, or question your character. They will consistently judge you into believing they need to fix you, as you are not good enough, which could lead to fearing being at church services with them.

Sometimes, the severe judgment towards you or other family members leads to straying from religion and spirituality altogether and questioning or destroying your faith. Being able to celebrate your spirituality is supposed to be something beautiful, peaceful, and loving. They turn it into something ugly, judgmental, and hateful.

Legal Abuse:

Legal abuse is a strategy used to prevent you from leaving or, after you leave, to threaten and instill fear, along with continued abuse. They still want power, control, dominance, and to break down your boundaries. Examples include:

- Threatening or extorting your children, threatening custody, or threatening child support.
- Blatant lying to their attorney, temporary mediators, mediators, and the entire court system about their finances to represent that they can't afford what is a fair and equitable settlement. They will purposefully take a job making less money, and if they own their own business, they will falsely represent their business as failing.
- Stalling to deplete your financial resources while increasing your attorney fees to instill fear into settling with less than a fair settlement.
- They will drag out legal proceedings until you give up by continued postponements, unnecessary motions, hearings, or sending unfair or threatening settlement offers. This is commonly known as vexatious litigation.
- Preventing the sale of assets or hiding money or assets in any way.
- They seek revenge and want to win at all costs because you left them. They will prevent you from moving on and continue trying to hurt you because you are still their target. They welcome the drama because it feeds their ego and agenda. If their new relationship or any of their friends see a red flag from them, they can dismiss it by blaming you.
- They are willing to spend tens to hundreds of thousands of dollars to fight you while accumulating tens to hundreds of thousands of dollars of debt. They will be wining, dining, partying, and taking trips while you struggle to pay the bills.

Unfortunately, the judicial system does not protect you from these strategies. Because they are not recognized in any way as abuse, the abuser can lie under oath and can basically get away with their deceit. All of this is considered post-separation abuse. In the United States, you are just a case number. No one recognizes any trauma you have been through unless you possibly have a physical violence police report or injunction, and even then, the truth doesn't matter. What matters is your judge's opinion, case law, and how aggressive an attorney you have the financial resources to retain. They will take you back to court for sport to hurt you for as long as they can get away with it. As one of my survivor friends says, the justice system is their playground.

"It's Still Domestic Violence

They don't have to hit you, choke you, or slam your head into a wall in order for it to be domestic violence.

They can degrade you, humiliate you, blame you, scream at you, lie to you, cheat on you, and withhold finances, or even just try to control you +

It IS still domestic violence."

Morgan McKean

The Cycle of Abuse:

Although there are many interpretations of the cycle of abuse, and all have validity, the original was developed in 1979 by Dr. Lenore E. Walker to explain behavior patterns in an abusive relationship. The cycle doesn't always lead to physical violence and repeats until the relationship ends. Over time, the length of abuse diminishes, and the actual abuse increases. Dr. Walker's four stages in the cycle consist of Calm, Tension Building, Incidence, and Reconciliation.

The Calm Stage

Also considered the Honeymoon Phase, abuse doesn't occur immediately in a relationship. In the beginning, the abuser needs to show kindness, connection, and intimacy. They prey on vulnerabilities through "love-bombing," an overwhelming show of affection and attention. They will give excessive gifts, trips, compliments, and other strategies to lead you to believe they are the love of your life and that you are the luckiest person in the world. They also "mirror" you with the same likes, feelings, and opinions. They will do or say whatever is needed to make you fall in love with them. In actuality, they are wearing a mask, really aren't that person, and it's a fabrication to win you.

After your relationship continues, and the cycle of abuse goes full circle, they will use this phase to further manipulate you into believing they really are that person. It will again be affection, gifts, trips, and a representation that things are perfect and normal. They will even gaslight you into believing you are at fault and caused whatever happened, or it wasn't that bad, or it didn't even happen at all.

You may believe them for many years and are happy during this stage. Unfortunately, the relationship is a complete illusion, and the person you fell in love with never truly existed. Over time, this stage gets shorter and less 'sincere.' The only goal in this stage is to fool you into not leaving them for all other stages.

The Tension Building Stage

In tension-building, they lose power, control, attention, affection, or superiority. They may seem annoyed and will give you the silent treatment, sigh, pout, and give you looks of disdain. You wonder what you did wrong to cause this behavior and know it's only a matter of time before you are confronted. You feel the need to keep conversations light and happy and not talk about anything important or substance, agree with everything they say so they are less annoyed and feel like you're walking on eggshells. They will try and isolate you from others. They will do whatever is necessary to ruin friendships and family connections because other people caring about you threaten them, as you would have people to turn to for care and guidance.

The Incidence Stage

In the incidence stage, they attack verbally, physically, or both. You may even be relieved to get it over with to calm your anxiety. For my platform, I will provide an example of a nonviolent verbal attack:

In a verbal attack, they will accuse, blame, project, threaten, gaslight, intimidate, and manipulate you into believing you are to blame for everything wrong in your relationship and are a terrible person. They want you to believe your character or your children are flawed, and their job is to fix you. They will accuse you of cheating and anything else they see fit. During the verbal attacks, they will have you miss work, miss meeting friends, or do anything else. You will be forced to stay and take it or be threatened. You are required to hear their assault on everything about you. They also want you to react to the attack so they can blame it all on you. If you try to defend yourself, they will call you a victim to fool you into believing it's your fault. You feel hopeless and alone and have no idea why the person you love and who is supposed to love you is hurting you in such an evil way.

The Reconciliation Stage

The attack is over in the reconciliation stage. You go through a wide range of emotions. You feel a sense of relief, but at the same time, you are a nervous wreck. You feel incredible sadness, hopelessness, helplessness, anxiety, and exhaustion from what happened. Because they have entirely put down everything about you and blamed you for the entire incident, you are left confused and in despair. Am I really as awful as they say I am? Do all of those people really hate me? Would a counselor tell me I'm just as horrible as they did? Does my child think I'm a toxic parent? Was this my fault? Did I deserve this? You relive the incident in your mind over and over and over and wonder if there was something you could have done to prevent it. The abuser is happy with themselves. They attacked and blamed you, so they have no accountability. They know you will now try and make it up to them, which gives them the power, control, dominance, and breaking down your boundaries that were their goal. They will continue by gaslighting you into believing they did nothing wrong without evidence otherwise. They'll have "forgiven" you; everything can be wonderful and normal. The honeymoon phase starts all over again.

The cycle of abuse is a circle and is never-ending. A classic strategy of an abuser is, in the beginning, they also paint a perfect picture to the outside world, and then slowly, over time, they manipulate and smear the victim's reputation. So, when you are abused and go to others, your name is already tarnished, and they won't believe you. It's calculated and premeditative. It's so difficult as the true victim even to believe the person you thought loved you would go to all the trouble to destroy you piece by piece, day by day, year after year. It's even more of a tragedy when they do the same thing to their own children. They want to make sure people think you are overreacting, lying, or that you are confused, exaggerating, or crazy. What makes it worse is when people also think and believe that if it were really happening, you would have left because, obviously, to them, no one would stay in a situation that sounds like what you are describing. People say things like it takes two to make a relationship a success or failure, which does not apply to an abusive relationship. Abusers play the victim and martyr to you and others and accuse you of their actions. I have learned this is the closest thing you will ever get from them that's an actual confession, an admittance of guilt. Then they will treat you well, making you doubt yourself, so you will work harder to please them. It's part of a cycle of abuse, so you feel loved then, unloved, happy then sad, worthy then worthless, and so on. It goes around and around until you have no sense of self-awareness; you feel broken, beat down, dazed, depressed, filled with fear, or emotionless. They make you feel like your memory is slipping, you have mental issues and need help.

Whether diagnosed or not, abusers have a personality disorder. Here are the main types of personality disorders. This is not everything; just a brief summary:

Narcissistic Personality Disorder (NPD):

Individuals with Narcissistic Personality Disorder (NPD), according to the DSM-5 (Diagnostic and Statistical Manual of Mental Disorders, 5th Edition), exhibit five or more of the following, which are present by early adulthood and are on a spectrum from mild to severe:

- A grandiose sense of self-importance
- Preoccupation with fantasies of unlimited success, power, brilliance, beauty, or ideal love
- Belief that one is special and can only be understood by or associated with special people or institutions
- A need for excessive admiration
- A sense of entitlement (to special treatment)
- Exploitation of others
- A lack of empathy
- Envy of others or the belief that one is the object of envy
- Arrogant, haughty behavior or attitudes

These individuals can be easily upset by criticism or defeat and may react with disdain or anger—but social withdrawal or the false appearance of humility may also follow, according to the DSM-5. Most have secret feelings of insecurity, shame, vulnerability, and humiliation. The severity of symptoms varies, along with the type. There are several types, but below is a brief description of the difference between Overt and Covert NPD:

Overt – more common and much easier to spot, as they externalize their arrogance, are outwardly demanding, and display extreme character traits, and their confrontational communication style does not go unnoticed. They are obsessed with power and image and want attention at all times.

Covert – wolves in sheep's clothing and are trickier and more dangerous. They are underhanded, deceptive, and act behind the scenes. They pretend to be lovers, givers, altruistic, loyal, and kind. They are projecting a calm and patient mirror to the outside world, but on the inside, they are as deeply selfish as overt.

Sociopathy and Psychopathy = Antisocial Personality Disorder:

Psychopathy and sociopathy are now largely used interchangeably. The DSM excludes both in favor of Antisocial. All sociopaths and psychopaths are narcissists, but not all narcissists are sociopaths or psychopaths.

- Superficial charm and good intelligence
- Absence of delusions and other signs of irrational thinking
- Absence of nervousness or neurotic manifestations
- Unreliability
- Untruthfulness and insincerity
- Lack of remorse and shame
- Inadequately motivated antisocial behavior
- Poor judgment and failure to learn by experience
- Pathologic egocentricity and incapacity for love
- General poverty in major affective reactions
- Specific loss of insight
- Unresponsiveness in general interpersonal relations
- Fantastic and uninviting behavior with alcohol and sometimes without
- Suicide threats are rarely carried out
- Sex life is impersonal, trivial, and poorly integrated
- Failure to follow any life plan

They can be witty and fun to be around but lie, exploit others, and are uncaring. They can act rashly and destructively without feeling guilt when it hurts others. Modern diagnostic systems consider ASPD to include two related but not identical conditions: A "psychopath" is someone whose hurtful actions toward others reflect calculation, manipulation, and cunning; they also tend not to feel emotion and mimic (rather than experience) empathy for others. It is a severe form of ASPD. They can be deceptively charismatic and charming. By contrast, "sociopaths" are somewhat more able to form attachments to others but still disregard social rules; they tend to be more impulsive, haphazard, and easily agitated than people with psychopathy. ASPD affects 2% to 4% of the population and is more common in men.

After I learned all this information, I diagnosed my abuser as a covert, malignant narcissist with sociopathic and psychopathic tendencies!

For reference, I will briefly explain some of the terms, tactics, and strategies used in nonviolent abuse:

The Mask - There are 6 common masks that abusers and narcissists will wear to go undetected. They will play the VICTIM (Woe is me - look at what you/they did to me), the MARTYR (I tried so hard to help you/them but rejected me), the RESCUAR (I am the hero and look at all the good things I've done for you/them), the LOVER (I'm the most passionate, loving person you/they will ever know and I will love more than you/they have ever been loved – their actions are called Love-bombing), the WORKAHOLIC (Look at how hard I work, what a great job I do and you/they should be grateful and give me praise), or the ELITEST (I have so many friends; people always like me and want to be like me; I am good; therefore everything I do is good). The mask they wear at any given time depends on their audience or agenda. It's like they are a chameleon or an actor putting on a show.

Future-faking - Future-faking is when a person lies or promises something about the future to get what they want now. It could be as basic as promising that they will call you later and never call, promising to go on vacation or an outing with you, and then never taking any steps to make it happen, or if you were in a relationship, you would never have to work. Future-faking during the love-bombing phase makes you think they really want the same things you do in life. They lead you to believe your life with them will always be as wonderful as they represent. They will also use future-faking as a way to threaten, and if you don't comply with their demands, they will tell you that the relationship is over. They will take everything from you, including your children, or if you leave them, no one will ever want you, so you may as well stay.

Mirroring – Mirroring, as I mentioned previously, is another trick to fool you and a tactic to lead you to believe they like the same things, will act like you, have the same opinions, dreams, and beliefs so you think they are your perfect match. Once the relationship becomes serious enough, they will slowly change, and you'll be left wondering why.

Gaslighting – Gaslighting is manipulating your mind and reality to gain power and control. This manipulation leads to you questioning your own reality and not questioning the motives and actions of the person "gaslighting" you. They will tell you that you or they said something that wasn't said; a scenario happened when it didn't and will lead you to believe your memory or mind is slipping and you're going crazy. They use gaslighting so you won't remember or question what they've already done to you or what they're currently doing. It is to fool you into second-guessing yourself and relying on them for what is right and wrong, so you stop believing in yourself. They want to create cognitive dissonance where there are two different realities, the one that is true and the one that is a lie, and confuse you into believing the lie. If you have never watched the movie "Gaslight," I would recommend watching it to get a clear perspective on what this means.

Isolation - Isolation is a premeditative method to remove you from family and friends so they have greater control over the relationship. They don't want other people to care about you or have people to turn to for guidance, influence, or strength; want to limit the fun you have without them and for you to be dependent on them for all of your needs. They will strategically and calculatingly ruin any relationship they deem a threat in your life. They will make up stories for you to end your relationship or about you to them so they end your relationship.

The Silent Treatment – The silent treatment's goals are to manipulate, control, dominate, and get what they want. They will ignore, sulk, pout, and sigh to let you know you've done something wrong, and you have to guess what it is and make it up to them, even if you've done nothing to provoke it. Unless they have a specific agenda, they won't want to tell you what you did because then you would focus on that one thing, as they want you to focus on everything. They also use this strategy if they want you to cater, give extra attention, or work harder to please them, especially if they are around people they want to impress. Even though this is considered abuse, if you are in an abusive relationship for a long enough period of time, you'll get used to it and accept it. It could become a form of peace, as you know they'll be ignoring and not communicating with you, and as long as they're not communicating, you aren't being attacked.

Projection/Blame-shifting- Projecting and blame-shifting are the closest things an abuser will do as their own confessions. They will target you to blame, accuse, shame, belittle, and judge to deflect accountability and responsibility. It's a defense mechanism, and they will use this strategy if their "mask" slips and they feel either you or anyone else may be onto their abuse or behavior. They will accuse you of anything they are doing, like cheating, lying, deceit, stealing, spending, addictions, abuse, or even someone not liking them, either to you or anyone else in your life, so you look like the abuser they look like the victim. They won't acknowledge anything wrong within themselves, as they don't have the capacity to feel vulnerable, and how other people view them is much more important than their true character. To make themselves appear vulnerable, however, they could strategically bring up a minor imperfection or trivial flaw to make them look genuine and humble.

Supply – The supply of a narcissist/abuser is having people or things in their lives to feed their egos. They need constant approval, praise, adoration, affection, and attention. It's a psychological addiction, and supply is their drug. The supply can be you, children, or any other person/thing that feeds their needs to be put on a pedestal. They are never satisfied, and it will never be enough. They will start emotional or physical relationships with others if they feel they aren't getting enough from you. They can have several simultaneously and will almost always have someone to replace you immediately if you leave them. If they aren't getting enough supply from their children, they will turn to other children for the validation they crave. They purposely target those drawn to their charm, are naïve and vulnerable, and will use whichever of their masks to manipulate their target.

Triangulation – Triangulation is adding a third party to manipulate and control you for their agenda and to coerce you into actions or feelings you wouldn't otherwise do or feel.

- They will dangle someone they are cheating or having an inappropriate relationship with (supply) to make you jealous/ insecure, to work harder in the relationship, to win them back, or to change you into what they want you to become.
- They will try and manipulate someone you care about into agreeing with them on an issue to put a wedge in your friendship and/or to change your mind about something to convince you they are superior as the other person agrees with them.
- They'll talk highly of someone to purposefully raise your insecurities, comparisons, and self-doubts.
- They will try and convince you to do something for them that you normally wouldn't do by comparing what others are doing.

Flying Monkeys – The term flying monkeys came from the movie Wizard of Oz, describing the Wicked Witch using them to do her dirty work. Abusers/narcissists will surround themselves with other people they have manipulated, believe their lies and charm, and for loyalty. They will strategically pick people by what they can do for them personally and professionally, to make them look more educated or successful, as an extension of themselves to carry out schemes or abusive behavior, and even with other abusers/narcissists/cheaters, etc. to feed off of one another to validate the behavior.

Scapegoating and Smear Campaign - Terms to describe the premeditative, calculated, and strategic devaluing of you to others. They will lie, belittle, accuse, blame, character assassinate, and discredit you as a setup. For someone who is being abused in any way, to have the courage to seek help or support from friends or family and not be believed is both a travesty and a tragedy. There are three main reasons they scapegoat/ smear. First, they want to distract people from the truth by accusing you of doing the things they are actually doing, along with accusing you of being the abuser and they are the victim. Secondly, it's for their reputation if they think they may be suspected or caught. Thirdly, it's to isolate you from others if they suspect you are about to or have started going to other people for comfort, assistance, or guidance, and will discredit you immediately. They will also use this strategy after you leave them to everyone in your lives and through the court system.

Stalking – Stalking occurs before, during, and after a relationship and is a way to control, intimidate, and cause fear. Examples:

- Frequent phone calls and texts, and being upset if you don't answer immediately.
- Insisting you call or text to check in with them.
- Questioning your activities and insisting on knowing whom you are in contact with, questioning others to find out what you are doing or who you are in contact with.
- Not allowing you to keep communications private and requiring you to show them call and text logs, emails, mail, and photos, and will also do this with or without your knowledge through hacking/spy apps or your phone carrier account.
- Not allowing alone time, or you going somewhere without them.
- Will go through your personal possessions, either with or without your knowledge.
- Showing up at your place of employment and activities, without warning or invitation.
- Following you or having someone else follow or watch you, as well as having a tracking device on your vehicle.
- Cyberstalking your social media, restricting social media accounts, following your friends on social media to keep tabs on what they are doing while purposefully not posting to go

unnoticed, starting fake social media accounts to stalk you, or as a sneaky way to message people secretly.

- Video or audio taping you without your knowledge or watching you if you have a home security system.
- Accusing you of something you've done or somewhere you were in hopes you will "confess."

Children and parenting - Having a child is the greatest gift you could ever receive. Our children deserve love, affection, care, and guidance. As parents we try our best, but we are far from perfect and make many mistakes. There is no mistake in this world that is worse than a parent abusing their child(ren) in any way, shape or form. Children are easy targets of abuse because they're helpless and look to parents for all of their needs. It's easy for an abuser to have power, control, dominance, and to break down children's boundaries. Besides physical or sexual abuse, there are so many other ways a parent is abusive to their children. Abuse happens whether the parents are together or apart, and unfortunately if the parents are apart, an abuser has more of an opportunity to abuse, neglect, or use the child against the other parent. They will also use them as pawns or weapons to control the other parent. Narcissistic/abusive parents look at their children as extensions of themselves and expect perfection, and they will:

- Think and express the worst about their child's character and quickly blame their child before anyone else's. They will consistently remind them of their flaws and everything they've ever done wrong to shame, which destroys their self-esteem and self-worth.
- Highlight their child's flaws to blame the other parent, and will severely judge the other parent's parenting.
- Try and ruin relationships within the family if they feel slighted. They will play children against each other to create sibling rivalry for their affection, attention, or possessions. They will have a favorite (the Golden Child) and one they blame (Scapegoat Child).
- Severely judge that the child will rebel against things the abusive parent wants them to do, believe in, or care about.

27

- Not letting the child act their age and will require they act like an adult.
- Require the child go to them for love or attention, and will only initiate when it suits their agenda or if they have an audience to impress.
- Exploit the child's talents to look like it's their influence or to impress others.
- Extort or threaten in order to purposefully hurt them or the other parent.
- Withhold food or water, medical treatment, or any other essential need.
- Imprisonment or restraint of any kind.
- Witnessing abuse to a sibling, parent, pet, or anyone/anything else.

When a child feels unloved by a parent, chances are they won't hate the parent, but themselves, and this could lead to emotional, mental, and psychological trauma, as well as thoughts of self-harm. Some children will try harder to please the abusive parent in hopes they will show them love or even blame themselves for the abuse, feeling they are not good enough.

Why does someone abuse? Abuse should never be rationalized, but understanding why is key to possibly ever being able to change behavior. All abuse, whether physical, sexual, verbal, emotional, mental, financial, spiritual, or legal, is about power, control, dominance, and breaking down boundaries. Abuse escalates over time, and they choose this behavior. There are many different reasons: they have a personality disorder or grew up with someone who has a personality disorder, were abused, have anger issues, watched or witnessed abusive behavior, grew up with an addict or are addicts themselves, have control and/ or boundary issues, are afraid, lack empathy, are defensive, or are exhausted and at the end of their rope. I've read and experienced that abusers are filled with low self-esteem and shame and seek targets they believe are more easily manipulated and less likely to be able to defend themselves. Inside themselves, they feel powerless, unintelligent, and worthless. Their reputation and how others feel about them become their main goals in life, and they'll try to impress people to feed their ego, lie about anything to look better or hide their faults to escape exposure or accountability. They tend to judge, blame, and project onto others, especially their families, because of how they secretly feel about themselves. They must hide who they are from the public, so they need masks.

They are in their own self-induced prison, and with their abuse, they convict you, so you'll also be "doing time" with them. It's devastating that abusers want to abuse those who love them the most and have power over you to ensure you don't leave (entrapment); however, their abusiveness becomes the dysfunction and destruction that makes you want to leave. Most abusers won't recognize they have a problem and need to change. They will lie about it to get you to stay with them and to others to blame-shift but need extensive counseling and the desire for them to change abusive behaviors.

Help/What to do - If you or someone you know is in a violent relationship, please contact a domestic violence organization or shelter as soon as possible. They have the resources to direct you to the proper authorities or safety. If you suspect you are in a nonviolent abusive relationship, start by making a plan. Talk to someone you trust that will support and help you. Find a therapist specializing in domestic abuse if you feel like relationship counseling is an option. If the abuser will not take any responsibility and continues to blame-shift everything onto you, or what they do claim responsibility for is non-genuine, the likelihood of your relationship getting better is almost non-existent, as they will need the desire to change their behavior. Leaving isn't easy, takes a lot of courage, and is both stressful and terrifying, especially if you've been threatened in any way if you leave. Take any step necessary to protect your safety. Leaving an abuser is the most dangerous part of the relationship.

Start taking notes on what you've been through and are currently going through, as this is a reminder when they try to stop you or get you back. If possible, carefully and safely try to audio or video any abuse that's going on. Gather as much evidence as you can and secure any important documents. Do not tell them you are leaving, as this will only lead to them trying to convince you at all costs to stay and will remind you of every good time and none of the abuse. The absolute last thing an abuser or narcissist will tolerate is you leaving them because that takes away their control. They are capable of anything to gain it back, including physical violence and murder.

Make a timeline of when you can leave and the needed resources. You will at least need the following:

- A safe way to leave
- Money to start a new life, possibly a vehicle, a job, availability to credit
- A new place to live/furnishings, if necessary
- An attorney if you are married or have minor children
- Counseling with a therapist specializing in domestic abuse for yourself for recovery and healing

What abuse does to a victim/survivor – Abuse victims will suffer a variety of emotional, mental, and physical symptoms:

- Depression, anxiety, and lack of self-worth:
- Helplessness, anger, fear, emotional numbness, and the feeling of being alone and withdrawn.
- Loss of sleep/exhaustion and other physical symptoms such as IBS, jaw clenching, rashes, physically slumping over, and other illnesses.

Abuse can lead you to believe you are crazy or are losing your mind and memory and cause cognitive dissonance, PTSD, panic attacks, eating disorders, substance abuse, and possible thoughts of self-harm. Victims/survivors of all types of abuse need years of counseling to recover and heal, as wounds go much deeper than the surface.

Trauma Bonding – Trauma bonding is similar to Stockholm Syndrome, in which people held captive develop feelings and trust for their captures. In an abusive relationship, at first, the relationship is loving, but over time it changes, and you don't know why. You may blame yourself for the change, hope or are promised it won't happen again, try to change yourself so it doesn't happen, don't realize its abuse if it's nonviolent, feel stuck or helpless, are afraid of their threats, or just afraid to leave and be on your own. You also don't want the relationship to fail, and remember the person you fell in love with and don't realize that person doesn't exist because you fell in love with their mask. During the cycle of abuse, you have periods where the relationship is really good, which is confusing when the relationship is really bad. Trauma bonding is compared to being on a drug because, during the relationship's ups and downs, your body reacts with high levels of the stress hormone cortisol, paired with dopamine. With that back and forth, the body becomes addicted. This is why some victims take such a long time to leave, some never leave, and some wait until the abuser leaves.

No Contact – Going No Contact when you leave an abuser is a strategy to break free from them and includes not meeting in public or private and not talking on the phone. No Contact is because an abuser will use any of their strategies to manipulate, coerce, threaten, pursue, and love-bomb you into coming back to them, like a "Hoover vacuum" to suck you back in. The best way for them to do this is if you are in person or on the phone because they will try and control the conversation, twist your words and reasons, gaslight you, and for violent abusers, you could be in physical danger. If you need to communicate with them, the better ways are through texts or emails, so at least you can control the communication and have everything they say in writing. In extreme cases, you may need to block their messages, emails, and social media. When you finally have the courage to leave, the last thing you need is for them to manipulate you back into the relationship.

After you leave/ The divorce/custody process and still the target - After escaping, an abuser still wants control and will punish you to gain revenge. After you leave, the most important thing to remember is to take any steps necessary to secure your safety, especially if you were in a physically violent relationship or believe they can harm you. Victims of violent abusers are up to 75% more likely to be murdered than if they stayed in the relationship. If an abuser was suspicious, you spoke about your relationship abuse, or you were leaving them, or if they left you, they will have already blame-shifted, scapegoated, and smeared your name. This is so you look like the abuser (or anything else they lie and accused you of doing), and will continue trying to convince people they shouldn't like or communicate with you and will play the hero or the victim card for sympathy.

If you are married/have children, the abuse continues through the court system – Legal Abuse (post-separation abuse). You are still their target, and they will go to great lengths to lie, deceive, and threaten your financial well-being and custody just to hurt you further. They will manipulate the system to drag out legal proceedings to deplete your financial resources, to continue controlling you, and to prevent you from moving on with your life (vexatious litigation).

Commonly, they will be in a new relationship fairly quickly to feed their need for admiration and affection and for others to look at them as the one who is worthy of love. Most likely, they have replacements lined up before you even leave and don't believe they need to go through the grieving process. This is while you are the one who's grieving and needs counseling to heal and recover from what you've been through. Counseling helps process the abuse you've experienced and your emotional and mental scars. Connection really helps through friendships, support groups, church, etc. It hurts, is lonely, and is hard, but it's worth returning your self-worth, spirit, and happiness.

When you talk about domestic abuse, and even when you think about it, what comes to mind are the things that are seen. Bruises or physical proof from a physician or the police are what you envision. Nonviolent abuse is hidden. You have no idea what's going on behind someone's closed doors, and that's one of the main reasons I wanted to write this book and let the public know exactly what's happening. Abusers choose whom they abuse and carefully choose when and where they abuse. They will stop their behavior when it benefits them or when they are in public. Most of the information I provided is from extensive online and social media research. I posted much of this information on my Facebook in October 2020 during Domestic Violence Awareness Month to bring awareness and understanding to these hidden evils.

I want to educate the public on nonviolent types of abuse, and most of the information in this book is to bring this awareness. Even though most of this book is about nonviolent abuse, all abusers are capable of physical violence. Nonviolent abuse is much higher than violent because not all abusers are physically violent, but all are nonviolent. Recognizing these as abusive behaviors is much harder unless you are aware of the different types and tactics. Some abusers act overtly abusive towards others, therefore, are easy to spot. They don't really care about their behavior and are fine with showing it to the general public. But some abusers hide it covertly so that no one would ever suspect it. They can be even more dangerous. They are wolves in sheep's clothing or Dr. Jekyll and Mr. Hyde. They are two different people, one that is real and one that was created. My husband was that kind of abuser, and he was masterful. He had a mostly good reputation. He represented that most people liked him and thought he was great. That's what I thought. Some people could see right through his act. Those people could spot who he was because they have been exposed to that personality before. Those people are few and far between, and most of the time don't speak up.

"the most painful lessons are delivered by someone masquerading as a soul mate."

Steve Maraboli

3

MY RELATIONSHIP

Sleeping with a Monster

I DIDN'T SEE THE HIDDEN PART OF HIS PERSONALITY. I DIDN'T HAVE THE best relationships with men in general, was naive, and had been taken advantage of several times, but I always knew one thing. What you saw was who they were and you take that person at face value. An asshole is an asshole, and someone good is someone who is good and decent. That's why he was so dangerous, I didn't see it coming until it was too late. He painted a picture to me that my life with him was going to be perfect. The person I believed was my knight in shining armor turned out to be a monster – the boogeyman. So, let me start at the beginning. Dennis and I actually went to middle school and high school together. We were not friends, just classmates. From what I remember, which isn't much, he had a decent reputation as a jock and preppy.

On a Saturday night in January 1998, I was with friends at a few bars in my downtown area. Out of the blue, I ran into Dennis with another high school classmate and their friend. The other classmate said – "Hey, isn't that Jeanelle from high school?" They spoke with me for a few minutes, and Dennis asked me to lunch, and I accepted. We went to lunch and had a connection. He seemed nice but unlike the guys I was used to. We started dating, but something was different about him. He was very intense and overly affectionate. At that time, I felt uncomfortable and found myself pulling away. I hadn't felt that from anyone before. He questioned why I would pull away from him, and I blamed myself and my unfortunate past with other men. It became so intense and uncomfortable that I broke up with him after less than a month. I again blamed myself. I told him I wasn't ready for a relationship but wanted to remain friends. I still regarded him as a good person, so we remained friends and saw each other now and then. I dated other guys that year, and at the beginning of 1999, I realized I was ready for a family. Looking back, that put me in a vulnerable position, so my defenses were down. I thought about the men I knew, and I thought about Dennis. It was long enough from when we originally dated that I didn't remember how uncomfortable I was around him while we were dating, so I contacted him to hang out. I was vulnerable, naïve, and craving love. So, I was looking in the wrong place, and I sure did find it. I had no idea what I found was the worst place possible, which was in the hands of an abuser.

It was February 7, 1999, and we attended an art festival that Sunday. It was a beautiful, sunny day, and we had a great time together. I remember wearing a sundress and was glad it was warm for that time of year, even though we live in a southern state. He was supposed to go out with his parents that night for his mom's birthday, but it got canceled, and he asked me out for dinner (I wonder if it really got canceled, or was just what he told me? – now I'm not sure it was the truth). After dinner, we went to a bar to listen to one of my friends play guitar and sing. Everything seemed perfect that day, and I told him I was ready to settle down and wanted a relationship with him. He said he was dating someone else and needed to talk to her about breaking up first. It was after midnight, so we agreed our dating anniversary would be February 8, 1999, even though he technically was still with someone else. I excused his intense affection as love. I had gotten laid off from my place of employment right around then and started helping him with his sales job. I had repeatedly told him that I wanted an old-fashioned family, and because of the way I had grown up, it was really important to me to be a stay-at-home mother for my children. He agreed and even made a snide comment about working mothers who put their careers before their families. He seemed really happy about it all, which made me really happy. All I had ever dreamed of was having a happy family and children with a trustworthy and loving man. I felt like the luckiest woman in the world and envisioned our wonderful life.

At that time, I lived in an apartment with a roommate, Noella. She and I joked a little about him that he was preppy and geeky, but I thought those qualities made him a decent person and not a jerk. My relationship with Dennis progressed quickly. I didn't realize then that our relationship's intensity and acceleration were huge red flags. Now, I recognize that he "love-bombed" me and "mirrored" everything I wanted. He represented himself as the most loving person I've ever met while being humble, decent, trustworthy, and everything I have ever wanted in a person. He was my knight in shining armor, and I was completely swept off my feet. Things continued progressing very quickly, and I was head over heels in love with him. What really happened is that I fell in love with the person he represented to be (his mask), but he wasn't that person at all. It was a huge lie, and that person didn't exist. I was so ready for love and a family that I excused any red flags. The saying goes, "If it seems too good to be true, it probably is."

I had been married twice before Dennis. When I was 18, I married someone who was completely destructive and physically violent. He fits the commonly known description of a domestic abuser. That lasted 2 years. I stayed in the relationship because he threatened physical harm to me, my family, and anyone I dated after him ("If I can't have you, no one will"). I finally left him when I realized that one of us would end up dead and the other in jail. At 20 years old, I obtained a restraining order, filed for divorce, and escaped while he was at work. Then I was married for 6 ½ years to someone 17 years older than me who made me feel safe and was more of a father figure. When I turned 30, I realized I wanted a family but knew he wasn't the one, that I wasn't in love with him and wanted to be in love with the man I had children with. I did not have a great history of picking men and thought at this point that I was a better judge of character. What I realize is that my vulnerability and naivete guided my choices. I was searching for love. I wanted it so badly and thought I found it. I wanted to be happy and wanted my children to be happy. My desires were so strong that they clouded my judgment. Dennis was also previously married. He said they were divorced because his wife was an alcoholic and cocaine addict, hung around people who enabled that behavior, and she picked that life instead of their life together. I was sworn to secrecy about both of our previous marriages. He said people were judgmental and would think badly of us. I would ask him why he cared, so many people have been divorced, and I really didn't want to lie. He regarded what others thought of him and his reputation as the most important things in his life. I disagreed with that decision, but repeatedly, he told me he always made good decisions and that I needed to trust him. So, I chose to trust his decision and avoided telling people the truth (so, lie).

Dennis told me not long after we started dating that he knew both of my husbands cheated on me after I told him I wouldn't have been surprised if they had. I asked how he knew that information, and he responded that he knew people who found out that both cheated. Wow, I feel stupid now for believing him (since he was really lying), and it should have been a red flag, but I wanted this to work so badly that I excused it and chose to believe him. He also told me he spoke with the guy I last went out with to make sure he knew things were over between me and him, which I also chose to believe (most likely another lie). It may as well have been a test to see if I was still communicating with him. I started noticing other things which I excused. When we were going out somewhere and meeting other people, if we ran a few minutes late, he would make up a whole story that we needed to tell them about why we weren't on time. I didn't understand and questioned why we couldn't be truthful and just said we were running behind schedule. He didn't want anyone to think badly of him, so we had to lie to blame someone or something else out of his control.

He often considered himself a good Christian man who grew up in a typical Christian household with very Christian parents. Sometimes, he would say his parents were the best, and sometimes, he would say, "You can pick your friends, but not your family." He would purposefully ignore his parents and then talk about how much of a good son he was. It was confusing, but again, I dismissed it. His brother was an atheist, and Dennis didn't like him very much. I initially felt sorry for his brother and tried to include him in some of our activities. After a while, his brother showed enough oddness that I stopped trying to include him. At one point, his brother trashed his parents and Dennis on Facebook, saying he was beaten as a kid, and said many negative things about both their dad and Dennis. Dennis flat-out denied anything his brother said and made sure everyone knew their childhood was completely normal and his brother was lying. Now, I bet it was true, and if I had to guess, Dennis's brother was the scapegoat child, and Dennis was the golden child.

He almost immediately told me he wanted to take me on a trip to go snow-skiing because I had never been. When I asked a couple of weeks later, he seemed like my reminding him was making him do it like he wasn't going to, but I painted him in the corner. He joked about it numerous times. On so many occasions throughout our relationship and marriage, he would make it a point to invite someone to do something, even though he knew it would never happen. He claimed it was a strategy, so he looked good for extending the invitation. I believe he never intended to go on that trip, but since I reminded him, we went, and it was wonderful and extremely romantic.

After dating for a couple of months, I thought he was the one and told him I wanted to be with him forever. He was very humble and said he would have never had the confidence to tell me, so he was glad I told him first and that he would have never had the courage to set himself up if I didn't feel the same way. I also told him I loved him first, and he said he would have been too afraid to tell me before I told him. He also repeatedly told me that he was "painfully shy." That was part of his setup; I didn't see the red flags! He was the person who would exchange numbers with someone within 10 minutes of meeting them, and they were then invited to everything from that moment forward. He needed to be liked immediately and would do whatever it took to gain a new friend. He also said he disliked surprises because they focused on him (surprises take away control). These things were to make me think he was humble. He continually sold himself as extremely well-liked and more intelligent than most, with a high IQ (can't remember what number he said, but would always say that it was at least 20 points higher than normal), and that he always made good decisions and people would come to him all the time for his advice. His idol was Ronald Reagan, and he collected his books through the years. He always said how he admired Ron as such a good husband and sent love letters to Nancy. He would even get emotional about it, which made me believe that was the kind of husband he wanted to be. Let's just say that he didn't write love letters to me.

When we started discussing marriage, he knew my grandmother was the most important person in my life (deceased in 1991). Her birthday was November 11th. 1111 has significance and is supposed to be the time of day because the numbers point up to the heavens, the angels sing, and I refer to her as my angel. He said we should get married on 11/11. I beamed with excitement. I know now that that special day was manipulatively taken from my love for her and replaced with our wedding anniversary. That was a subtle way of stealing it from her, which he had to do because she was so important to me, even though she was no longer alive.

At that time, I had a huge group of friends, most of whom were male. We always had such a fun time together. They all seemed to like Dennis because he made sure everyone knew what a great guy he was. He was different from my group; they were pretty casual and laid-back, while Dennis was preppy and seemed strait-laced. While everyone would be in jeans, he was in khakis. I was perfectly fine with that because it gave me a false sense of him being above everyone else, including me. Dennis also had a group of friends. From what I remember of his group, they were nice enough. One thing about them was that Dennis usually picked up the check when he went out with them (I realized he had a hero complex). I remember him saying that when he was out partying and felt drunk, he would pay the bill and just walk away and go home without saying a single word to anyone. He would just disappear. Now I understand why he did that so no one would see him being less than perfect or not in total control while looking good because he paid for all of them. One day he invited me to go to the opening of a bar downtown because he knew the manager. He brought along a guy friend, Pat. While we were out, Dennis said all the girls usually flirted with Pat. I did not. I think back and believe it was a test to see how I acted around his friend, whom other girls apparently liked and flirted with. Later in our relationship, when Pat had a girlfriend and then when he had a wife and kids, Dennis would say Pat had to do everything, and his girlfriends and wife didn't do much. He went so far as to call them lazy. He said Pat did most of the cleaning, cared for the kids, and did everything at their parties. He made sure to mention it every time we were with him. I always wondered why, but now I believe Pat was just a nice guy who liked to help out, and Dennis wanted to make sure it was looked at as a negative.

I broke my apartment lease with Noella because Dennis and I wanted to move in together. I convinced the leasing office to let me out of my lease as long as she found another roommate, which she did. I moved into the small house downtown he was renting. It was so small that there was barely enough room to walk around when my furniture and possessions were added. We started looking for a larger home to purchase in anticipation of our upcoming marriage and having a family. There were a few instances that concerned me. If he asked me a question, and I didn't give him the answer he was expecting, he kept asking me the same question over and over. I didn't understand why he was doing it, which made no sense. Was he expecting me to change my answer? It felt like I was being interrogated. Once, he asked a question about one of my friends, and I said I didn't know. He wouldn't take that as an answer. He pressed me over and over for an answer until I started crying. I again didn't understand but excused it. He also started setting me up early in our relationship by making jokes with our friends that I was an airhead. He would lift the hair over my ear, blow in it, and then lift the other side, acting like the air had gone through. I thought it was an innocent joke, but now I realize every little thing he did was part of his manipulation and strategy, and he was conditioning me to doubt myself and to believe he was more intelligent. Another concerning thing he said to me was that when he was growing up when his dad came home from work, no one was allowed to speak to him until he was ready. I can't remember if it was to read the newspaper or watch something on TV, but it sounded odd. His dad was an elder in the churches they attended and would visit people when they were in the hospital. Dennis would go with him as a child. He said their family would prepare the church before services and clean up afterward. He mentioned their humble lives and how his parents always tithed 10% to the church, no matter the sacrifice. He said they gave up drinking completely, never cursed, and always had many friends. He also spoke highly of one of the couples that were friends with his parents, who owned a business and were very wealthy. He would mention them often, always with admiration. While Dennis was growing up, he told me some things about his mom. He said that his mom was his biggest fan when he played sports, but at one point, he forbade her to come to his games because she embarrassed him. He also said that when he played sports, he had extra laundry, and his mother wanted him to do his own. He said he told his mother that she was shirking her responsibility as his mother, then he put his clothes in the washer, pressed the button, and then the dryer, pressed the button and asked her if that was so hard she had to complain. Looking back, it showed a pattern of disrespect for women if he treated his mother that way. She was very sweet and mild-mannered.

Dennis hated tattoos, and anytime he saw someone who had one, he looked down upon it. He said openly how much he despised them and that the only tattoo he ever accepted was when his friend's child died and got a tattoo out of remembrance. He also said he believed his friend's wife's negligence led to the death, and that's why they divorced. He sounded so believable, but why would he say that? To lose a child is such a heart-wrenching tragedy. For him to cast blame and judgment on the mother was such a disgusting display of misogyny, and it was not the only time he blamed a mother for a child's death. He said other odd things to me. He said that he learned through a mental health professional that you take the strongest trait of both parents, multiply it by 10, and that's what their child would be like. He looked at his friends' kids and would actually say that. He also claimed that 100% of marriages end because one of the spouses was unfaithful to the other. He would say this expression, "Someone doesn't take the lead off of first base unless they were going to steal second" (or something like that). It didn't dawn on me when he was married before; was he talking about himself and his first marriage? He also said he quit basketball in high school because he wasn't coachable. He said he disagreed with his coach about something and quit. I never questioned what he said, and boy, was I dumb for excusing all of these crazy things!

He didn't want anyone to know about his education and kept it a secret. He didn't graduate from our high school as he claimed. He said something about a dispute over his credits, so he finished with a G.E.D. from a local community college. He also only took a handful of college classes and stopped going. Sometimes, he said he quit because he was making too much money waiting tables and then in sales. Then sometimes, he said he quit going to college because he paid for his wife to go and couldn't afford to pay for both of them. He said that one to look like a hero. That contradicts when he said at another point that she was a dancer and had a scholarship. He told people the entire time we were together that he has a Bachelor's Degree in Business Management. If I ever questioned him about why he lied, he said he knew people would judge him. I commented that he should be proud of whom he was and making a success of himself, and not worry about what other people thought of him. When I said that, he was mortified and strongly disagreed. I was sworn to secrecy and had to lie for him. He also was an avid fan of a certain college football team. People would ask if he graduated from that university, and he would say he went to the university in our area but would travel to see friends every weekend at the other one (but some people were under the impression he went there, so I wonder if he went back and forth). He was highly focused on a pristine reputation and would say that people would tell him they wanted his life but would change their minds if they knew the truth.

We spent a few months looking for the right home. We settled on a house that was being sold directly by the owner. We made an offer, and the owner tried to say later that we agreed on a higher price. Dennis was so angry that he wanted to pull the entire deal immediately. I tried to reason with him, and he just wanted to kill the deal. Even though it was definitely a dick move, I wound up talking to the owner myself and telling him he was trying to screw with us, and if he was not going to agree to the correct price, we would walk away. Things worked out, and we bought the house, but Dennis despised the guy from then on and would bring it up now and then. Since we weren't married, he said the house would only be in his name to protect me. I questioned why it couldn't be in both of our names, and he claimed it couldn't be because we weren't married and to trust him. I was suspicious but trusted him and gave him all the money from my savings, which happened to be half of the down payment. This was an incredibly premeditated set-up and the very beginning of his financial control.

We decided that we wanted a family right away after our wedding. We went to my gynecologist in June to make a plan. I was on birth control and also wanted to quit smoking. I started taking medication to quit and stopped taking the pill. The doctor said it would probably take my body six months to a year before I could get pregnant. I wanted to quit smoking before I had children, but Dennis took it upon himself to take credit. My smoking didn't bother him when we were first dating, and he constantly complained about it after we were in a committed relationship. We moved into our house in July and celebrated with terrible pizza and a bottle of Dom Perignon champagne. I didn't get my period that month, and we bought a home pregnancy kit. When it tested positive, he made a point to comment on the expression of happiness I had on my face when we found out I was pregnant. Why was he more focused on the expression on my face than our excitement at the moment? It was odd, and I excused it. Then, when we started going to an obstetrician, they tested to see if you've ever been pregnant. Again, Dennis commented that he was relieved I had never been pregnant before, even though I told him I hadn't. I guess he didn't believe me and needed proof?

Again, he said something odd that I excused because it could have been legitimate, but looking back, I know exactly why. He said he wanted us to keep our pregnancy completely a secret from everyone, including our parents, for the entire first trimester. He claimed the reason was that if we lost the baby, most likely, it would be during that time. I hesitantly agreed because he was always so convincing that his way was best, and it was also something couples did when they thought their pregnancy was high-risk, even though ours was not. So, we hid it from everyone. I hated that. I wanted to share our joy with friends and family. After the first trimester, we went to tell our parents. Remember, we became pregnant in July, and our wedding wasn't until November 11th. My mother and stepdad were very happy for us. He was terrified about telling his parents because he feared being judged. He commented that he felt like a teenager going to his parents to tell them he had knocked up his girlfriend (well, we weren't teenagers, we were in our early 30's). They were not nice about it at all and were shaming. They did judge him and were disappointed. I was disgusted by their self-righteousness. I understood where he got it from, but I excused it as usual. Now, after over 20 years, I realized it was a scheme. He only wanted to keep our pregnancy a secret to protect himself from his parents' and others' judgment. How disgusting! He took that time away from me and my joy of being pregnant because he was afraid. I learned much about his strategy and calculating schemes after leaving him.

Dennis began asking questions about my friend group. At one point, he asked me if I had dated any of them and if I slept with any of them. I did, but I also already felt his judgment and knew if I told him yes, he would make me give them up. I would have to choose between him and them, and I didn't want to give up either, so I lied and said no. It was the time when Friends and other shows were on, even Seinfeld, and it wasn't taboo any longer, so I didn't think it should have been an issue. It was also none of his business because it was in the past, and never once did I ask if he dated or slept with anyone from his friend group. I didn't even ask him if he dated one of his female friends from his childhood who called our house after we moved in. He was on the phone with her for a long time before I went and checked on him. While he was still on the phone, I casually asked if he was still talking to her. He lied and said he wasn't while the phone was to his ear with her on the other line. I didn't ask him why he felt the need to lie. I wasn't going to accuse him of anything. One weekend that October, I visited my sister Madison, about a 3-hour drive, to let her know about our pregnancy and to visit her new baby boy. Dennis went out with my friends one of those nights. I woke up the following day to a voicemail from him. When I listened to the message, I was horrified. He found out I lied to him and left me a horrible and very long voicemail. I wish I still had it; it was in the evilest voice I had ever heard and gave me the chills. I left my sister's house and raced home at dangerous speeds. When I arrived, I apologized for lying and explained why. He didn't want to hear why; that was an excuse, and excuses weren't allowed. In that evil voice, he gave me a 'lecture' that lasted for hours. My heart dropped, and I didn't understand what he was doing to me. I knew lying to him was wrong, but my intentions were never malicious. I loved him, and I loved my friends. Yes, I made a mistake by dating and sleeping with 2 of them over a couple of years, but does that mean I had to give them up forever? Maybe so, but his attacking me wasn't normal – we could have discussed it as mature adults. I blamed what he did, 'the lecture,' on myself since I caused it. However, I felt his evil that day, and if I weren't already pregnant, I would have left him. He showed me who he really was, which wasn't the guy I fell in love with. I knew and felt it at that point. However, he already had me as helpless as a person could be. That day I lost the very first piece of my spirit.

I was pregnant and had no money, job, or other place to live. This little baby inside me didn't ask to come into this world, so I needed to do whatever I could for her best interest. I felt such an incredible amount of fear and wanted to protect her at whatever cost. I didn't want her to grow up with a broken home that didn't even make it to her birth. In a split second, I was reminded of my childhood, and would never want that for my child. I remembered how much my mother struggled, was frustrated and in anguish, keeping a roof over our heads and having food on our table. I also remembered how it affected me and my dysfunctional and destructive behaviors. He also threatened to ensure a judge gave him full custody, making me more afraid. So, I begged for his forgiveness and gave up my entire friend group. I not only had to give them up, but I also had to get rid of all pictures and traces of them. I blamed myself; it was my fault. And what he did that day was my fault as well. Even with my worries, I still thought he was a good guy, and it would never happen again if I were good. Originally, all my friends loved Dennis, and my best friend Stan even joked that he would marry Dennis if he could. They also called us Barbie and Ken because we looked perfect together. Now, they were all gone from my life, and we were very far from perfect, not knowing what would be to come. Besides having to get rid of all those pictures, he also didn't want me to continue my friendship with Noella and made me get rid of those pictures. I had to remove all pictures of my ex-husband and said he did the same with his ex-wife. Now, I'm sure he was lying and was probably hidden somewhere. His elimination of all my friends at this point was crushing, but I realized that if he didn't eliminate them this way, it would only be a matter of time before he found another way. It wasn't an if but a when. In getting rid of pictures, I believe his motivation was to erase my past and memories so it would be easier for him to mold me into what he wanted if I forgot who I was and the friends who cared about me. I wish I could have those pictures back, and I miss being able to see those memories. In addition to my friends and pictures being eliminated, he went even further by combining our cell phone plans. I don't remember the entire situation, but he was able

45

to keep his old phone number, but mine had to be changed. This was also before smartphones, so you would write down phone numbers you wanted to keep and re-enter them on your new phone. Of course, many other friends were omitted because now I would be married and have a family, so it was 'inappropriate' for me to keep those phone numbers (he specifically said that to me). That strategic plan eliminated the possibility that anyone from my past would be able to contact me and vice versa, essentially erasing almost everyone from my life. I had no understanding that I was already shackled and put into a cage. They were unseeable but definitely were there.

"I'm going to groom you to believe that I am everything you want.

But in reality, you're ALL I'm looking for.

I will mirror you and make you believe you have found the love of your life.

I will end up with EVERYTHING I want.

And you will lose EVERYTHING you ever were."

#narcissisticabusenearlykilledme
@narcissistic_abuse_is_real

Dennis bought me an excessively large engagement ring. Don't get me wrong, it was beautiful but way larger than it should have been. It was a 2.12 caret, pear-shaped diamond, with 6 baguette diamonds (then the wedding band added 3 more baguettes). He purchased it from one of my friends who owned a jewelry store. We were allowed to keep him as an acquaintance because he was our jeweler (in other words, he was useful to Dennis). One year I sent a Christmas card to him, and was scolded and reminded he was only our jeweler and an acquaintance. Our wedding was going to be small. We were paying for it ourselves and didn't want a traditional wedding, since we were both married before and pregnant. We decided to get married at a small outdoor chapel with mostly family and had dinner afterward at a charming Italian restaurant. Our wedding was on a Thursday because that's the day November 11th fell on in 1999. We had a party with our friends at our favorite bar on Saturday night. After I gave up my friend group, it was smaller. It was fine. I liked where we got married, went to dinner with our family, and the Saturday night party. He had me create all of the wedding invitations instead of getting them made because it was cheaper and he made sure I spent as little as possible on my wedding dress and accessories. I think my dress was about $100. He also insisted on coming with me to pick it out! At least it was pretty, and I liked it. I did feel a sense of sadness at the wedding and during every moment of the events and I was also hurt that I no longer had my friends. At one point, he even said his boss and wife questioned him about marrying me and discouraged it. Why did he need to say that to me? It was a hurtful thing to say to your soon-to-be wife. Dennis decided on an elaborate honeymoon. Now, I'm guessing he didn't want me to spend money on my wedding dress because that was something for me, but the honeymoon was as expensive as he saw fit since it was exactly what he wanted. First, we spent a couple of nights at a charming boutique hotel in our area, then one night at the airport. I distinctly remember our very first night as husband and wife, the moment we walked into the beautiful and charming hotel room and the fear I felt for the future (it was an omen of prophetic significance). From there, we went to three different places in Canada and were gone for at least another week. It was nice, but in the back of my mind, I felt uncomfortable and nervous about our relationship.

At first, he allowed us to have someone clean our house. It was something that I always wanted but never had the opportunity to do. I was thankful it was through my pregnancy because it kept me away from the fumes of cleaning products. As soon as our daughter was born, he made me give it up, and I needed to clean the house myself. He said he didn't want people to think I was spoiled. Then, years later, when all of our friends had a cleaning service, he allowed it again to make sure he looked good to them. It was yet another instance where his reputation with others was more important than mine and our relationship, along with not wanting to spend money on something relating to me or my happiness. And, speaking of the birth of our daughter, that was such a joyous day and quite sad. While we were pregnant, we took parenting classes and CPR classes and were going to be co-parents. He learned with me all of the normal things first-time parents learn. He seemed so happy during all of it. The day she was born, everything changed. That day, I asked him if he wanted to take a turn changing her diaper. He said no, he was not going to be changing diapers. He told me he had a job; our daughter was now my job. He turned our having a child together into her being my chore, which was so unloving. I completely understood that he had a job and that I would be taking care of our daughter by my choice, but the way he said it, along with his tone on the day our daughter was born, was a setup for our future. The happy family I thought we were going to have seemed like it was already gone, but I was so happy to be her mother and was going to make sure she felt enough love to take his place if necessary. I was devastated and knew I would never have another child with him. We originally wanted to have two children, and I made whatever excuse necessary to convince him one was best. I'm very glad he agreed. After Harlow was born, our family and his friends visited. Within the first week, my old best friend Stan came to the house. He just wanted to meet the baby and say congratulations. I was sad and heartbroken and again told him I wasn't allowed to be his friend, and at the same time, I was afraid I would get in trouble with Dennis. A few more pieces of my spirit were taken away.

So, our precious little baby daughter was my responsibility, my job. I took care of her if she cried, needed changing, feeding, bathing, or got up in the middle of the night. He got annoyed when she cried, would question why, and wanted me to figure out what was wrong and fix it, and even said those exact words. He worked out of the house, so the three of us were usually together. If she cried, he came out and asked me to get her to stop because he was working. I knew how much of a burden it was getting up from our bed in the middle of the night to tend to her, and his judgment was already when she cried, so I devised a plan. I slept on the couch with her for the first six months, with her in my arms, propped up with the boppy pillow. That way, she could breastfeed and return to sleep when she woke up. He was okay with that because then he wasn't disturbed. He seemed only to hold her when he wanted to and showed her affection and care when he chose to or when we had company over (agenda or audience). I have mostly tried to stay physically fit, so when I was cleared to exercise again, I started immediately and had equipment in our bedroom. Dennis watched Harlow while I worked out in the mornings and complained about it. Instead of being happy to spend time with her one-on-one, it seemed like he was her babysitter, and was annoyed. I stopped asking him as soon as I figured out something she could do to keep herself occupied with me in the bedroom.

He made me feel like something was wrong with me, that if I wasn't in a perfect mood all the time, it meant I was ungrateful, and there was no reason for it. No matter what was happening, I had to always be in a good mood. I couldn't defend myself or have opinions when we disagreed about anything. He was always right, and I was always wrong. He always wanted me to agree with him, whatever the reason. It was like he was trying to brainwash me into believing everything he believed in and thinking everything he thought to be exactly who he wanted. I said to him one day that it felt like he wanted me to be a Stepford Wife and like he was trying to brainwash me. He immediately denied it, but that was how he treated me. I became so sad and confused that one day, I told him I wanted to see a counselor. He reluctantly agreed. I made an appointment with a Christian counselor at our church, but they no called or showed. He told me that I didn't need a counselor but to change my behavior, and I wouldn't like to hear what a counselor would say about me anyway.

One day, he asked why I wasn't in a good mood. I said I didn't know that it may be PMS. He told me PMS doesn't exist and that it was just an excuse women used. I shouldn't be in a bad mood because I should be grateful we had such a great life. If I was in a bad mood, that meant I was ungrateful. He continually used the word "victim" to describe me. He would say to me over and over not to play the victim. Pieces of my spirit continued breaking off little by little. When he wanted me to do something, anything, he wouldn't ask but instead would say, "I'm going to have you do this," "You need to," or "I need you to." He did that throughout our marriage and was fine inconveniencing me to have me do something for him. He would grossly underestimate how much time it would take me to help him but grossly overestimate what I was doing otherwise. He referenced how long it should take to do something, and I would think, "This isn't UPS!" He would constantly tell me that everyone liked him, he had so many friends, they'd always go to him for advice, and he knew so many secrets because people trusted him. Again, he would say he always made good decisions, and I needed to trust him because he knew best. He said that everyone should make good decisions once they become an adult. I believe he said all of that so much to manipulate and confuse me into thinking he was always right and I was always wrong. I kept asking myself why he treated me this way, and if I really was this horrible person he was trying to change, why did he want to be with me in the first place?

He would refer to each of his guy friends as his best friend. He liked to name-drop any of his friends with status or wealth and would work it into any conversation, even if he was talking to a stranger. Once he told someone that the president of our local community college, a neighbor, was one of his best friends, and he was part of his Saturday golf group. He wasn't one of his best friends, just a neighborhood friend, and he golfed a few times when he was filling in for someone else and by no means was part of the regular group. I couldn't understand why he continually needed to lie and misrepresent himself. When trying to impress someone with his knowledge on a subject, whether about travel or a restaurant or whatever, he would always say, "You HAVE to go there; you HAVE to eat this; you HAVE to try this; you HAVE to ...." You could see the uncomfortableness on people's faces, and I felt embarrassed.

We were hanging out with friends he introduced to me during our pregnancy and early marriage. One group was from when he spent one year attending another high school. I already knew one of the girls, Kip, because she also went to school with me before transferring to the new high school. She and her husband Tim had their son six months before Harlow was born, so we had much in common. I wonder now if Dennis wanted to be friends with them because Tim was a contractor and did some renovations at our house at a low cost. They had a second son, and Kip and I had playdates for years with our kids, attended our kids' birthday parties, and went out as couples. Our dentist, Kurt, and his wife, Melissa, were part of that group as well, and let's just say that throughout our entire marriage, most of our dentistry was free (useful?). Dennis said at the beginning that Melissa didn't like him, but after a while, he changed that to her not liking me so that we wouldn't hang out with them anymore. I questioned why he used to say she didn't like him and now me, and he said he was protecting me. That wasn't the only wife when he said about not liking him, then switched to them not liking me. He initially said those wives didn't like him because they were feminists, and he didn't like feminism and would complain to me about it. He must not have liked that these women could have their own opinions. He also didn't like Oprah Winfrey. He would say, and said many times, that she was the anti-Christ because she glorified victims. I used to watch her show and felt the need to stop because of his opinion of her. I didn't want to get in trouble because I watched a show "that glorified victims." I realize now that he didn't want me to watch that show to get an education and expose who he was and what he was doing. Oprah was a strong woman who helped those in need and educated the public, so her power threatened him, and he couldn't have that.

We started going to church as a family, but if we were in the service and our daughter fussed at all, he would immediately walk out, and we had to leave. No matter where we were, he would do that in a restaurant, a store, or anywhere else. His child would not publicly cry and possibly annoy anyone and embarrass himself. I found this behavior excessive and unnecessary. Most reasonable people understand when a child cries because it's a normal part of having a baby. I could see if a baby's crying didn't stop after a few minutes, but he wanted to leave the moment it began. More and more, I felt helpless, alone, and sad. I started talking to two ladies at church for advice about what was happening. They were so lovely to me, but they truly didn't understand. Dennis had started telling me that my past was affecting our relationship, and he was taking the beating for what others did to me. I didn't think I was doing anything like that and was so confused by all the things he was doing and saying. I started my friendship and mentoring with these women because I thought I was damaged, and my wonderful

Christian husband was trying to help me. They were very supportive, and I took bible study classes to improve myself. Maybe he would like me more if I was more of a Christian woman? I also spoke about what was going on at home with our pastor. He and the ladies encouraged me to pray about it daily, so I did that. I hoped things would improve and told them I believed God had a reason why we were together. We also wanted our daughter to go there for preschool, so we joined the church to move up on the waiting list. You were given envelopes with your name for your tithe as church members. Dennis said he would never use them because he didn't want his tithes to be tracked. The real reason was that he didn't want to be judged by how little he wanted to give and always had an excuse. The Bible says you are supposed to give your first 10%. Dennis never did that and barely tithed anything. I always wondered why he claimed to be such a Christian but didn't do one of the most basic and essential parts. We became somewhat involved with our church. I was baptized, our daughter was baptized, and we went to a small couples' bible study group. We also volunteered. I was a church greeter, and Dennis was an usher. When we went to our couples' group, all of them would share their struggles, but we kept our mouths shut. We pretended we were perfect and everything was fine. I felt like a fraud because that's exactly what we were, and I would fight back the tears during group discussions. I tried to hide it, but I wonder if they ever noticed. We were not perfect, and it was a lie. I was still consulting my two ladies for advice but said nothing to anyone else. He was also continuing to represent to me that I needed to work on myself and become a better person.

When our daughter was a toddler, I took her to Gymboree and several other things. The times at Gymboree were some of my favorite memories of being the mom of a toddler. It was also nice getting out of the house and meeting other moms. We spent a lot of time together, and I felt great when she and I weren't home. We could be ourselves. Two moms and I became close friends, and Harlow with their little girls. We had so much fun going to the park, Chuck E. Cheese, the library, and several other things. One of the moms and her husband began going out sometimes as couples with Dennis and me. When she turned 30, she had a group of girls go out, and the guys went out separately, and then we all met up later. Unfortunately, her husband frequented strip clubs, where the guys went. When we met up later and danced at a club, she was pretty drunk, and many guys were hitting her. I had Dennis dance with her so those guys would leave her alone. Her husband's best friend got angry at Dennis and accused him of coming onto her, and they almost had a fistfight. I defended Dennis, and we left. He suggested I end my friendship with her. I agreed and ended it the next day.

He regularly let me know his decisions were always better than mine. He set me up to question my decisions and parenting. He made me feel obligated to parent his way because he was superior. A few things he did while she was a baby and toddler made me angry. He would throw Harlow into the couch. I kept telling him she could fall off and get hurt. He continually said it was fine and knew what he was doing. One time she did bounce from the couch to the floor, and he dismissed it as a fluke. He also threw her up in the air. Of course, a baby would love the feeling, but I was mortified. I was so afraid he would drop her. He also would hold her in his arms and skateboard around our neighborhood. All I could think of was that if the skateboard hit something in the road, Harlow would fly out of his hands. Thank the Lord, nothing like that ever happened, but I still feel it was a dangerous, irresponsible risk he felt entitled to take with a helpless and fragile baby. He expected her to act like a miniature adult. If we were at a restaurant or a friend's house and she started acting up, he continued to freak out and wanted to leave immediately. She wasn't allowed to be a normal kid, and he also expected her to speak adultlike and not like a child. When we were at my parent's house, and she was playing and running around with her cousins, Jenny and Zander, Dennis didn't like that and would make her stop. My mother saw him call her over, grab her arm, and give her that evil look that meant she had to stop. Just like he wanted me to be perfect, he wanted her to be perfect. It broke my heart and was such a shame, so I was always glad when he wasn't around so she could be herself and act her age.

I still wanted our relationship to work and be a happy family. Once we started going out when our daughter was a baby, I wanted us to have 'date nights.' We started going out just the two of us and went out with couples. One time, we went out with two other couples. One was Stevie and Lainie, and the other was Bette and Joe. Stevie was Dennis's childhood best friend and knew everyone through golf, as he was a golf professional at a local golf course. We had a nice time out to dinner and had a lot of fun that night. When we returned to our house, Dennis wanted everyone to stay longer and have drinks. I was exhausted because I had a baby to take care of. So, when I said something to him, he got mad at me and had everyone stay regardless of how I felt. I was exhausted and unhappy, and I'm sure it showed. After that, for the rest of our marriage, he reminded me that Bette wanted to "throw me away." He said he begged her not to and asked her to mentor me, which never happened. We all remained friends for many years, but I was always reminded of those words: "She wanted to throw me away, and he begged her not to." Of course, more pieces of my spirit were lost, and I continued not understanding why he was treating me that way and cared more about his friends' feelings and enjoyment than his wife. He invited another couple over on another occasion, and I asked to cancel because I felt sick. He didn't care and had them come over anyway, and I had to entertain them even though I felt horrible.

When I did anything not up to his standards, he would give me those 'lectures' that sometimes would last for hours. He always worked in how flawed I was and how Christian and good he was to shift the blame. If I tried to defend myself, it was an excuse, and I had to "own what I did wrong" and not be a victim. Most of the time, I didn't know what I did wrong because he spoke in circles. If I got upset or yelled in reaction to what he was doing and saying to me, he called me cruel. One time I burst out crying and said, "We are not getting a divorce!" I didn't want to fail, especially since I had a child I was responsible for. Her well-being was my number one priority. So, most of the time, whatever it was, I ended up apologizing so he would stop lecturing me. His demeanor instantly changed when he was done, and I gave him what he wanted, from evil one minute to loving the next. It was so confusing, which was just the beginning of my confusion. Did he believe that treating me with love afterward would make me believe that what he did didn't happen, wasn't that bad, or maybe it was me and not him? He would say something mean to me and then say it was a joke. He eventually stopped because I told him that if a joke hurts someone, then it's not funny. He claimed he liked dark humor.

"IT WAS JUST A JOKE. LIGHTEN UP!"

"How many times has the Narcissist maliciously teased you about your supposed lack of humor? All because you didn't laugh at the caustic nature of their jokes that were always aimed at you.

Narcissists will gaslight us and tell us that we can't take a joke. We know full well that their "jokes" were meant to cause us harm. And when we don't react like they want us to, they turn to their buddies and say, "Looks like someone can't take a joke. See what I have to deal with?"

@FreedomFromNarcissisticAndEmotionalAbuse2021

He kept threatening me that if I ever left him, he would make sure a judge wouldn't give me any custody. He said all he needed to do was bring up my dysfunctional past. I was terrified. Of course, that made me feel even more helpless. He wanted me to fear leaving him, and used our child as ammunition. Then he would make me feel sorry for him by saying if our marriage didn't work out or if I ever died, he would never remarry again. He continued to confuse me by saying how much he loved me with all his heart and needed to help me. .As all of this was going on, we continued representing we were the perfect couple, lying to people about our past marriages and his education. I could not express my feelings if I wasn't happy, so I started my fake smile. I pretended to be happy when I felt so much pain inside. I tried my best to love and cater to our daughter and be a better person. One day, when she was about four years old, he told me something negative about her, which was heartbreaking. Who taught him to think so twisted??? It was just the beginning and a set-up, as it reflected and projected how he felt about himself. She was an AMAZING child, kind and loving, and his judgment and unkind words about her had nothing to do with her and everything to do with him – remember that! She was such an incredibly caring child. When a little girl cried on her first day of Pre-K 3 because she feared being there without her parents, Harlow walked right up to her, hugged her, and told her it would be okay. This was then and always what represented her character. I just wanted her to be happy, and would always try to show her all of the love I possibly could, so she could feel it. I felt like he treated her like an object and treated her well only when it was convenient for him, depending on his mood, needs, or audience. He accused me of not parenting her properly or punishing her enough when she did something he deemed wrong. It got to the point that I was overly punishing her for anything so I wouldn't get in trouble. I felt horrible; this was no way to parent a child and it was so unfair for her. We were not on the same page, and he regularly told me his way was best. I preferred when she and I weren't home with him. For each piece of my spirit that was taken from me, knowing we would never be the happy family I always wanted took the most. I also hurt so much for Harlow, wondering if she didn't feel love from her father.

Dennis, being in sales, worked for a successful marketing business. For a while at first, he worked in their small office. Then the owner told him he would rather Dennis work from home. That was a red flag, but Dennis said it was because his boss was an asshole, and no one liked him. I'm betting that Dennis created a hostile atmosphere and couldn't take authority, so he started working out of the house. He was an excellent salesman, earned a good living, and, in 2004, decided he wanted to start a business. He said if he started this business, he would need me to do the bookkeeping, which wouldn't take much time. I was helping him already, and he said it wouldn't be much more. Growing up, my mother was a bookkeeper, and that was something I told him I never wanted to do. I reminded him that I wanted to be a stay-at-home mother, and he agreed, continuing to say he needed my help and it wouldn't be much and would be only a few hours a week. I said I would do it, but he wouldn't have taken no for an answer. It turned out to be much more, and when I told him what he said, he denied it and told me a few days a week. When he asked me to do something, I did it. I didn't want a 'lecture' and tried to stay 'out of trouble.' Through the years, I felt sad and envious of all my friends who didn't have to work, stayed home with their children, and I hated bookkeeping. When he noticed that, he reminded me how grateful I should be for him giving us such a good life, and he gave me a job to help our family. I also felt sad and envious when we were around another couple or family that seemed happy. All I ever wanted was to have a happy family.

I can't remember how we found out, but his boss was about to sell the company and wanted him to sign a non-compete around the same time. He had a previous draft of a contract without a non-compete from a while before, and I casually told him that it was too bad he never signed it. Well, his boss had signed it, so Dennis decided to sign it with a fraudulent date and represented it as a valid contract. So, when we opened our business in the same industry in September 2004, Dennis's boss was livid. Dennis was his most successful salesperson, which would severely affect the sale of the company. Dennis presented the previous contract his boss knew he had never received fully signed. Dennis was sued, and they went to mediation. He wanted me to lie for him, and I wouldn't dare say no. I'm so lucky it turned out I didn't have to. Dennis lost and had to pay his old boss for several months, and that company was eventually sold. He swore me to secrecy. The business became increasingly more successful year after year, and I had to work a little more. I continued as the bookkeeper and helped him with special projects. Our daughter didn't like me working because it took time away from her, and I felt terrible about it. We worked out of the house for at least a few years, and he hired an assistant/customer service person and a couple more salespeople. I really liked his assistant, Melony; we were great friends and enjoyed working together. She saw how he treated me at some point, and I could talk to her about it regularly. It was comforting and therapeutic getting to vent to someone. I cared about her a lot. We wore cute slippers when we worked together and had lots of fun, especially when Dennis wasn't home.

Since I still cared for the home and our daughter, I avoided working more than 25 hours weekly. I felt burdened because I never wanted that for our daughter. I wanted to be there for her whenever she needed me, and when I was working and had to tell her I couldn't spend time with her, it broke my heart, and she had to play by herself and be quiet. He knew how important it was to me to be a stay-at-home mother, so he had to take that away. He didn't care about my wishes or our daughter's, just his. It continued to take a toll on my emotional well-being. The business continued to grow and invaded our entire house. After a few years of our house being a complete mess, we bought a building and moved our office. I forgot to mention that when we started the business, Dennis told me all the business paperwork would only be in his name to protect me. I questioned it and was silenced. He was protecting me, and that was it. So, when we bought the building, it was also in his name. And, when we bought two other buildings, they were in his name also. When we paid ourselves, every penny was in his name. I never earned a penny the entire time I worked at our company. I had no title, and the only thing with my name on it was that I was a signer on the business bank accounts since I cut all the checks. I joked that I was the volunteer wife because I didn't feel like a part owner. He joked to his friends and customers that he had me doing the bookkeeping because he could never trust another person not to steal, and at least if I stole from the business, I would be stealing for our family. I not only didn't like what I was doing, but I also disliked working with him. He didn't care that I didn't like what I was doing. Sometimes, I would tell him that if I had to work, I'd rather do something I enjoyed, like studying to be a nutrition and fitness coach. He discouraged it and said I needed to do this for the success of our family. He said whatever he could to make me feel guilty and do what he asked. He made me feel like if I didn't do this for us, I would be the reason it would all fall apart. He continued to say that the business and our family would fail miserably if I didn't do the bookkeeping. He needed me to work with him to control my time and what I was doing and to prevent me from earning income.

I had grown to loathe him because of all he was saying and doing. I had planned to leave after Harlow finished college but realized there was no way I could stay that long and would go when she started. I never once changed my mind. Of course, I would have liked to leave him earlier, but I stayed because I felt it was best for Harlow. Besides threatening that he would take her away from me, he also threatened that if I ever left, everything was his, and nothing was mine, so I could leave with nothing. He said that during our entire marriage. I took his threats seriously because I knew and, at the same time, didn't know what he was capable of. I felt his evil. It was at least a consolation that we were doing well financially. Almost immediately after we got married, he bought me a BMW (of course, in his name and part of his love-bombing), and then, through the years, I also drove nice Mercedes'. When I got my first Mercedes, it was the car of the year. It was hot and fast, and I said it was the most beautiful car on the road. He liked people thinking we were doing well, so when I got that Mercedes, I knew it was so he looked good. I was fine with that.

Throughout our marriage, he would name-drop wealthy or successful friends, what they had, and what we had. There would be times he talked to a stranger and told them who our friends were, the cars we drove, our travels, our business, and every room in our house. I would get so uncomfortable and embarrassed by it. Occasionally, he talked about his parents' wealthy friends and almost seemed to want our lives to be like theirs. He kept mentioning that they owned a business together, and the husband ran the company while the wife did the bookkeeping, just like us. He had us only use cloth napkins, real plates, and silverware, and would be mortified if I wanted to eat using paper. I wonder if that rich couple did all of these things. He also wanted particular items that I also wonder came from them. He wanted a Remington bronze statue of a cowboy, along with other collectibles like Armani statues and Waterford crystal. He wanted his mother's China, crystal, and silver, and we started collecting wine. He also bought me certain jewelry pieces and gifts that seemed more like status symbols than presents from a husband who loved me.

We had many friends in our neighborhood. I would consider Sue Ellen and Dan as our best friends. We hung out a lot with our neighbors. Besides them, there were Sharon and Len and Deidra and Bill. The guys would go golfing, and the girls played Bunko. Sue Ellen, Sharon, and

I had close birthdays, and we usually celebrated together, once during a hurricane. Sue Ellen and Dan would watch Harlow regularly, they loved her, and she loved them. It was adorable that she called them Sue See and Big Dan. When Sue Ellen was pregnant, I was so excited for them, and they would make wonderful parents. I told her that whatever she needed, I would be there for her because I appreciated how much she was there for me. When I would go to Bunko, I noticed when I got home that Dennis treated me differently. It seemed like he was pouting, quiet towards me, and would usually already be in bed. It got to the point that I didn't even want to go anymore because I didn't want him to treat me that way. So, I quit and told him it was because the girls were gossiping, and I didn't want any part. Any time it would be brought up, that was the story I stuck to. It made me sad that I had to give it up. I didn't realize that the silent treatment was to punish me and to change my behavior. He wanted me to give up Bunko as part of isolation and because he didn't want me to do anything that made me happy, especially with other women.

We had Harlow's fifth birthday party at a park and had many kids, their parents, and our families. After the party, we received a call from Kip that her husband Tim had a heart attack at his softball game. She called back later to update us and said he didn't make it. We were stunned and were there for her for whatever she needed. I cried and prayed for her for years. Dennis took it upon himself to tell me that since he was a Christian man, it was his duty to help her get her finances in order and do things a man would do for her. He even told me his Christian duty was to take her out occasionally since she no longer had a husband. He said he would take her on friend's "dates." I thought it was odd, but I grew up Catholic and wasn't sure if other denominations did things differently. So, I chose to accept it. If nothing else, I already knew he was judgmental and self-righteous, so I trusted he wouldn't cheat on me. He would say that he grew up avoiding the appearance of evil and always did everything as if Jesus came back and would he approve of what he was doing. I kept going on playdates with her and our kids, but at some point, she backed off from me. Dennis said she had a huge support group and that I shouldn't worry about our friendship anymore (huge red flag I didn't see). I was hurt but had to understand as she continued to deal with her husband's death. Now I wonder if she had feelings for Dennis and was ashamed to continue our friendship. I wondered if they had an emotional relationship or if anything else had happened. One thing that always bothered me after Kip's husband died was when Dennis was helping her with her finances, she continually said that she recommended to everyone that they should have a will. Dennis would always dodge preparing a will, almost like it would give up some of his control. I would ask him about it, and he always had an excuse to put it off. Other people even advised us to prepare one, but we never had one. Once, he was pressured into doing it by our accountant, and we started drafting it; he never followed through, even though he was the executor of his parent's will and a friend's will.

Towards the holidays that year, our neighborhood had a holiday party. I went home early to take care of Harlow, and Dennis stayed. When he got home, he said he defended my honor, but Sue Ellen called me shitty for calling the police on a new neighbor that had very loud parties, many continued very late into the night, and it would affect Harlow's sleep. He said a few times that he defended my honor. I was confused and hurt that she would say something like that about me, so I went to talk to her the next day, and when I mentioned I was there to discuss what she said the night before, she seemed to dismiss it. I told her I guess we weren't friends anymore. I stopped seeing her days before her son was born and was so sad about it. Dennis said he wanted to grab a beer with Dan and told me he called him. He claimed Dan didn't want to get in the middle of it but changed it later to Dan saying he knew how I was, and Dennis had to agree with him. Dennis also said Deidra and Bill agreed with Sue Ellen, so we wouldn't see them as friends anymore. Throughout the rest of our marriage, each time he "lectured" me, he brought up how Sue Ellen thought I was shitty; Dan said, "You know how your wife is," and that Dennis had to agree because he knows how I am, and Deidra and Bill were right there with everyone. Every time he said that he was stabbing a knife into my heart. Remember this story because it will come up again later.

After that, we started hanging out more with a gay couple across the street from us, Wayne and Ronald, and became very close with them. They were Harlow's Tooth Fairy, which was incredibly sweet! We went there for Friday happy hours and holidays. Dennis was closer to them because he wanted to do business with Ronald's company, and I was okay with that. I had Harlow to take care of, and that was definitely my priority. He and they joked that Dennis was just another gay hanging out with them. There were always many people at their house, and it was fun. At first, Sharon and Len participated regularly, but then Wayne decided he didn't like Sharon for a trivial reason, so not only did Wayne and Ronald stop inviting them to their house, but Dennis had us back off from them as well. Ronald loved NASCAR racing and would go to some of the races, and was good friends with some NASCAR people. Dennis hated NASCAR and would say it was white trash, although he was perfectly fine hanging out with those extremely wealthy people. He knew I used to like NASCAR and enjoyed reminding me that I used to be white trash. He never said to Ronald or anyone in that group that he hated it, but he voiced his opinion when he was in a group that didn't like it. It hurt when he put down things I used to or currently liked to do.

We also had friends through Harlow's school. I was always happy to have friends, even if it was just couples going out together. One night, when we were on our way out for a date night, and no one was available to go out with us, he told me it wouldn't be enjoyable without another couple. His saying that to me hurt so much that I started crying and asked to go home. That was such a hateful thing to say to your wife. He didn't care what he said and would say that he spoke in facts and truths and that feelings didn't matter and weren't the truth. He said that as a strategy to make me believe he was truthful and to invalidate my emotions. He killed two birds with one stone with that statement. I don't even know how many times he lied to me. I would like to know all of the lies I still don't know about so I can continue putting the puzzle pieces together. I also believe that feelings are the backbone of a relationship. Any 'feelings' he had were fabrications, just more lies.

He told me about his guy friends when they cheated in their marriages or relationships. There were many. I always wondered why he remained friends when he knew his friends were not only being unfaithful but sinning since he was such a Christian man. In his telling me that information, the biggest cheater was his childhood best friend, Stevie. Stevie was Harlow's Godfather. Had I known back then, I would not have approved him as a possible guardian for our daughter, although it may have been made up since he was lying about so much. Before Dennis told me about his cheating, he would tell me he grew up in the church with him and would be a good father figure. I think now that he told me about all the other guys' cheating to throw himself off of the scent. He would accuse me of cheating on him the entire time we were married, so I'm pretty sure he was cheating. He used his fake Christian reputation and projecting to lead me to believe he was faithful and would repeat that he would never do anything that would appear evil if Jesus stood right next to him. It was funny because he could have an excuse for a man who cheated, but if a woman cheated, he would flip his lid. Many friends lived in this neighborhood, and he told me some wives were cheating. Dennis would be livid and couldn't stand any of them. I avoided any invitations to go out with those girls unless it was as couples. With one of our closest couple friends in that neighborhood, Dennis told me Janice had been cheating on Blake and was caught several times. Dennis said he consoled him several times, but I was confused she never once said anything to me. Dennis said she got caught and confessed to Blake that she had met the love of her life and was leaving him. Because from what Dennis told me, I did not hesitate to give up my friendship with her, just like Dennis wanted. We watched all of the seasons of The Americans. When one of the FBI characters was cheating on his wife with a Russian informant and had an apartment for her, his wife knew he was cheating. They would fight about it often. When she decided to leave him, she moved in with another man she met through support group meetings. The Russian informant was shipped back to Russia, and the FBI agent finally realized what he had done to his wife. He apologized to her and called himself an asshole. Dennis physically jumped up and yelled at the TV, "You weren't an asshole; she was doing the same thing." She left him because he was cheating, but he had to yell at the TV to defend the husband! I never once considered cheating on Dennis, even though I was unhappy most of our 19-year marriage and didn't love him. My concern wasn't for myself but for our daughter's well-being. I wonder if he wanted me to cheat on him, so he could validate and blame his behavior on me. Because of his accusations, I was afraid to talk to men. If a man said something to me at the gas pump, grocery store, gym, or anywhere, I was mortified because I didn't want to be falsely accused. One time, we were at a dance club with Stevie and Melony, and Dennis went to the bathroom while I was dancing with Melony. A guy started dancing with me, and I leaned over (because the music was extremely loud) to tell him I was married and had a child. Dennis walked up at that moment and accused me of being inappropriate. I tried to explain, and he wouldn't believe me. He interrogated and accused me, and at that time, I didn't even know he was gaslighting me, so I was always confused, and he made sure to twist my words and use them against me. If while explaining, my story changed even a bit, if I remembered more of what happened, he would say I was lying because I was changing my story. He made me apologize to Stevie and Melony (in tears) for ruining the evening and humiliating him. I knew I didn't do anything wrong, but he obligated me to apologize to make me look guilty. I was so upset and felt helpless and afraid. When Harlow was in school, she had a friend whose mother had passed away from breast cancer, and we were friends with the dad. I treated him just like I would treat a girlfriend, my daughter's best friend's parent. Pretty quickly after his wife passed away, he was juggling many women. At one point, Dennis accused me of flirting, which was the furthest thing on my mind. I thought it was disgusting to date so many women simultaneously. I treated him nicely and friendly because of our daughters. After that, I was terrified whenever I spoke to avoid getting in trouble or having him mistake my friendliness for flirting. Dennis told me numerous times that guys and girls could not be friends. If a guy was friends with a girl, it was only because he wanted to fuck her. He had so many 'girl' friends; does that mean he wanted to fuck all of them? How many did he actually fuck?

"most harmful abuse sometimes does not look like abuse at all.

Manipulation, insidious insults, conditioning and brainwashing, gaslighting and mentally abusing will hurt a person where it hurts the most, in their soul.

Don't underestimate an abuser's ability to destroy you without ever lifting a finger."

Maria Consiglio

He continued giving me those 'lectures.' Like I said, sometimes these lasted for an hour, and sometimes hours and hours. On more than one occasion, it was spread over an entire weekend. I was nervous on a daily basis, afraid of when the next one was coming. I never knew what was going to set him off. I never knew what he was going to accuse me of, blame me for, who he was going to say didn't like me, or what horrible things he would say about me. Sometimes I found myself holding my breath in fear (which I now know is part of having a panic attack or PTSD). There were many times he would give me the silent treatment, sigh out loud, 'huff and puff,' and I had no idea what he was dreaming up in his head. I knew he was stewing inside about something, but I was so afraid to talk to him about anything, so I would keep my mouth shut with a fake smile. When he gave me the lectures, I couldn't defend myself. He said the reasons why were just excuses. In his eyes and words, I was playing the victim, or the martyr, or just gave excuses. He would repeatedly say I had to own what I did and apologize so he could help me grow, mature, and become a better person. I had to listen no matter what I was trying to do; if I was trying to sleep or getting ready to go somewhere, no matter what, I had to listen and stay there and not walk away and barely say a word. If I tried to walk away or told him I was going somewhere, he would say that meant I didn't want our marriage to work and it would be over (and to walk out the door with nothing). I felt like I was being held hostage (nonviolent physical abuse besides verbal). So many times, I didn't even understand what I did wrong. So many times, he would twist something innocent and normal just to be able to accuse me of something. He also made a point to remind me that I "grew up white trash," was like my mother, was like my sister Madison's dad, and would also say that men always take a beating from their wife or girlfriend's past relationships. He reminded me how many people didn't like me and would mention them by name. If I had enough and got angry or reacted to him, I was called cruel; how dare I yell? This was just a discussion and not an argument. He would make me feel like it was my fault (this was reactive abuse – to get a reaction from me to be then able to blame the entire attack on me). He continually had to "put up with me" and said numerous times that people wanted him to leave me, but he was a Christian man, and it was his duty to help me and not give up on me. He went around and around and around with his words so that at the end, I was so confused and sometimes couldn't even remember what was said. I would question myself all of the time. He would manipulate, gaslight, accuse, blame, project, and make me feel crazy. It was so premeditative, strategic, and calculating. I would remember what a great guy he was when we were dating, and where did that person go? Then I would blame myself, while at the same time, I knew what he was doing was evil, wrong, and also lies. He would say to me he wasn't the boogeyman, but he really was, he really was the boogeyman. He was a narcissist, and what he was doing was abuse, but I didn't know this yet. I started taking notes every now and then when I remembered.

He would ensure I knew everything was always my fault – blame shifting. He would question my memory by saying something and moments later saying he never said it or would say he told me something that he hadn't - gaslighting. Even if I repeated his exact words, he would say he never said it, and he would also say not to put words in his mouth. He used the word 'insane' a lot. He always said I needed counseling but would never admit I was wrong and wouldn't want to hear what a counselor would tell me. He would repeat the same things over and over throughout each lecture. He would also say that, unlike me, he would never hurt Harlow or me. If I had a different opinion from him, he would say opinions don't matter because only the facts and the truth matter, not opinions. If I said that he was trying to control me or that I wasn't allowed to have feelings, he would simply say that wasn't true. He believed and said that everything that came out of his mouth was the truth, so I would believe it, while every word was a lie. He always thought he was right and would say he always makes good decisions and would repeat this often. He would try and prove me wrong so that he could be right. He would argue until I gave up and did this to other people. He would have knock-down, drag-out arguments with people he disagreed with until they gave up, too. If someone disagreed with him, he would attack their character and to others. I used to say to him that "he could out-dick anyone." He actually took it as a compliment. While doing this, he usually threw in one of two minor things he had done wrong in the past, so it appeared like he was normal and humble. In him always being right, there were so many times he argued with our daughter and me about things that shouldn't even matter. She and I had Apple products, and he had Android and other non-Apple products. He constantly put Apple down because we liked them, and he didn't. He would say that everything is black and white and gray didn't exist. There was no compromise. He would jump to conclusions and go to great lengths to prove us wrong. He would google everything. If you said something he disagreed with, he would immediately research it to prove him right. And, if he was wrong and Harlow and I researched it on the internet, he would even say that you could prove or disprove the same thing on the internet with enough research. He magnified himself as being better than the general public while he magnified our faults.

Once, on a guys' trip, he argued with one of his friends. From what he said and others told me, he argued with this friend so viciously that he made him leave the trip when the fight ended and shredded his character. It reminded me of the lectures that he gave to me. They felt like attacks. The other guys on the trip felt bad for the guy who left and remained friends with him, although they hid it from Dennis. Most of Dennis's guy friends recognized you don't argue or disagree with him. And his friends, knowing how judgmental and opinionated he was, continued being friends with him because he also manipulated them

into believing he was the kind of friend that would give you the shirt off his back. From what I know during our relationship, he also did the same thing to a friend who helped us with some computer work, and when we received the bill, Dennis was livid and believed we were being overcharged. He sent this guy an attacking email and shredded his character to his neighbors and friends. He also verbally attacked a couple of our employees and his friend, who lived in another country. I wonder how those people felt when attacked and if they realized what it was. Did they feel his evil, judgment, manipulation, and gaslighting? I wonder how they would feel knowing Dennis did it to me hundreds of times and hundreds of hours throughout our marriage. At least they could defend themselves, argue back, or at least walk away. He regularly gaslighted, intimidated, and invalidated me so much that I didn't know what to say to him daily. I couldn't have an opinion, and if I made the mistake of having one, he put me in place immediately by jumping down my throat. I was confused, in shock, afraid, and didn't know what to feel at any given moment. All I could do was pray and prayed so often every single day.

He started online gambling by playing poker. At first, he was obsessed with it, then lost a bunch of money, enough that he had to confess to me. He said he would never play again. Then he took it back that he would only play friendly games with his buddies as a social function. But then he went to poker rooms and sometimes would be out all night. I wonder if he was playing or doing something else since it would always be overnight. He would also do it when he or we were in Las Vegas. I had no idea if he was telling the truth about his winning or losing. He continually excused his behavior, but I wouldn't dare say to him that excuses weren't allowed!

Harlow recognized how he treated and judged us early, but out of respect for her, I won't go into any detail from her point of view. Her experience is completely different from mine as she was a child and I was a mother and wife. Dennis was a monster behind closed doors, but I couldn't comprehend the damage he was causing because we pretended to be a happy family. I was happy, however, that she was getting a good education at a preparatory school. This also brought status to Dennis, which, of course, he wanted. During this time, we often went out with

Mike and Sarah. They were our 'go-to couple.' After a couple of years, they met another couple, and we also started going out with them. Mike and Sarah also went out without us. That's normal, I had no issue with it. One day, Dennis came to me and said that Sarah didn't like me and didn't want to go out with us anymore (remember this story as well). That contradicted what he had said previously, that he didn't think she liked him, and commented how she was a feminist – which I knew he didn't like. I wonder if part of the reason he would call women feminists was that they could have their own thoughts, feelings, and opinions, which Dennis couldn't accept and needed to put down to make sure he kept me in line. I also think he was jealous and felt threatened by the other guy friend, who was younger and more successful.

Whenever he 'lectured' me, he would remind me of all the people who didn't like me. "You know how Sarah and Mike stopped going out with us because she didn't like you, and you remember Sue Ellen and Dan and how she said you were shitty, and Dan said, you know how your wife is, and I have to agree with him – I know how my wife is, and Deidra and Bill were right there with them and Bette wanted to throw you away and I begged her to give you a chance." He would go on and on and on to tell me who didn't like me, over and over and over again for hours, as well as call me a victim and tell me what a bad person I was, how no one liked me, and everyone liked him, and I needed to be a better wife and mother. He didn't like that I wouldn't work for our company full-time and said I didn't do enough to help our family. It didn't matter what the subject was, I was put down, and it would last for hours. He would read into my words and make assumptions, but I wasn't allowed to comment on his, and if I did, he would say that's not what he said or don't change his words. There was neither my opinion nor his opinion, I either believed in what he said, or he accused me of being against him, not trusting him, or not having faith in him. He said we didn't have a marriage if I didn't trust him. I had no choice but to trust him or pretend because of his threatening consequences. No one is perfect, and we all make mistakes. Still, he told me that once you become an adult, you should automatically know how to make good decisions consistently, and he claimed he always made good decisions; that was also why I needed to trust him because he said I didn't know

69

how to make good decisions. He continued saying he avoided the appearance of evil and that if Jesus stood right next to him, he would approve. He had to remind me of things I was ashamed of in my past. I would ask him why he was doing this and why he was constantly confronting me about something. His answer to that was that it wasn't a confrontation but a conversation. After he was done lecturing, blaming, accusing, and confronting me for hours, he hugged me, told me he loved me, seemed as though everything was fine, was in a good mood, and then suggested doing something fun. His demeanor changed in an instant. I would be left in shock and confusion and felt so broken.

When we would go out with others, he would do or say something that put me in a bad mood, so I wouldn't have that great of time, and so others would think I wasn't nice. He didn't want me to have a good time, just him. It irritated him if I had too good of a time unless he was trying to impress someone or if it fits his agenda. He wanted others to see him happy and in a good mood socializing and wanted them to see me grumpy and quiet. He wanted others to like him and not like me. He also didn't want me to get too close to anyone, which was a threat to him, and he had to eliminate that person. Once, we were on the way to a grand opening party for a restaurant, and he reminded me that no one wanted to be around me and made me cry. I wanted to go home, and he said some things to cheer me up. He didn't want me to have a good time, but once I started crying, he had to do something to stop it so we could still go to the event. I fought back the tears and wanted to cry the entire time we were there, and I even went into the bathroom to cry at least a couple of times. I had to hide my pain from him and everyone else. I had the fake smile on my face, and I felt defeated and hurt. I felt myself stop liking and doing things, almost like I was afraid of liking them. If I liked something he liked, he would obsess and try to force me to do it more than I wanted. If I liked something he disliked, it was put down. So, I didn't want to do or like anything. The one thing I always enjoyed was going out to dinner on Friday and Saturday nights. Almost every other meal during the week, I made myself, so it was nice and relaxing to go out and having someone else cook for me. I wouldn't let him take that away from me, but it didn't stop Dennis from constantly complaining about taking me out because he went all the time with his buddies, plus he didn't want to see me happy. When we walked into a restaurant and they were on a wait, he would want to leave immediately and say something nasty to the hostess. So many times, we would leave place after place when he didn't feel like waiting. I wonder now if it was because I was excited to be at those restaurants but also because it's a distinct trait of narcissism to be mean to people in the service industry and be above waiting for a table.

Once, we were at the 50th birthday of one of our neighbors at her house. A lot of our gay friends were there. We all were having a great time until the dancing started and I was dancing with one of the guys. I was having fun and laughing, and then Dennis decided he was leaving. He acted mad at me but said he was tired and wanted to go home and insisted I stay. I knew what that meant – I was in trouble, so I left soon after that. When I got home, he was in bed, gave me the silent treatment, sulked, and sighed. When my stepdad's niece got married, Harlow was about 8, and she and I were in the wedding, as well as Harlow's cousins, Jenny and Zander. Leading up to the wedding, Dennis seemed fine. But, at the wedding, he was anything but happy. He was in a bad mood the entire time, especially at the reception, because I was sitting with the wedding party. Then, there was a lot of dancing, and I was having fun with the other bridesmaids, which annoyed him. He decided to leave. When I got home, again, he was in bed and giving me the silent treatment, sulked and sighed. He just couldn't be happy that I was having a good time. When Harlow and I were at the beach with Harlow's friend, Kerri, it was so much more fun when the guys weren't there staying at their condo. A few times when Dennis, Kerri's dad, Joe, and his new girlfriend, Lana, also went to the beach, I tried having fun anyway. We couples would go out later to a bar and dance. Lana and I had so much fun dancing and would laugh and have a good time. When that happened a few times, according to Dennis, Lana told Joe that she didn't like me and didn't want to go out with me anymore, that I said something to her she didn't like. So, I texted her about it and apologized if I said something that offended her. She responded that she had no idea what I was talking about. I told her Dennis said Joe told him, and she answered that it never happened. I brought it up to Dennis, and he said she wouldn't tell me and was lying, but I had to believe him. So, after that, we rarely saw them anymore, but Dennis could keep his friendship with Joe. That happened a lot – he could keep the friendship with the guy, but we couldn't be friends as couples anymore. At this point, I guessed he didn't like me dancing. For each new person he said didn't like me, it took an even greater toll on me. As much as I caught on that he was making it up, I couldn't shake the feeling that maybe I wasn't liked, and he was right because I heard it so many times for so many years. As usual, I was confused and hurt. I also started wondering what Dennis said to them when we stopped going out as couples since I was somewhat clued in on his lying to me, so what was he lying to them about me? Don't get me wrong, it wasn't always horrible; we would have fun times, nice things, a nice house, and travel. Also, owning a business had perks because I didn't work full-time and took off when needed. I also drove an amazing car. Harlow got to go to a great school and was always involved in cool extra-curricular activities. What ruined all these things is that I never knew when he would strike, which made every day stressful, waiting for the next lecture or unkind words woven through the good times.

In 2006, we turned 40, and Dennis suggested we take a trip to California to Napa Valley, Pebble Beach, and San Francisco. I thought that was great. He made all the arrangements, and I should have known he had an ulterior motive. He wanted to be able to golf at a Pebble Beach course, and we stayed at a ridiculously high-priced hotel on the property so he would be able to play a round at Spanish Bay. During this trip and the enormous hotel bill he chose, he complained about everything I wanted to spend money on. When we were in Carmel shopping, he guilted me into not buying anything for myself. When I decided to purchase a silver leather jacket (which I still have), he made me give it to him to give to me for my actual birthday, even though he spent so much more on his rounds of golf. He also knew I didn't like driving in a convertible car because I have long hair, and it would get really messy, especially with it being windy, chilly, and damp. He didn't care. He said he was renting it for us and that I should be grateful and like it because he was doing it for 'us.' It was like he wanted to ruin the trip for me and make sure I didn't have a good time. I really enjoyed the vacation, but it did cause tension, and he reminded me for the rest of our marriage that it was my fault and that I ruined the entire trip. Not long after, he even purchased a convertible BMW, and as he said with the rental, he bought it for 'us' to enjoy, and I needed to enjoy it for the good of our family. He didn't care that I didn't like convertibles and was trying to force me to like them because he said so. Whenever he wanted to put the top down when I was in the car, it created tension, and he did it purposefully. He liked breaking down my boundaries by getting me to do things I didn't like by saying it was for our family or us.

When I started having issues with my menstrual cycle, I decided it was time to stop taking the pill and do something permanent (considering I would never have another child with him). I asked him if he would get a vasectomy, and he flat-out said there was no way he would ever do that. I started researching my options, and I had an IUD for a year, but it didn't work. I was planning on getting my tubes tied and a procedure to stop my continued bleeding. He was all for it, even though it was major surgery. Once I told him it would be thousands of dollars for me to get my tubes tied and only hundreds for the vasectomy, he decided to do it because of money (and so many of his guy friends already had it done). He cared more about money than me and my health.

Dennis made snide remarks to me all of the time. Once when I was driving his SUV and the brakes wouldn't work, he commented that it was a user error. He belittled what I did each morning to prepare Harlow for school and said what took me an hour only took him 7 minutes. When I had a meeting, and he was taking her to dinner, he said it would be better because I wasn't there making a production. Once, when one of our customers owed money on three different invoices, he said that because of the way I received their previous check, he would have to write a doctoral thesis to explain it to them. He continually said I was only doing league minimum and that I didn't do anything more than everyone else "in the world." He said I wouldn't be marketable much longer if I left him, so he knew I wouldn't leave. He also threatened that I wouldn't get much in the divorce if I left. Everything was his, nothing was mine, and if I left, I needed to leave with nothing. When he referred to his dad being in a wheelchair, he said he couldn't wait to be old and in a wheelchair so I could take care of him. He asked me to rub or scratch his back most nights, and it was almost always when I finally sat down to relax. There were even times he wanted me to rub his hands or knees. Those confused me because he could rub his own knees more effectively because he would know where it was needed, and if he wanted a hand rubbed, he could rub it with his other hand. It was like he was purposefully trying to inconvenience me. Once when we had friends over to our house for dinner, they liked Mustangs, and I mentioned I had a few when I was younger. Under Dennis's breath, he said, "White trash." When Harlow was a baby, I told Dennis I wanted life insurance on myself for her, and he laughed, saying I was a liability and not an asset. When he said I was pretty a lot of the time, he would also add, "Even though you have a big nose." If I even had a tiny bit of garlic, he'd make a nasty face towards me and say I reeked. He would talk someone else up as he put me down, so I would compare that person to me (triangulation). When he told me I wasn't liked, he added that he was well-liked.

We enjoyed going to charity events and galas. I LOVED (and still love) dressing up. We went to a gala with our friends Bette and Joe. They also invited 3 other couples. One of the items up for auction was a trip to the Bahamas, using someone's plane, house, and boat. We all bid on it together and won the trip. One couple couldn't go, so it was 4 couples, us, Bette and Joe, and new friends through them, Skye and Mike, and Otto and Petra. We had much fun on that trip, but Dennis went entirely out of his way to impress everyone, especially Otto. At one point, they had a kayak race, which was ridiculous and unnecessary. Nevertheless, we all became friends, and the four couples saw each other when we could get together. Bette, Mike, and Otto were all in the hospitality field. They were also fairly wealthy and successful, which was a big motivation for Dennis wanting to be friends. Dennis always had an agenda when he became 'best friends' with someone. They had to serve a purpose in his life. He made sure to have certain people in his life by what they brought to the table: an accountant, an attorney, a dentist, a jeweler, timeshare and hotel executives, the wealthy, etc. He also had certain friends who were only around to be his minions, for attention, or for his agenda. When I was friends with someone whom he didn't think they had value, he would ask what they brought to the table and put them down if they didn't have anything of use to him. He actually said he liked having friends who were "CEOs and Captains of Industry!" He also gaslighted his friends by telling them he would never ask to do business with friends or make money off them to make himself look humble, leading many of them to do business with him. Let's just say he makes an incredible amount of profits from the friends he does business with.

He liked that Bette and Joe, Skye and Mike, and Petra and Otto traveled extensively and that Otto and Petra were from France and had a house there. When Harlow was 10, they invited her to stay at their home in France, and later I joined Petra, their kids, and Harlow. We later met Dennis and Otto in Paris. The last night before we met the guys, I felt sick and was sick the entire Paris portion of the trip with a food-born-bacteria. It was disappointing, but I tried to make the best of it. It was very apparent Dennis was not sympathetic to how I felt and didn't do much to take care of me. I muscled through it as best as possible during the day, and at night, I would stay back at the hotel while Dennis took Harlow for dinner. Finally, I got medicine to kill the bacteria, but it was one of the worst health experiences in my life. In many European cultures, children can drink at their parents' discretion. Before I joined Petra and the kids, she allowed Harlow to drink cider, which is alcoholic. We then adopted that it was okay on occasion. Every now and then, we allowed Harlow to have a small portion of wine. I was okay with adopting this philosophy because it wasn't a forbidden fruit. Dennis seemed okay with it because our friends were okay with it but would go back and forth. If we were with people who were okay with it, he was okay, and if we were with people who weren't okay with it, it was either a secret or he blamed me

2014 was a huge travel year. We went skiing in Utah, Rome for Skye's 50th birthday, Iceland for a wedding, and a long trip to Europe in the summer, going to France, Switzerland, and Italy. Before going to Rome, Dennis wanted to address his thinning hair and decided to get hair plugs. When I was 45, he allowed me to have some plastic surgery he called my "45,000-mile tune-up," so I was totally fine with him wanting to do something for self-improvement to make him feel better about himself, even though it cost $12,500 for just hair plugs. Around the time he was to get this done, his best friend Stevie's dad died. Dennis told Stevie he was sick and couldn't help or see him with the arrangements. He tried to get Stevie to hold off with the funeral and to have a celebration of life at a later date. He was mortified about someone (even his best friend) finding out he was doing this. He also told our office that he was helping Stevie with his dad's death so they didn't miss him not coming in. I found this disgusting and deceiving, but I kept my mouth shut and was sworn to secrecy. I couldn't understand why he had to keep it a secret, especially considering Stevie's dad had died. He said he couldn't tell anyone because he didn't want to be judged or made fun of. For goodness sake, Stevie was bald, so I'm sure he would have understood! After trying so hard to get Stevie to move a service to a later date, the funeral service was set. It wasn't long enough after the procedure for his hair to grow out, so he was extremely nervous and paranoid that someone would notice. He made an excuse that he got a buzz cut and kept asking me if his plugs were noticeable that day. On another note, when I had my plastic surgery, Dennis asked me what feature I liked the least. I told him it was the bags under my eyes. It is genetic and always bothered me. He used this information to tell me and others that he would never allow me to get my eyes done. He only wanted to know so he could use it in his abuse; the one thing that bothered me the most was never going to be fixed to make me feel bad about it. Also, I believe the only reason I was allowed to have plastic surgery in the first place is that it was pretty typical for many of our friends, and if he didn't let me, it would make him look bad.

The Rome trip for Skye's 50th birthday was my favorite trip I'd ever been on. Italy was beautiful, charming, and historic, and I loved the food. Skye and Mike were incredible hosts! We stayed at the Rome Cavalieri Hotel, which was gorgeous and luxurious and overlooks the Vatican. Not only did we have a private tour of the Vatican, but we also went to a winery, Florence, and to a very charming little town called Orvieto. If I remember correctly, about 15 of us were on this trip, and everyone had a fantastic time. I love Skye very much and appreciated celebrating with her. We went to Iceland for our friends' wedding. What a beautiful country! I loved not only our friends but both of their families. Everyone was so nice, and the wedding was one of the most charming I'd ever attended. The family has a chapel on their property, where the wedding was held. It was wonderful. We knew them through Dennis's first wife, who was related as a cousin (although she oddly was not invited – weirdly, Dennis was closer to her family than she was – hmmm). While we were there for the wedding, Dennis treated me poorly the entire trip. He gave me the silent treatment, pouted, and sighed. It made the whole trip stressful and tense. He blamed me for this and said the whole trip that I was cruel to him ("cruel" was definitely one of the main words he used to describe me). He kept going on walks with the groom to smear, blame-shift, and scapegoat. I tried my best to pretend I was happy and had my plastic smile on my face, while I felt like crying the entire time and did cry several times in private. I believe he acted this way because he wanted to ensure he was well-liked, and I wasn't. He knew these people for a very long time and couldn't have them think highly of me. I believe he was jealous of my spirit (even though he already took half of it away from me), and if I was liked, it threatened him.

Our Europe trip was nice but long. We stopped in Berlin during our layover, and then over the next few weeks, we went to France, Switzerland, and Italy. I loved the places we visited, the food we ate, and the friends we traveled with. It didn't stop my anxiety traveling for so long with Dennis; at one point, Petra witnessed how he treated me. I could tell she felt sympathy, but Otto put her down regularly, so it wasn't too unusual for her. A few other stressful incidents in front of our friends added to my anxiety and unhappiness. When we were at Otto and Petra's house in France, the girls were heading to Paris, and the guys were going on a golf trip. Dennis had rented a car that I was to return to Paris. Petra decided she didn't want to drive to Paris and wanted to take the train instead. Dennis took me aside and was furious that she was acting spoiled because we would not only have to pay a huge penalty fee to return the car to a different location, but it would also cost hundreds of dollars more to buy train tickets. He already had me fear to spend on this trip, and I tried to talk to Petra to get her to change her mind. Otto was angry with her and upset her enough to cry, and my voicing our concerns added to it. Dennis then pretended in front of everyone that he disagreed with me, blamed me for the entire thing, and even got mad at me! Most vacations with Dennis were equally stressful and unrestful because he needed to pack as much into them as possible, with us traveling overnight, getting up early, and going to bed late. I'm sure it was, so the trip was less enjoyable on purpose. I also knew that my work piled up at the office every day we were gone. I asked during this trip if the customer service rep could help, but when Dennis found out, he stopped most of it. On our way home from one of our trips, on the plane, Dennis's abuse escalated to physical violence. The airline wanted to take my carry-on luggage, but I didn't have a lock for it and it contained all of our valuables. I kept asking the flight attendant if I could please keep it because of those reasons, and Dennis told me to stop because I was embarrassing him and shoved me twice. I looked him right in the eye and told him I'd leave him if he ever touched me again. Harlow was sitting on the other side of me, and I can't remember if she noticed any of it.

Mike's (of Mike and Skye's) birthday is the day after mine, and we have celebrated together a few times. 2014, we celebrated at their house while Harlow was at a friend's. When we got home, all the lights in the house were on, and we discovered our house had been robbed. Most of what they took were Dennis's watches he had collected and a watch we were holding for Mike's company that Dennis sold him worth over $20,000. Because it was a business claim taken from our home, it was not covered by either insurance. Earlier that week, I went to lunch with Bette, Skye, and Petra, as we would for each of our birthdays. When I was about to leave for lunch, Dennis said he needed me to drop the watch off at Mike's office. If I said yes, I would be at least 20 minutes late for my birthday lunch, so I told him I could take it afterward. He said no, I had to do it before lunch, so the watch didn't sit in my car. I told him I would bring it in, and again he said no. So, I told him I couldn't do it. He was extremely annoyed with me. I knew he just wanted to inconvenience me and take away some of the time with my friends, especially because it was my birthday celebration. Because he brought the watch home with him and set it on the kitchen counter (instead of locking it in our full-size safe), it was stolen. Weeks later, he blamed me and made me apologize to him, and would also bring it up during 'lectures.' In the back of my mind then, and even now, I recognize he is a schemer, liar, and is capable of anything, and I wonder if he set it up to punish me for not taking the watch as he asked. Besides it, most of what was taken were his watches, my iPad, and Harlow's laptop. They never discovered who did it, but at one point, the police found a couple of his watches and pieces of clothing, and my iPad was recovered. It was unfortunate that it even came into my mind that he could do such a thing.

Up to this point, our business ran very well and successfully, and we had accumulated a good amount of money in the business bank account, which was around $200,000. Dennis hired Bette and Joe's daughter, Hope, because he was sure they would hook her up with many of their contacts, and she would make us a lot of money while looking like a hero. We had only paid salespeople commission only but agreed to pay her a salary. It was way more than we could afford, but he was so sure her sales would be huge for the company and didn't care that I was concerned. Then, he decided to hire Otto's oldest son's girlfriend, Yvonne (again to be a hero), at a salary not long after hiring Hope and didn't care about my concerns. Let's say that it didn't work out, and the business suffered completely. Most of the money in the business was gone, and sometimes I feared making payroll. When Hope came to work with us, she noticed I wasn't myself. I apologized to her. I told her how much I hated working with Dennis and that I was a completely different person when I was at work. The moment I pulled up to the office, my demeanor completely changed, like I was going to prison (from the prison at home to the prison at work). I couldn't help how I acted and how I treated everyone. I felt horrible and would try to be nice, but I couldn't help but resent being there every minute. I felt awful about it and still wish I could apologize. Hope saw how he treated me at work. She also identified that he was a male chauvinist and often treated her and Yvonne with disrespect. Yvonne was one of our employees that he verbally attacked and made cry when he didn't agree with her on something, and she tried to defend herself. One day, she fainted in the office, and Dennis didn't even try to help her. It reminded me when shelves and heavy binders from above my desk came crashing down on my head, and it was bleeding; he had his assistant take me to the emergency room instead of him. When his assistant Amy worked with us, he also wanted to be her hero because her family couldn't afford for her to attend college. He took it upon himself for us to pay for her four-year degree and didn't even ask me if it was okay. He said she could study whatever she wanted, and he expected her to give him at least a few months' notice when she graduated and would finally leave. It's funny because she gave her two weeks' notice to take another job the semester before graduating. I thought it was a slap in the face. Also, I know she felt Dennis was judgmental because she had gotten a tattoo and kept it secret from him because she knew how he judged people with tattoos. She showed me and asked me not to tell him.

After the robbery, he wanted to move out of our neighborhood, and I agreed. He was so paranoid that he wanted to live in a high-rise condo, luxury, with a doorman and security. We looked at a very expensive condo for what we would be getting, which also needed a complete renovation, plus monthly condo dues of about $1,700. I told him that we could afford a much nicer house instead. So, he started researching houses on the internet and found one downtown. When we went to look at this house, he was obsessed with it immediately. We went to look at it with our friend Russ. Dennis said he loved the house and wanted to buy it, disregarding me. It was a very old historic house, built in 1919, and had a lot of charm, but it needed tremendous work. I turned to Russ, who had many concerns, and he would talk to Dennis about the possible money pit it could become. Dennis didn't listen to a word; he was in love with the house and said he would put in an offer on it. He didn't ask me how I felt about the house or if I even liked it. He said he loved the house, and my answer to that was that I knew he was. Luckily, he offered list price for the house, stipulating that they would fix any work an inspector said it needed at their expense. They agreed. Even though all the repairs were done, including the house being tented for termites, it still needed much renovation and updating. I knew I would only be in the house for a few years before leaving him, so I didn't resist. When I went to lunch with Bette, Skye, and Petra, I did say I liked the house but that it wasn't my dream home, and Dennis and Harlow liked it much more than I did. Before we moved, Dennis took the deal off the table because he disagreed with the repairs that needed to be done. Then he told me that he really took the deal off the table to see if I liked the house. He had a scheme that we parked at the house and walked to dinner to see if I liked that lifestyle. He said both Skye and Otto called him to tell him I hated the house and not to buy it. I called Skye and thanked her for caring enough about me to do that. She had no idea what I was talking about and said she never called him. I told him what she said, and he told me she was lying, and I had to believe him or our marriage was over. I told him I believed him, but I really didn't. He had done this enough times that I no longer trusted him. Even though he let me keep my friendship with her because of her and Mike's status (a CEO and captain of industry!), it didn't stop him from trying to ruin it on several other occasions. He would remind me how she lied, as I knew he was lying. I was annoyed with Petra. I felt like she tattled on me to Otto. It wasn't the first time I said something to her that got back to Otto, that got back to Dennis. I was mad at her, but after a while, I realized she was not only naïve, but the things that she told Otto were relatively normal and innocent, and of course, Dennis would turn into something ugly. He twisted whatever he felt like to be able to confront, lecture, accuse, and blame. We moved into the house, and I grew to love its charm and having that downtown walking lifestyle. We updated a few things in the house, but Dennis had so many crazy ideas I thought were very tacky and expensive, and I was thankful they never happened. Because we had a game room with a second kitchen, he did spend $5,000 filling up those cabinets with liquor! He insisted that we have any type of liquor possible for anyone coming over. That fit his agenda to be excessive and impressive.

Russ passed away suddenly from an aggressive cancer just before we moved. Dennis took it upon himself to help his widow, Jenny. He had to be her hero, just like with Kip (and all the others – it was definitely showing a pattern with women other than the two he was supposed to love the most). He helped her sell her house and get her finances in order. He was annoyed when she decided where to move without his input, which seemed suspicious. He told me that very soon after Russ passed away, he told Jenny not to feel guilty when she was ready to date. In the timing, it was highly inappropriate and made me again suspicious. I thought he secretly saw Kip on a social level and was pretty sure he was doing the same with Jenny. Jenny was diagnosed with breast cancer about a year before all of this. Dennis decided to make a meal to bring to their house (hero?). I didn't like him in the kitchen because he didn't practice good hygiene. He didn't wash his hands and didn't wash produce. He refused and would say he knew what he was doing, but he made this meal alone while I was busy with Harlow. On the way to Jenny and Russ's house, Dennis wanted to stop at the mall to pick up a blazer at Neiman Marcus. When we got to their house, he immediately started setting up the food. I mentioned that he should wash his hands. He replied that his hands were clean. I said we were just at the mall, and since he was serving food, he should wash his hands. He looked at me with an evil look and repeated, "MY HANDS ARE CLEAN!" I was stunned, upset, and disgusted while needing to have that fake smile and pretended I was having a good time while wanting to cry and excused myself a few times to actually cry in the bathroom. I didn't even want to eat the food, but I knew I had no choice. After the meal, I said something to Jenny about how he was treating me and that I planned on leaving him when Harlow went to college. On the way home that night, he verbally attacked me about how cruel I was to him and humiliated him in front of them. That lasted at least a few hours. So, my reminding him to simply wash his hands before serving food led to a verbal attack. I never knew what would set him off, and I became terrified to say anything. I was nervous and anxious about every word that came out of my mouth, so I tried saying as little as possible.

After Russ died, Jenny spent the night at our new house for New Year's Eve because Dennis insisted she was invited to a neighborhood party with us. Was this also triangulation? The next day, we were having our annual New Year's Day party. Dennis opened some pretty expensive wine that night to impress Jenny, and the three of us drank for hours before we went to the party. He liked to be impressive and excessive. At the same time, I was at the point in our relationship that I liked to at least have a buzz at night because I was so miserable. Something happened at the party, and Jenny said something to Dennis, unaware of the events that would result. However, who knew at that point what their relationship was? When we got home and got ready for bed, it was close to 1:30 a.m., and we had about 100 people coming over the next day for our annual New Year's Day party, and I only had one person coming to help me. I always had to cook most of the food, which took about a week before the parties, and I was exhausted. He wanted sex, and I told him no because I needed to get up early. He asked how I felt about having the New Year's Day party. I told him it was a lot of work and wished it wasn't as big. Whether we had any dinner or party at our house, he was obsessed with everything being perfect and excessive, which always resulted in days of extra work for me. He then said we would never have another party at our house. I had reached my point and was okay with it. I felt so burdened about the amount of work that I didn't care anymore. It was all or nothing to him, so I called his bluff, and it would be nothing. I think it was a threat, so I would immediately change my mind. I was so over it. From then on, he constantly reminded me that we couldn't have people over at the house ever again because of me. Whatever! Speaking of New Year's Day, every year we were together, he would say to me on the first day of the year, "You know, next year you'll be........" and say the age I will be the following year. For example, if I were turning 40 that year, he would say the age I would be the next year, 41. It was like he wanted my year to start off negatively. He always claimed it was a joke.

Months later, we were at the dinner table, and he started burping in front of Harlow and me. I asked what he had for lunch, and his reply was just "soup." When I asked if he was at the office, he said a local restaurant but didn't say another word. A couple of days later, that Friday, he went out with a client to happy hour and didn't get home until after 8 p.m. when we already had plans to go out to dinner (It may have been a client – but who knows what kind of 'client/vendor relationship' was going on). He wasn't hungry but took me somewhere so I could eat, and he just got a beer. When discussing his happy hour, I casually asked whom he went to lunch with. Then it poured out of his mouth, "Jenny." He started rambling and said she needed products for her company, and she still kept in touch with Russ's family and was fine at her job. I asked if she's dated, and he said it didn't come up. I knew what a nosy body he was, and it would have absolutely come up. That definitely made me even more suspicious. Why was he trying to be secretive about their lunch? Jenny also backed off from my friendship around this time. Hmmmmmmmm. He had become very secretive about many things. For all of the years he accused me of cheating, I believe he was cheating throughout our marriage. Especially towards the end, he showed so many red flags that he was. He was very secretive with his plans, whom he was texting, and who he was on the phone with. He put a very long passcode on his phone and changed the settings, so when a text came in, it made a noise, but there were no pop-ups of part of the message like it used to be, which is a setting you must change. He started shaving his whole body from his neck to his feet suddenly a couple of years before I left him, even though he knew specifically I had no issue with his body hair – he didn't care. I had already been shaving his back and neck for him almost every week, and now he was shaving his arms, legs, and EVERYWHERE else. I'm all for self-improvement and taking steps to feel good about yourself, but this was definitely way beyond that. He started wearing his fun weekend underwear (that I would get him), cool jeans outfits during the week, and regular underwear on weekends. I would find random loose keys in his pants pockets. There were times I heard him whispering on the phone at home, and when I got close and he heard me coming, he would put his phone down and pretend he was watching TV. If we were together in the car and someone called him on Bluetooth, he seemed paranoid, and the second he answered the phone, he would announce that I was in the car with him. Sometimes, when he got home from work, instead of coming right up to me and kissing me (like we were required to do according to him, or he would get angry and accuse me of withholding love), he would secretly take a shower in the guest bathroom before he came upstairs, or would quickly go straight to the master, saying he needed a quick shower. Again, he continually accused me of cheating throughout the marriage. I read something that some people had said that when their spouse was cheating, their side of the bed smells, and they have to wash their sheets more often. Well, his side of the bed smelled nasty, and I had to clean the sheets and even his pillow more often. I was repulsed and disgusted when he touched me! Maybe subconsciously, I didn't want to catch him cheating because then I would have left him and wouldn't have met my goal, and he would have made good on his threats to take Harlow away from me, along with me having to leave with nothing.

He complained about me spending too much money all the time. I knew that I wasn't; he just wanted to control me financially, even though he would deny it, plus he almost always needed to have something to blame or accuse me of doing. He would say I controlled the money to make it appear (gaslight) like I was. But, as I've stated, he made sure nothing was ever in my name the entire time we were married. I never earned a penny in my name and only paid him what we needed to cover the monthly expenses, and everything else stayed in the business. He made me make spreadsheets of what I spent (once on a debate trip to inconvenience me and the other moms thought it was crazy). Each time, it validated that my spending was in order, but he complained anyway. He was absolutely blame-shifting and gaslighting me. When our local basketball arena opened, he spent over $30,000 per year for the first two or three years it was open for two seats to lead people to believe we had more wealth and status. You could add everything I spent on myself for 19 years, and it wouldn't have added to just that alone. When he had me working for the business, he would guilt me into staying by telling me our business would fail, our family and marriage would fail, and it would have devastating financial consequences for my bad decisions (he used those exact words). He would claim that he didn't need much in his life and that our success was for Harlow and me, and I had the power to make it continue or fail. When I brought up retirement accounts or wanted a paycheck, he claimed we would wait until a few years before retiring to pay me and put money in my retirement account. That was another strategic way of manipulating me not to leave him and continue financial control.

Many years ago, we went to New York and bought fake designer purses. When I used them, I always told people they were fake and actually thought it was fun. I didn't want to act like a fraud and pretend they were real. Dennis wanted me to represent that they were real and would be annoyed if I told someone the truth. He even gaslighted me and guilted me into not wanting real designer purses by telling me I said once that I respected a friend only because she had designer bags. I knew I'd never say anything like that and told him. He was so adamant that I did, so I believed him but was confused by not remembering something that didn't sound like what I'd say. For my 50th birthday gift, I wanted a real Chanel purse. Needless to say, I never got it. He guilted me to buy inexpensive clothes by saying I wore cheap clothes well and knew the value of things because of our industry. I spent the least on myself out of everyone we knew, was always nervous about buying something, and sometimes wouldn't tell him. It was funny when I did buy something, Dennis would comment like, "Did you need that?" or "How much was that?" Then, he would buy something for himself, and usually more. If I bought a shirt, he would order a dozen. He ordered at least a few if I bought a pair of shoes. He was constantly online shopping. I would always catch him on his computer looking at watches, cars, sunglasses, shoes, belts, houses, and trips, and he was obsessive about wanting things, especially status symbols. He rationalized his spending and purchases by giving his items to me to give him as gifts. I had two huge bins filled with things I was holding to give him. He could then say he didn't buy things for himself. When I reminded him of all his purchases, he could say they were gifts, which didn't count. It's funny he always complained when I asked for something as a gift. He only wanted to get me what he wanted to, instead of what I really wanted, while he was doing that exact same thing, except his volume was much higher. He would often make me hand over what I bought myself so he could give it to me as a gift later on. He was very much into dressing himself. Besides having pants in every color of the rainbow, his closet was fuller than mine, he had more shoes than me – over 100 when I left him (I counted), and he was dressed in a way that his outfit had to match his glasses, his belt, his shoes and right down to his watch (with a couple of my friends, we joked that he wore his Garanimals for those who are old enough to know what that is). He had a collection of watches, cufflinks, belts, glasses, etc. I think he had over three dozen pairs of glasses alone. It was ridiculous and excessive, and it felt like he needed to have more than me out of jealousy (maybe he was overcompensating for my purses or jewelry). He spent hours in his closets organizing everything. When we went out somewhere, it would take him longer to get ready than me; he would change his outfit several times and always complained that I was too dressed. He had to look perfect, and he was complaining about my dress! I admit I also had a lot of clothes, but I accumulated mine while he regularly purged and replaced his. He was obsessed with us matching when we went anywhere; our colors always needed to coordinate. He wanted us to match as a couple and a family when we went somewhere together and was insistent.

During High School, Harlow was in the school debate program. I volunteered as a judge and a chaperone and truly loved being a debate mom, loved the kids, and loved taking care of them. Plus, it kept us out of the house. When I went on debate trips, I could be myself and be at ease. It was nice getting to know other parents and enjoying myself without fear. He also didn't know most of them, so I didn't have to worry that he would ruin my friendships with other debate moms. The first time I went on one of the trips was during Valentine's Day weekend, the year all of Boston shut down because of a snowstorm. At one point, because everything was shut down, the kids didn't have food to eat or even water to drink. From that point forward, the first thing I did on trips was to make a run to Target, Walmart, or the local grocery store to ensure we had enough water and snacks for the kids. It made me so happy when the kids were cared for and they appreciated my effort. It was also such a blessing that the debate teacher was so kind and caring towards Harlow; I was so glad she had him in her life.

Since she was a little girl, I tried my best to show Harlow as much love as possible, loved spending time with her and doing things for her. Any time I could make her happy, she deserved it and made me happy. As much as I tried, hoped, and wanted us to be a happy family, one day, she said something to me that changed everything, even how I was her mom. From that moment on, I did and gave her anything I could. She was always taking different lessons, from swimming, ice skating, singing, guitar, dance, etc., to participating in volleyball, track, and debate, and made sure she took fun summer camps. I even loved it when we went to Starbucks, the cupcake place, movies, or Target. I felt our home was like a prison, so it was a pleasure whenever we could be out. When it was just the two of us at home, we liked cooking and watching TopChef and Ellen. We enjoyed spending time with and loving our sweet kitties. We smiled and laughed together, which was priceless instead of fake. One day, I found a letter on the floor in my closet. It said:

Mom,

Thank you so much for everything you do for me. Thank you for always having food in the pantry & fridge, and for having incredible meals prepared every night we eat at home. Thank you for being cool and letting me be myself. Thank you for always making sure I have clean clothes & sheets & towels. Thank you for buying me nice clothes & shoes & books & makeup. Thank you for being so kind, especially on debate trips & just every single day. You mean the world to me and I LOVE YOU

(she drew a heart) Harlow

I felt so loved and it melted my heart, but at the same time it was incredibly sad that I was so afraid of what Dennis would think, I immediately hid it. What I didn't know was he already saw it. Later on, when he brought it up, he was mad and said he was the one who did all of those things. Really? He may have earned the money to pay for all those things, but he had no real love in his heart. Harlow and I always truly loved each other, always did, and I hope always will. During his verbal attacks, Dennis told me that Harlow would abandon me at some point because I was a horrible mother and prevented a relationship between her and him. He also told me she told him I was the most toxic part of her life. So, besides trying to play us against each other, he needed to destroy our love for one another. He was a vulture picking away at our spirits. He was coldhearted and got pleasure from our pain. I would see it in his eyes.

The 'portrait' of our life seemed like a pretty picture. We lived in a lovely house, drove nice cars, owned a business, our child was in a prep school, and we took nice vacations. Dennis made sure the outside of our house always looked pristine to give people the impression that everything was equally pristine on the inside. We always matched as a couple and a family when we went anywhere to provide a false sense of unity. It's funny; when we took actual pictures as a family, all I could see was unhappiness in our eyes and smiles. If I even mentioned to someone a little bit of what was happening behind closed doors, it was unbelievable because they saw a picture of a happy family, and those things don't happen to happy families. Behind our fake happiness and nice things, I felt like I was in prison and was being psychologically tortured and terrorized.

"The worst prison in the world is a home without peace.

Be careful who you marry or fall in love with."

Unknown Author

I found out that Dennis was stalking us on social media, as well as tracking our phone calls, texts, and my emails. On Instagram, he would go into our accounts and see who liked our pictures, then go onto those people's accounts and look at their pictures. Instagram eventually changed its security, so people like him couldn't be social media trolls. He regularly checked my LinkedIn profile and went onto some of my followers' profiles. I was also not allowed to be on Facebook. He said Facebook was a marriage killer and made me agree that we shouldn't have accounts. My cousins asked if I could open one with a fake name to be in contact with them, but he said no. I personally think it was just another way for him to control who I was in contact with. Facebook isn't a marriage killer; untrustworthy people are marriage killers. Abusers are marriage killers.

I continued to keep whatever I could from him. If we were a typical family, and Dennis was a typical husband and father, I wouldn't hesitate to tell him things, but I knew his judgment and blame. He continued to want Harlow's and my relationship to be ruined and blamed me for being a horrible mother. He hated and was so jealous that we were close and of our love for each other. I think that's why many of his verbal attacks concerned her; he would say such awful things. Each day, I had no idea what he would say or do, which created such an atmosphere of stress and uncertainty, and I always felt anxious and heartache. OUR HOME WAS EMOTIONALLY AND MENTALLY UNSAFE.

His tireless quest to hurt me finally broke me down and made me believe that I was a horrible person, a terrible mom to Harlow, and ruined our marriage, so we started seeing a Christian marriage counselor, Mary. While we were there, all Dennis would do the entire time was bash me and blame everything on me, and I could barely get in a word. He trashed me as a mother, wife, and person, and at the same time, he said he had to help me and would marry me all over again. I said in front of Mary that he was saying that to make himself look good, which he, of course, denied and represented he was highly offended. His strategy was to make himself look like a saint and manipulate her. I told Mary in front of Dennis that if I had not been pregnant, I would not have married him in the first place. I told the truth! It was because of that first 'lecture,' but at this time, I didn't realize that it was a verbal attack, so my description didn't label it for what it was. All I knew was that I felt his evil and was terrified of his threats.

"The only reason a narcissist goes to therapy is to manipulate the counselor. POTENT narcissist supply is gained in the attention, empathy and sympathy from a professional who unknowingly supports their abusive façade."

Nova - @novas_narcissistabuse_recovery

He continued making me believe I was a horrible mother. He had us all go to the counselor together, and it was an absolute disaster, just like when I was going with him. He tried so hard to get Mary to believe him, and he manipulated her like a puppet. When I saw Mary alone, I told her the truth about what was going on behind closed doors and finally got her to believe me. She advised me to leave him, but then Dennis would come in and manipulate her into believing him. He was incredibly charming toward her, and I wouldn't doubt Mary had a crush on Dennis, which may be why she believed his bullshit. She was also a Christian Counselor, and I'm sure she couldn't comprehend that evil people in this world use manipulation and a mask of Christianity to hide who they really are. Even though going through this entire experience was disastrous, it was really a blessing I'd learn later.

That Valentine's Day in 2017, he insinuated that I had a boyfriend twice because he couldn't trust me, that I'd kept things from him, and that I couldn't blame him for thinking that way (I wonder whom he was really projecting about?). Then he bashed my friend, Whitney. He didn't like our friendship because she was single and had a great career, which was a double threat to him. Then he said he would teach me how to be a friend. I needed to start with lunch. I said I'd rather do something over the weekend since I didn't really like going to lunch. Usually, I ate lunch at my desk at the office to get my job done to be over with it (plus, I didn't want to eat my lunch with him anymore, so working through was a good excuse). That was wrong, according to him, that I needed to go to lunch because people have things to do over weekends. For my Valentine's gift, he got me sexy nighties (I wonder how many others he bought them for?), and I told him I really didn't want them (the thought of even trying them on disgusted me). He falsely apologized to me and said he wasn't sure if that was what I wanted to be now. He said I had cleavage and that I told him I rocked my jeans. Now that I'm 50, he said again that he wasn't sure if that's what I wanted to be (I had cleavage one day because of a shelf bra and hated cleavage, and a server we knew told me one night that I rocked my jeans – a female server – which was an extremely nice compliment seeing I was put down so much). Then he said he didn't want me to be mad at him for telling me this, but I was too skinny right now, and he didn't know if I was doing it for myself, him, or someone else, but that I was too thin and needed to put on a couple of pounds. I told him I wasn't trying to be too thin and probably was because I was stressed (besides, when I was pregnant, I stayed within 5lbs. of my goal weight our entire relationship); boy, was I stressed!!!!! I can't even imagine if I gained any weight, would he have called me a fat chick, like he always talked about other women? When he got home from work the next day, he gave me a sticky note, and I asked what it was. He said it was a list of 25 names of people I could be friends with. I was very confused, considering all the friendships he tried to ruin or ruined. Then, later, he asked me if I was upset about the list. I told him I thought it was like he was trying to pick my friends. He immediately jumped up, asked where the list was, and took it back from me. He then asked when we were seeing Mary again and then remembered we didn't have an appointment with her together. Then he pouted, gave me the silent treatment for five days, accused me of holding out love from him (projecting), and started lecturing me. I kept telling him that whether it was an hour or five hours, I didn't want his verbal beatings (I was finally seeing it for what it was – it was a beating). He said it was me not wanting to grow and have a good marriage and that it was my daddy issues coming out, and I would need to hear it from Mary. He wanted me to return to bed to finish the "conversation" and then have sex. The last thing I wanted to do was have sex with him, especially after his attacks. I said I didn't want to. He then told me he couldn't talk to me about anything, and I said I didn't want a lecture and was told I was wrong until I agreed with him.

Dennis and I almost broke up around this time. At one point, he made up this elaborate plan to commit suicide because he said Harlow and I didn't want him to be around. You talk about playing the VICTIM!!! He said he was going to skydive, and when it was time to pull the parachute cord, he would plunge to the ground. That way, it would look like an accident, and we wouldn't have to be with him. I felt sorry for him and also knew it wasn't time yet. I still knew Harlow needed to finish high school to get to college. If we left him then, things would have drastically changed financially, and in my mind, I knew we had to suck it up for another year and a half. We were so close to the end that I needed us both to hold on. Dennis insisted that Mary was on his side and knew everything was my fault and that he was good, so I said she was fired. He reminded me often that Mary knew what I was, and I couldn't hear the truth. I told her the truth, but if she believed his lies and if he was going to try and manipulate her continually, she was out of the equation. As I said, she couldn't comprehend what he was doing because she was a Christian counselor, and he manipulated her into believing he was a good Christian man. It was also apparent that she never had training in the types of nonviolent and narcissistic abuse. Dennis continually told me that every counselor in America would tell me the same things about me, including Mary. He said that during the rest of our marriage. He also completely denied ever saying he was going to commit suicide. When I told him the exact story he told me about jumping out of a plane, he said, "I only said how I could see how someone would want to." Saying that was purposefully to make me feel like someone would want to kill themselves because of me. When he threatened suicide, he reached the point where he spoke about the end of life. It's horrifying to think that if he was willing to talk about ending his life, taking any of our lives was possible, even if his motive was just getting me to stay with him. I learned this is very common; when an abuser begins losing control, they will threaten suicide. Certain abusers will carry it out and, in some cases, take their victim and children with them for ultimate control that can never be taken back, along with the prevention of accountability (murder-suicide – which is tragically happening more and more each day). He continued telling me that Harlow told him I was the most toxic part of her life and that another counselor told him she would abandon me when she turned 24. Sometimes, he said, when she was 22. He notoriously changed his numbers when he accused me of something. I guess he was so wrapped up in remembering the story that he couldn't always remember the numbers. The things that would come from his mouth were absolutely vile, hurtful, and evil. I felt so helpless, fearful, and heartbroken every moment of every day.

"I won't survive without you"

"Threatening suicide if you leave, and other things of that nature, are ways for them to control you and keep you where you no longer want to be."

Unknown

He finally allowed me to leave working at our (his) company in mid-2017. I was so relieved, and knew at some point I needed to leave the company if I was leaving him. He hired his old assistant to take my place. Funny, he put her through 4 years of college so she could be a teacher, and now she was back a few years later as a bookkeeper. I didn't care. I was happy that I didn't have to work with him anymore. We agreed that I could stay home until Harlow went to college. He played nice for a few months, but that's as long as he could take it. Then he was worse than ever because he knew he was losing control and needed to regain it. I was glad Harlow got a job as a hostess at a restaurant and was out of the house a lot more. She worked as much as possible, and I was glad for her, but it was much more stressful because I was with him alone more often.

Someone finally told me that Dennis was emotionally and verbally abusive, and things started clicking into place. I learned the terms 'gaslighting' and 'narcissist.' I read several articles, and little puzzle pieces started fitting together. He really was the boogeyman, a monster. I discovered that Dennis told his friends certain things, so he could look like a victim and blame me. I even have a butt-dial message I still have saved of him talking about things and blaming me. He also represented that I wanted everyone to feel sorry for me and that I needed help (HE WAS THE ONE WHO NEEDED HELP!). He had to tell people things, even if it was made up, so he could blame his wife and look like a victim, while he hid everything about himself so that he wouldn't be judged or exposed. It's hard to understand why a grown man would need to make his own wife look so bad to everyone he decided. He was falsely accusing me, as usual, to make me the bad guy while telling me I was trying to make him out as the bad guy. All of this was to project, blame-shift, and smear me to escape exposure and accountability for all the horrible things he was doing.

On my 50th birthday, Harlow was so sweet and thoughtful. She made me a bubble bath, lit a candle, and poured me a glass of white wine. When I told Dennis how nice that was, his only comment was "day drinking," with a smirk. It's so funny that he could go to a bar with buddies on a Saturday or Sunday afternoon and drink while watching sports, but he had to put me down every chance he got and ruin what Harlow did for me (he was jealous and had to make it a negative). I had loved watching sports with my friends before I was with Dennis. So many nights and weekends were spent watching at a sports bar or someone's house. But I pretty much gave up because I didn't enjoy being with Dennis and was focused on Harlow's well-being. I would occasionally hang out and watch a sporting event, especially the Superbowl, but mostly when we were with a group, and I could socialize. I also used to like playing board games, cards, video games, bowling, putt-putt golf, pool, darts, etc. Whenever I played with Dennis, he would automatically say how competitive I was to immediately put me on the defensive. It got to the point that I rarely played games anymore, which was so sad because we always had a game room. I felt like I stopped liking many things and grew more negative because of my extreme unhappiness and pain. It was just more pieces of my spirit taken away.

In 2016, when we turned 50, he wanted us to take many of our friends on a trip. I said that was excessive, and I just wanted a party for my birthday. He insisted that we were treated to Rome for Skye's birthday and France for Otto's birthday, so we had to do this. Because it was a special birthday, he needed to make sure all of the focus wasn't on me, which is why we had to celebrate together, just like our 40th. He said we were going to an island because he got a deal from a friend. I said that I didn't want to, that if it were my choice, I would pick New York. Of course, it wasn't my decision, it was his, so we went to the island. It was okay, but Dennis tried to monopolize all of the activities on the trip, which he knew I didn't like, so I didn't participate in them. He wanted me to participate in things I didn't want to, and I decided I wouldn't. For all I know, that could have been a set-up to break down my boundaries or make me look bad in front of our friends, so I was unhappy and didn't have a good time. At one point, a group of us (without Dennis) went running a couple of errands, and they were all surprised at how much fun I was just in the car for that short time and made a direct comment about it like I was a completely different person (go figure). It was so nice, even for a short period, to let my guard down and enjoy myself. During that trip, he also got furious at Bette for ordering expensive wine at the birthday dinner and made me agree that it was horrible for her to do. I tried not to. I actually found it funny, but he always made me agree with him on everything and most times, it was just easier to agree with him than not, even if I didn't agree with him. Oh, and we all day drank each day! He didn't realize Skye was near when talking about Bette, so he later told me we both agreed about her, just in case we were overheard. He even tried to manipulate Skye into believing I was a horrible mother and that she needed to mentor Harlow since she was a Christian woman (he conveniently forgot he previously said she was a liar, and now he wanted her to be a mentor). He told me he was trying to have Skye do this because I was ruining Harlow. Because we secretly spoke about it, he didn't know that Skye was once married to someone similar to Dennis, so she knew what kind of person he was. Like so many others said, she admits that Dennis was way worse than anyone they have known – a master manipulator. He tried so hard to end this friendship, as with all of the others, and I was just thankful she saw through him and was so supportive of me. I'm sure he thought that if he were successful, it would have killed two birds with one stone because he wanted so much to ruin my relationship with Harlow and also with Skye. Skye supported me every step of the way, and I couldn't be more grateful to her; at least one of his schemes didn't work.

Dennis got so jealous that I wasn't working, so not long after I left the business, he wanted me to get a job. I took a really cheap online nutrition class to try and go in that direction, and Dennis not only said it was worthless, but he also kept pushing me to find a job. It was interesting how he waited to say that to me until after I finished the course so he could put me down. He also told Harlow that I would spend all her college money on my mid-life crisis to upset her and try again to put a wedge in our relationship. I knew when I left him that I needed some income to take care of myself while we divorced, so I began looking for an office job. It took several months to find one since I worked with my husband for no money for 17 years in a position I hated. Another motive in my getting a job is that if I left him, he would be in a better place if I earned an income.

Dennis's back went out mid-October 2017 (he said it was at the office when he got out of his chair, but now I'm wondering if it was because he was screwing around with someone). Dennis had been home all week with his back issue, and I was caring for him. On Sunday, 10/29, he came to the dining room table and asked, "What did you say to Bette about Teresa?" I told him nothing and was very confused. Teresa worked for a friend's company, and Bette was in Human Resources. He asked some more about it, and I said it had to be months and then, thinking about it, said probably a year since they became friends, and I just mentioned it to Bette. He interrogated, "Which is it, months or a year? You are changing your story." I didn't remember; it meant nothing to me then, just a mention. He said Bette told Teresa that her relationship with Dennis was extremely inappropriate and that she couldn't do business with him. Was he blame-shifting this on me to escape exposure and accountability? I excused myself briefly and, when I returned from the bathroom, asked why he accused me. He said he never accused me, only asked me a simple question (gaslighting). He said Bette fired his business because she wanted to hurt our family, which would cost us $40,000 annually. He also said Bette didn't have my best interest (she was helping me find a job), and I shouldn't be friends with her anymore. He said he recently went to lunch with Teresa and her boyfriend. He asked if I trusted him and I said I didn't know. He said I needed to believe him or not, one or the other. I said I didn't know, and he said if I didn't, there was no marriage, and it would be over. I said how he used to tell me all the time that he thought I had a boyfriend and was cheating, and he responded that he knew I wasn't (how convenient at this moment he knew I wasn't cheating on him because it was useful to this conversation). Then he reminded me that my decision to leave our business was costing such a loss, and his numbers kept changing as he went around and around with his words in his verbal attack. I was so over hearing all this crap that I screamed and said how much I hated him (reacting to the abuse), then went upstairs to shower. He followed me and continued through the shower, makeup, and hair, verbally attacking me. He said no one liked me, and people regularly called him and asked why he stayed with me and why they didn't like me. He said he was done telling me who they were anymore, just what they say (because he knew I now asked them directly) because it's his duty as my husband to help me change my behavior and grow. I said I was happy with myself, and he said that's why so many people don't like me. He brought up Bette and bashed her, Whitney, and Skye and how she lied to me. I mentioned he just wanted me to be a Stepford or submissive Christian wife. I was so upset that I started cursing. He then said I was mean and cruel to him, had taught Harlow to hate men, and gave her my daddy issues. He must have called me a victim and said that word at least 50 times during this attack. At one point, I said I wanted to be alone, and he wouldn't let me go anywhere. I said I wouldn't leave without Harlow, and he said he and Harlow now have a relationship, that they have had some great conversations, and that she doesn't want their time together to end when they had dinner a couple of times recently. She would want him to park in a parking lot and also walk around the lake to keep talking. Then he got right up to my face with his evil eyes and kept repeating that Harlow hated me. I screamed and started crying, and at one point, he was in my face trying to get me to hit him and kept saying over and over, "Why don't you hit me? I know you want to," and he said he never hit me and I reminded him that he shoved me twice on a plane and he said that wasn't a hit. (When he got in my face like that, it was to intimidate me so I'd react negatively, and he could blame me. He wanted me to hit him so he could accuse me of being abusive or validated to hit me back, which I believe he wanted to do badly. Part of his agenda was to upset me because it made him feel powerful. He got off on the negative attention as well as the positive). When I was fully ready and was putting on my jewelry, I didn't put on my ring. He asked why, and I said I wasn't in the mood. He asked where it was and made me give it to him. He said he knew I thought it was a gift, but it was a pre-marital contract. Also, at one point, he told me that if I left him, he knew he wouldn't have to pay me alimony for as long as I thought, and there wouldn't be much left anyway. He said he thought I married him for his money, and I said no, it was to raise a child. He mentioned Mary and how I wouldn't like to hear what a counselor had to tell me about myself, and she agreed with him; however, when I saw her without him, she agreed I should leave, and he denied that (that was one of the sessions when I told her Dennis said he was going to commit suicide and I was afraid for our safety as well). He said I never wanted to hear anything negative about myself and was like the original email he sent her, saying I was only happy when I was being praised and would never admit I did anything wrong (boy, would I love to see the email he sent her – I bet it was a doozy). Then, towards the end, he told me no one loved me more than he did, and he puts up with a lot with me but only wants to help me and wouldn't give up on me because he loves me and knows I love him too. I finally agreed, and he said he would help me become a better person and to trust him that he wanted to help me. I had enough, so I gave up. His demeanor changed instantly, and he asked only a few minutes later if I wanted to go to lunch and where I wanted to go. Then he asked what I wanted for our anniversary, to which I said nothing, and he asked where I wanted to go that night. I said I would come up with something. Harlow texted me that she wanted to meet at the pumpkin patch to get a pumpkin (she asked me alone, but I said he had to come along). He hugged me, kissed me, and gave the ring back. All of this was at least two hours. While we picked out the pumpkin, it took a lot of strength to fight back the tears; I was secretly a complete nervous wreck, and all I wanted to do was roll up in a ball in a corner.

You may be asking how I could remember such detail about all these things. I could be specific on what happened and the dates because a very special person for years told me to make sure I took notes. Every time something happened, she reminded me. I wrote them in the notes section of my iPhone. It was a good way for me to remember what happened because he regularly gaslighted me, and my brain would get foggy. So many times, I felt like I was in shock and couldn't breathe or think straight. I am so thankful she knew enough to tell and keep reminding me. Now, I can return to each attack and situation and relive what happened and how I felt every moment. Also, remember when he shoved me on the plane twice, and I looked him right in the eyes and told him if he ever touched me again, I would leave him that minute? He now had a boundary he couldn't cross because he knew I was serious. So, he never touched me again, but it didn't stop him from all of the other abuse, including getting right in my face and trying to bait me to hit him.

When Dennis's back went out, he was in bed for a week. His back had gone out before, and I played nursemaid to him both times. I did the same when he got his hair plugs and whenever he was sick. When I was sick, I cared for myself and was expected to do everything I always did. I did everything when Harlow came home from the hospital after she was born, except for my mother's help (because he already had a job, remember), when I had my surgery, and any other time I didn't feel well. After I had my surgery, one night, I had a very bad nosebleed, and when it got to the point that I needed to go to urgent care in the middle of the night, he was annoyed. I was thankful it stopped bleeding on the way so we could turn around and go home. I still cooked, cared for the house, worked, and cared for Harlow. If I didn't feel well, he was irritated. Every now and then, he offered to help me in the kitchen, and I declined because he didn't practice good hygiene. He started doing the dishes at some point, and I often had to rewash them secretly. Who knows, he may have done a shitty job, so I would tell him he didn't need to.

Petra and Otto's oldest son was getting married to Yvonne on 6/30/18 in France. Dennis had told Harlow and me at the dinner table one night that he didn't believe we were invited to the wedding, that it had gotten too big, and that they needed to cut costs, especially since they were hosting the bride's family. I was okay with that if that's what they wanted. Bette and Joe, and Skye and Mike discussed it at Petra and Otto's house one night over the summer, and then at my birthday lunch with the girls, Skye asked me if we made our arrangements yet for the wedding and I said that Dennis told me he didn't think we were invited. Petra was mortified, said we were invited, and was upset we thought otherwise. She did say that kids were not invited, so Harlow wasn't invited. I completely understood. She said something to Otto because he then forwarded the original save the date to me, copying Dennis, that was emailed to Dennis and the others on 7/30/17 (not long before we had the discussion at the dinner table). I told Dennis I guessed we shouldn't go since Harlow wasn't invited because this was supposed to be her graduation present. He asked who said that, and I said Petra. Then Dennis spoke to Otto, and Harlow was invited (very unfair to any other child not invited). He said to me that he never said he didn't think we were invited, and I told him he did but was dismissed. He also said he didn't receive the original save the date and had Otto send it to him again. In the months between the original save the date and the resend, I'm betting Dennis and Otto spoke about the wedding and plans at least a dozen or more times, especially because they spoke on the phone all the time. I wonder what his ultimate goal (scheme) was; it had to change because of what happened with Petra. On 10/28/17, while I was running errands, he tried to tell Harlow that Otto called furious that we didn't think we were invited and said to her he never said that, to which Harlow told him she was there at the dinner table when the conversation took place. He brought up examples about how he and Otto were best friends, that he was the executor of his will, and Yvonne worked for him, and Harlow reminded him she knew all of that because she was the one who brought it up that night why she thought we would be invited. He immediately dismissed the conversation. After that, he completely dropped any mention of the wedding until he started telling everyone that we couldn't go because I then had a new job and couldn't take time off. This was a new lie to make me look bad because when I was hired, I negotiated that time off already. He just wanted to blame me for not going and making himself and Harlow look like victims. It was also funny that Dennis and Otto had been close friends for years, but Dennis hid our previous marriages from him and kept telling me he knew Otto would judge us because he heard him judge people before who had been married and divorced. I think that was bullshit because Skye and Mike were previously married and divorced, and Otto never judged either. Dennis also hid from Otto that he had a GED and didn't graduate from college, and consistently said Otto would also judge him and not want to be friends with him if he knew. He just couldn't not lie and couldn't not scheme.

A couple of weeks later, we went to a charity event for our anniversary on 11/11/17. He was acting weirdly than usual. We ran into friends at the event, and at one point, he knocked over my full wine glass, and a lot of red wine got on my jeans. I told him wine spilled all over my knees, my jeans were soaked, and I was trying to wipe them with napkins. His only acknowledgment was that he said so matter of fact, it was a good thing my jeans were black, so you didn't see anything. He did not apologize or try to help; again, it was so hurtful and hateful. He made a big deal about him not wearing jeans that night and hated wearing them and wound up wearing a pair of colorful khakis (dare I say Garanimals?). I barely spoke a word with our friends; at this point, I was afraid of saying anything and was so unhappy that I didn't have anything good to say. The next day, I asked him if he would walk around the lake with me (our usual Sunday morning), and he said he was going to church with his goddaughter. He wore a stylish jeans outfit – jeans, a black button-down shirt, and stylish black sneakers. He hadn't said a word about it before that moment. How interesting that he refused to wear jeans the night before because he hated them, and now he was wearing them to church! Previously, he would never have worn jeans to church and would always negatively comment when someone showed up casually as a sign of disrespect. I was also guessing that was why he was acting more weirdly the night before because he was being sneaky.

He continually told me and others that I was spending a fortune and all of Harlow's college money. But the following weekend, he was out at the bars watching college football with a buddy 'day drinking,' later, I met them out as couples with Jenie and her boyfriend after I finished cleaning the house. He spent a lot that night ordering expensive wine to impress them. For years, he complained to me and others that I was ruining our finances; he continued buying for himself, even though he said he wasn't. He complained about me getting my nails done, but he had a more expensive massage membership. He complained about how much my hair appointments were, but he spent just as much on his hair; he got his cut and colored also. He complained about my gym membership until he got one. He bought himself a car wash membership, and to make it look good for him, he also bought one for me. But then I thought something was stolen from my car and something was broken. His reaction was abnormal (for a normal person); instead of supporting me, he just said he would cancel my membership. He would also complain that I earned Macy's rewards points. That's how I got a lot of my clothing and accessories to spend less money. He would get jealous and want to use them for himself or complain that we should earn airline points instead and that we were wasting them on Macy's. He didn't like that he wasn't in charge of them - I was for a change.

The next day, I was talking with Bette on the phone. She could only tell me that his behavior with Teresa was inappropriate. Teresa's boss went to management to let them know he was being forced to use Dennis's company as a vendor and was seeing Teresa inappropriately too much, that they saw each other several times within a month, and three times in one week and at one point was draped over her desk. I was told he was a predator and they could take legal action. That was all she could say. It was shocking, to say the least, that my friend told me my husband was a predator (which is another word for a monster)!

On 11/27/17, he wanted to "talk about our relationship." It was another hours-long attack that I needed to recognize and admit my faults and what I did wrong so we could move past it. He said he has a relationship with Harlow, and they are spending time together, that she is opening up to him, and she doesn't want their time to end (he had that story about walking around the lake and being in a parking lot memorized – I wonder how many of his friends heard that one?). He said he watched us on our inside security cameras and tried to accuse me of something (liar and stalker). In the middle of this attack, he said he found out why the company Teresa worked for thought his relationship with her was inappropriate, and it had to do with her title and level within the company (bullshit). He then said no one would tell him who he could and couldn't be friends with, and he was friends with all his clients and even the President of the company's (Mike of Mike and Skye) secretary. Then he said if I can't admit the things I've done, we would never have a good marriage, and if it's just that I was waiting for Harlow to graduate to tell him so he could plan for it and the business would only take three months to fail and we would have nothing left. And, I only wanted to marry him for his money (for the record, he didn't have much when we started dating and money was the furthest thing in my mind) and he provided a good living for our family by creating this business and creating a job for me with both of our lack of education (I at least have a high school diploma and 2-year degree, but he had to lump me in with him) and the fact I could come and go and take care of Harlow and take three months off a year and it was only three to four hours a day (gaslighting again) and even though I didn't like being a bookkeeper it was what our family needed to be successful and I should be grateful for that and not worry about not enjoying what I was doing and that he hates what he does also, but we are both un-hirable and the damage was done by my decisions that hurt all of us and especially Harlow with regards to going to college and our lifestyle and we can't go out anymore because we are $50,000 over budget and I misrepresented the budget and we spend too much and the only time he can go out is with a client for lunch (lies, as well as his words going round and round – that's called word salad). He mentioned how many people don't like me and don't want to go out with us because of me, and he doesn't tell me who anymore; he just gets those calls (except he would always remind me about Bette, Sue Ellen, Sarah, etc.). He wouldn't let me leave and blocked me from my car to run errands, and when I walked away from him, he followed me, continuing to attack me verbally. He said I misrepresented him to Harlow for the last five years and needed to admit I was wrong, and he's never done anything to her that she wouldn't like him, and I needed to admit that. And that I've held out love to him and won't tell him I love him unless he says it first (he hadn't either – I was responding to him not saying it to me and him holding out love towards me – blame-shifting but not a lie – I didn't want to show him love or tell him I loved him and only did it because I had to and not because I wanted to). Then, he also called me cruel and mean. Note: This is also when he was wearing all his fun underwear and cool jeans outfits to work and was manscaping and very secretive about his phone.

He finally ruined my friendship with Whitney. We were at Bette and Joe's Christmas party at the beginning of December, and Stevie was in town and stayed at our house. A lot was happening with Bette and Dennis, and we wouldn't be invited to their party. Bette and I discussed it and agreed with her due to the Teresa issue and other things. But Stevie came into town to stay with us to go to the party, so we wound up going. Dennis made sure of it. Whitney was there, and we were hanging out with her. At one point, Dennis was alone with Whitney and later told me that she was cruel to him (He just loved that word. Using overly strong words creates a sense of drama and theatrics, shock value, outrage, gaslighting and projection, and to attack and put the other person immediately on the defensive), that he tried to talk to her about our relationship, and she avoided the conversation. He then totally assaulted her character and wanted me to end my friendship with her since she was "cruel," and I shouldn't be friends with someone who treated my husband that way. I knew he just wanted to find some way to ruin my friendship with her, along with me going to dinner with her about a week prior, and he didn't like girls' nights. I called Whitney and told her I had to pretend not to be friends with her, and she was very hurt by all of this. It was hurting me, too, but I understood what was happening, and she didn't. Continually losing friends I cared about certainly added to my broken heart and spirit, and I felt like there wasn't much left.

Close to Christmas, he told me we weren't going to church as a family, that he was going to church with his goddaughter and her brother. Wow, every Christmas we were together, the three of us went to church on Christmas Eve, and he canceled it! Also, when he was out Christmas shopping for me with Harlow, he asked her if she thought one of us was being unfaithful. Lovely! Right around the holidays, our accountant (a friend, of course) told him that our earnings were right around prior years'. This completely contradicted him, saying that I cost the business $150,000 (he kept changing his numbers) by my decision to leave the business, that it was failing, and that it would only be a matter of time before he was out of business. He also said we were $60,000 over our personal budget and then said $40,000 in the same conversation. I started noticing him contradicting himself quite a bit. What he said was all over the place, even in the same conversation or verbal attack. When Amy first replaced me at our company, she was part-time and making $28,000, but then he raised her to $40,000 and then $50,000. Hmmmmmmm.

As much as he would complain that I was always spending a fortune, he would also say he never did anything for himself and rarely spent money on himself. That was a blatant lie (blame-shifting and gaslighting), because he went out with his friends to lunch, drinking, golfing, and on guys' trips. He especially complained during the last year and a half we were together because I left the company and eventually took a low-paying office manager/bookkeeping job. He had to make me look bad and feel bad. But he was going out more than ever with his friends and taking trips (including with Teresa, Jenny, and any other woman he was inappropriate with). He also had an inappropriate obsession with other people's sons, most of whom were teenagers or twenty-somethings. He loved hanging out with them and would call them his "golf son" or like that, and he loved the attention they showed him (this is considered triangulation, and he did this because he didn't feel like he was getting enough attention from Harlow). He paid the tab a lot when he went out, from before we even dated through our entire relationship. He liked being adored and admired and would go out of his way for that type of attention (I call that AAA – attention, adoration, and admiration, and you can add another A for affection with this cheating). I started making notes on all the times he went out with friends, golfed, and went on trips because he kept saying he wasn't going out or spending any money on himself. I knew he was lying, misrepresenting himself, and blaming me, so I needed what he did in writing so I had proof, if just for myself, while he was gaslighting me. I still have all of those notes as well.

So, while he was complaining so much that last year and a half, he decided to pay off my Mercedes out of Harlow's COLLEGE ACCOUNT, he purchased for himself a Mercedes and a newer SUV, and thousands of dollars of repair bills on that lemon convertible BMW before he finally got rid of it. Once he got his Mercedes, he said that he would always drive that model for the rest of his life and would just update it with newer ones. It definitely screamed status. I had ensured Harlow got a car for her 17th birthday so she could finally learn how to drive, which cost around $16,000. He complained the entire time she had that car about the expense. As he continued complaining, I suggested selling my car and that I would drive her car when she was at college or get a cheaper car. He said no, her Kia was a teenager's car, and he hadn't worked hard and built his reputation for his wife to drive a Chevy. I told him that my car was old enough at that point that it would start giving us issues, and he actually was going to make me buy the same model Mercedes in a newer year – about $60,000! He even started researching them online; we saw a few at dealerships. I kept making excuses about what I didn't like about each of them so he wouldn't buy it. How did that make sense? It didn't and completely contradicted him, saying I was spending all of Harlow's college money and we were going broke, as he was really the one spending it. I said we could sell the house, and he said no, again, his reputation. I canceled the maid service, cleaned the house myself, switched my nails to the cheapest service, and started painting my toes. He was still taking trips, golfing, and going out with friends even more. Now, he could try and hide from me how much he was spending and where he was going because he had the business pay for his entertainment. Sometimes, other people would tell me, and I regularly found receipts in his pockets in the laundry.

At the beginning of 2018, during Harlow's senior year, someone in her school's administration, I believe because it was anonymous, called the state department for Children and Families, reporting Dennis was abusive towards both Harlow and me. An agent left a message on my cell phone, and I was mortified when I called her back about the report. I tried to get her to call it off, begged her to ask her supervisor, and kept it from Dennis until I heard back. Unfortunately, legally, they had to interview me, Harlow, and Dennis. I denied the allegations because Harlow was so close to going to college and didn't want to ruin the outcome. And, of course, Dennis was as charming as ever to the agent. I was glad that the case was closed, but that didn't stop Dennis from accusing me, then accusing Harlow, and then blaming my mother for calling to accuse him falsely. He kept telling me he knew the truth and I needed to confess – that he "found out." He had done that so many times that he knew more than he really did, so he thought I would confess to something. After it was over, he continued to say that many neighbors and friends came to him about being interviewed by the department, and I discovered it was a complete lie because I have copies of the full report. He just wanted to look like more of a victim while he was accusing me of playing the victim. As he kept blaming me, I remembered having the voicemail saved. I could prove it wasn't me when I played it for him. At some point, the voicemail was no longer on my phone, and I think he deleted it since it was evidence that he had to get rid of it. I would have never deleted it, and I wish I still had that voicemail and would have transcribed it for the book.

This happened the first week at my new job. It definitely made it more stressful, and at some points, I felt like I could have a panic attack. But I was happy that I was free from him for over 8 hours daily. It was a relief when I was at work, and I didn't care that I worked 40 hours weekly. I was relieved when I left the house in the morning until it was time to go home. Of course, he accused me within weeks of screwing my boss and said that my entire paycheck HAD to go towards Harlow's college fund. He couldn't stand that I was making money, which gave up some of his control, so he needed to devise a way to control the entire amount. I would have been happy with that, but right after I started working, he strategically started paying himself less, which would burden our monthly expenses. Needless to say, not much was put in her college account because of that. He would be so angry when we were over budget, conveniently not remembering the budget was made before he bought his Mercedes (then later purchasing the newer SUV, both having car payments). He also got into a car accident that was his fault; Harlow got into a car accident; I took her on a couple of college trips he approved, he took her out of the country to look at a college, he went to the Bahamas on a guys trip, he went to South Carolina on a guys trip, he went to Las Vegas on a business trip (so he said because he conveniently forgot about it until a day before he was supposed to leave). He was just blame-shifting and complaining to me to make me look and feel bad while he was the one actually spending and over budget. He had me make a budget when I stopped working for our company. There were things I purposely left off, which he knew because the business always paid those expenses (which included all entertainment, eating out, and trips, among many other things). He also knew I didn't have extra amounts in the budget (this budget was made in March of 2017) for Harlow's college because we had no idea what was happening with that. She could have received a state award or a scholarship, we purchased pre-paid college tuition, and we already had a decent amount in savings and were still putting away $1,000 in addition to that each month (it would have been considerably more if he hadn't paid off my car and bought two vehicles for himself). He also told her and me that if needed, we would take out a home equity loan. He knew those things weren't on the budget; it was undeniable, and he just used it to his advantage to make me look and feel bad. If we were a normal couple that could communicate, we would have discussed it, but we were never a normal couple.

After the holidays, he was angry that I wasn't attending church with him, so I started going. I loved it so much, and although I knew he would use the sermons against me, I still wanted to go. Even so, I was terrified during church services because he would sigh, huff, puff, and angrily write things down in his notebook. I wouldn't sing and was afraid to participate, and many times, I was silently in tears and filled with anxiety. At church, there were so many sermons about God forgiving you of your sins, and once you are forgiven, it would never be brought up again, and only the devil reminded you of your sins. He would always say he was allowed to bring up anything he wanted to and remind me of whatever he needed to, and he was allowed to convict me. Well then, that settles it; Dennis is the devil!

> "Sometimes it seems that the louder someone claims sainthood, the bigger the horns they are hiding."
>
> Unknown

In February of 2018, coming home from church he confronted me and asked me questions about Teresa. He asked if I told Harlow anything and I said I mentioned it to her (of course I did - we talked about everything – we had to). He said he has a friendship with her, and they were still doing business together and had to meet in parking lots to hand over merchandise so she wouldn't get in trouble by Bette (shady – he was basically telling on himself), and I asked how she was paying for it. He said PayPal, and then said that if someone found out and she got fired, he would blame me. Then he said he was an approved vendor (contradicted himself) but that Bette was the kind of person who would make sure she was fired. I said it was Teresa's boss who went to Bette and said Dennis was draped over her desk, to which he denied and said she was in a cubicle, so that was impossible (was it really impossible?). Then he said they talk about very personal things, and she spoke about how when she was a teenager, she did cocaine one day, and then the next day she went to her dad and said if God put this on the earth, then he wanted people to do it and two days later (or something like that) she was in rehab, and she doesn't drink anymore, and she is so sad about her relationship with her dad and that even to this day they don't have much of a relationship and she would work the rest of her life to make it up to him (yeah right). Then he talked about her boyfriend and how when they were first dating a year and a half ago, he was only separated from his wife and was representing to her that he was getting a divorce but was still on and off with his marriage and that Dennis at one point sent her a picture of himself holding up his fist to make better decisions. So, their relationship was inappropriate and way beyond a customer/vendor relationship, and I told him he needed to end his friendship with her. He said he wouldn't stop doing business with her and that it was sad because he wanted me to be friends with her (triangulation – I think her name was on that list!). Then he talked about Harlow going to church with his goddaughter, and maybe she could mentor her because she had a character flaw and was going to college soon (a more disgusting projection). Then he asked me if Harlow should go to college in another country, and I told him yes (because I knew the best thing for her was to get as far away from him as possible). Then he reminded me if I left him that, I would be taking away money for Harlow. If we got a divorce, it'd be the last bit taken away from her. She wouldn't be able to go to college (leveraging and threatening our daughter's college to control me and prevent me from leaving). Then, she was going to hate me when she was 22 and wouldn't want me in her life anymore, and that was sad, and he felt bad for me. Still, I could fix it now if I admit I was wrong. He also admitted that he went into my email when I still worked with him and found an email to Bette saying that when he was accusing me of cheating on him probably the way I acted made him believe that I was (complete fabrication unless he created that email and sent it to her – I looked in my sent folder and didn't see it, and I wonder if he sent it to her and sent anyone else emails pretending to be me and then deleted them). Bette and I also discussed that Dennis would probably hide money from me if I were to leave him because many men do that. Dennis was furious by that, perhaps because he was actually doing it. Side note – one morning around this time, while I was at the gym, Teresa was there. I pretended I didn't see her, but at one point, I noticed she walked directly behind me while I was on the treadmill and then started working out a few down from me. Why wouldn't she have said hello or acknowledged me if I was supposed to be friends with her and there wasn't anything inappropriate going on? When I was at the gym with Dennis, she made a point to say hello to us. Was she trying to send me a message?

Dennis made sure he ruined my friendship with Bette. She was such a strong and successful woman, and he hated that. He even used Joe's friendship to try and gain information and also used Stevie in his schemes against Joe. Dennis would say Joe was such a great guy but could never keep a secret and said Joe would fill him and Stevie in on things that I know weren't even true and Dennis made up. He said Joe told him that Bette had a grocery list for me if I left him. I was so afraid of him finding out how I felt about him or about my future plan to leave him that I told Bette I would have to back off our friendship, but she was really still my friend, and I needed to pretend not to like her anymore so he would back off. Now I realize he lied about what Joe said, and he was reading my emails and blaming it on Joe. Unfortunately, Bette is one of my friendships I don't think will ever return.

On several Valentine's Days, he accused me of cheating on him (so what was HE really doing on Valentine's Day?). This year, he accused me of cheating with my new boss and wanted to see my texts from that day. I already knew he tracked my calls and texts through myVerizon, along with social media and emails, and obviously knew I was texting a lot that day. He read my texts, some of which were with the computer guy and my boss, and of course, had to insult the fact that I was now the "I.T. person," but then called me just a "gal Friday" at a shitty salary. He said he ended his friendship with Teresa, but not long after, he said no one would tell him whom he could and couldn't be friends with. In April, I needed to make up hours at work for a hair appointment and other things, so I went to work on a Saturday for 5 hours. He said he would go to work as well, but when I got home, he had been in bed for the entire 5 hours and said it was because he was so exhausted from all the bad decisions I had made for our family. That afternoon, when Harlow left for work, he verbally attacked me. It lasted for 3 ½ hours. During this attack, he told me Harlow told him I was the most destructive part of her life. He interrogated me on Harlow's college money and how it's not going to be enough, and I've put us in financial ruins, and we were going to have to sell the house because of me. Then he went into how much of a bad parent I was and how I misrepresented him to people, and I attack him. Then he reminded me that my job was lower than a bookkeeper and was a gal Friday, and I should have stayed as the bookkeeper at our company. He didn't even know what I did at work because I was careful not to mention it. After all, he was so angry, and I didn't want to get in trouble or be put down. Then he said if I went to another counselor I wouldn't be honest with them, and they wouldn't know what kind of person I was, and that the only one that could help me was Mary because she was the only person who knew the truth about me and Harlow (he knew he had Mary wrapped around his finger and could manipulate her at will). He reminded me about all the people I attack and all the people who don't want to be around me anymore, all the people who call him and tell him that they don't like me and they don't want to be around me, and they're surprised that he would be with someone like me and was staying with me. Then he reminded me about my parenting and how much of a bad parent I was because I wanted to be friends with my daughter and kept him from parenting her; then he asked me if I talk to her, and I just told him we didn't have much time to see each other since she was working. Then he threatened that she needed to pay for her college and said other horrible things (he was projecting, and everything he said was really about himself — absolutely disgusting). Then he brought up Skye and knew that she wouldn't mentor Harlow because she would have to tell me things about my parenting that I wouldn't want to hear and would ruin our friendship. So, he continued trying to put a wedge in my friendship with her. Then he reminded me how I attacked Sue Ellen, which is why she didn't want to be friends with me, and Deidra didn't want to either. I reminded him I was okay about losing their friendship because they were gossiping, so I quit Bunko. He continued telling me that people wanted to throw me away.

Harlow graduated from High School in May 2018. After graduation, we went to lunch with her best friend, Carlton, and his family. I was really good friends with his mom, Jenie. Earlier in the year, I told her that at some point, Dennis would tell me that she said something cruel to him or lied to him so that I would need to end my friendship with her and that he's been doing that for most of our marriage, and if he did, I would have to pretend we weren't friends until I left him. So, after that lunch, Dennis said that Jenie turned to him and said, "I told my ex-husband to pick up the entire check because you can't afford a place like this because you live paycheck to paycheck." I know she would never say anything like that, but I told Dennis I would talk to her about it. I really think Dennis was embarrassed that Jenie's ex-husband picked up the bill and was intimidated since he's a billionaire. I called her and reminded her about what I said earlier in the year, and she remembered. I said that he had done it and told her what he said she said. She was mortified and told me she would never say that to anyone ever, and I let her know I believed her and knew that Dennis was lying. On June 15th, he asked me if I talked to her. I told him I had and said she never said it. He responded, "Oh, Jenie, that's so disappointing; well, I guess you lost another friend. Why do all of these women lie?" Then he asked if I believed him, and I started saying he was my husband, and he immediately jumped up and said that meant I didn't believe him and, if not, our marriage was over. I knew I was being forced into saying I believed him, so obviously, I said I did. His verbal attacks were more frequent this last year, making it difficult to be home with him. Our home was an invisible prison, and I wore invisible chains when I was with him. When I left work each day, I felt anxious, and when I pulled up at home, and he was already there, my heart would drop, and I would subconsciously hold my breath. I never knew what kind of mood he would be in and whether I was in trouble for something. I continued to have the plastic smile on my face and tried to keep all conversations light and meaningless. I would dread Friday afternoons and wish they were Monday mornings. Even going out on the weekends was tense, to say the least; I always felt like I couldn't breathe, was in shock, and could hyperventilate at any moment (I didn't know it back then, but I was in an almost constant state of trauma, panic, and was suffering from Complex PTSD). Cleaning the house every other Saturday was a blessing because for the 6 hours it took me to clean, my time was occupied, and I didn't have to be with him. Yes, it would take me 6 hours to clean our house because we lived in a 5 Bedroom, 5 Bathroom, 2 Kitchen, 4300 sq. ft. house!

> "I was on the defensive every time he came home.
>
> The sound of his car made me sick to my stomach, because I knew I had to react to however he acted – and I never knew how he was going to act."
>
> Unknown

I never knew what snide remarks he would say. During the latest governor's race, he said that if the Democrat won, he would cancel my medical insurance and put me on Medicaid. When I was looking at a grocery store ad, he asked why I was acting distant towards him. He would guilt me to do things for him by saying everyone in the world does more than me and to stop doing league minimum. When I was on the phone with him and he kept asking me questions that each answer was yes, he asked why I was being short with him. When I asked how his day was, he replied that it was just like any other day (with a smirk). When we went to an art festival, he asked if his outfit was okay, and I said that the ball cap was probably a little casual for the rest of the outfit (which it was); he jumped down my throat and said he was a big boy and could dress himself (why did he ask then?). When I took that inexpensive online nutrition course, he said it was worthless. When he answered the phone when I called him, he didn't say hello; he said "Yes," and when we hung up, he didn't say goodbye; he just hung up. If he tried to reach me by phone or text and I didn't answer, he would then text or leave a message saying he was concerned for my safety to manipulate me to get back to him right away (I still have a saved voicemail from him with deep concern when he tried to reach me and

I didn't answer). He was notorious if you tried to get in touch with him, he just ignored it and would pretend he wasn't a 'slave' to his phone or would say he'd call back and never did. If I said he had been snoring the night before, he would say he didn't snore, that it was me, and that I kept him up all the time because of my snoring. Yes, he kept me up all of the time. In the middle of the night, besides snoring, he would sigh, huff and puff, move around, have the TV in the bedroom on, or would be in the bathroom on his phone (wonder with whom?). Once, in the summer of 2018, he met a friend traveling from his home out of state, and Dennis came home after midnight. When he came home late, I always pretended I was sleeping so I didn't have to deal with him. In the middle of that night, he startled me from sleep by yelling, "ARE YOU TEXTING?" I said, "No, I was sleeping." He responded, "Oh, I thought I saw a light," and didn't bother apologizing. For goodness sake, if a normal person saw a light, they would be concerned, not accusatory. For all the f'ing times I caught him on the phone in the middle of the night, not once did I accuse him of anything. It took me hours to get back to sleep, not that I slept well anyway – I was constantly up for hours because of my stress, sadness, and anxiety. I silently wept in bed for hundreds of nights with Dennis beside me. I always had tissues handy and would wake up in the mornings, either still holding one in my hand or finding it under my pillow. I don't think he ever noticed because my feelings or me, in general, didn't matter to him at all.

If I accidentally scared him by walking around the corner, he would jump out of his skin (total drama), get mad at me, and accuse me of doing it on purpose. He would always say to me that I was the person in charge, which was to confuse and gaslight me into believing that while he was really controlling me. When he said he was doing something for 'us,' I was automatically supposed to like it and be grateful and didn't take into consideration whether I wanted it or not because, again, he didn't care about me or my feelings. When we were going out for dinner, he would say he didn't care where we went and didn't care what we ate (we had to share everything – and of course, he always took the last bite without asking), but then wouldn't like my decisions and changed them. It was highly stressful when I came up with where we should go or what we should order, and I was anxious about what he said or thought. He continued to put me in a bad mood right before we went out with people, reminding me how they didn't like me. He also brought up negative things to me, so I would agree with him to make me look bad. My spirit was withering away, and I tried my best to feel numb instead of total anguish. One morning, he was going golfing and was leaving before I got up. Suddenly, he flipped on the bedroom light and nervously said he couldn't find his wallet. He regularly couldn't find his wallet, keys, phone, whatever. I always had to help him. This one morning, he had me get up from still sleeping to help him find it. He was not concerned that he woke me up and only cared about his needs and agenda. When we couldn't find it, he had me give him one of my credit cards and told me when I found it to let him know. Not only was it rude to make me get up at the crack of dawn to help him, but he also expected me to continue looking for it without regard for me or my time. He didn't apologize for waking me up or thank me for helping him look. He found his wallet not long after he came home, and I'm now wondering if he hid it purposely so he could wake me up to be mean (cruel?), among all the other times he misplaced something.

If he was driving and someone cut him off, he would chase after them and sometimes be very aggressive. He would tailgate if they were ahead and put on his brakes if they were behind. He wanted to intimidate and scare them (and me). What if they called his bluff and slammed on their brakes? What if someone had a gun? When we were running late, he drove recklessly. It was a blatant disregard for our safety. He also wouldn't use his blinker. He said that it was a courtesy and not a law. Yes, it certainly is a courtesy. He was such a male chauvinist, and I often felt his hatred for women, especially strong women. When the Me-Too movement started gaining popularity, and many celebrities and powerful men were called out, he got angry that all these men were being accused and getting in trouble. At one point, he made a nasty comment that he was sure many women were also about to be accused. Then, one woman was accused, and he got so much satisfaction and kept commenting about women doing the same thing. He couldn't acknowledge injustices against women and got angry about it. He even laughed about the tape of Donald Trump when he said, "Grab her by the pussy," and would joke with me about it and others in front of me.

He would tell rude male chauvinistic jokes in front of me all the time, and I had to pretend I was okay with it. He told his buddies that I liked these types of jokes. I pretended, as usual, not to get in trouble with that fake smile on my face. So many times, I just agreed with him to keep the peace or prevent a nasty comment or argument. He reminded me and his buddies that his childhood skateboard had 'no fat chicks' on it and was proud of it, which was demeaning and disrespectful to women. And remember, he was also a huge fan of really dark comedy, which a lot of it was misogynistic.

In June 2018, he told Harlow to get a student loan for college, and at the end of the school year, he would decide if to pay it back. He told her this the entire way to and from her Visa meeting. (This was to make her feel bad about herself, mainly because we were on the way to doing something special for her, and when he would do this in front of me, I tried my best to change the subject or the mood and conversation lighter by bringing up other things or something positive). This was a day to celebrate her accomplishments and the opportunity she deserved to go to a prestigious college abroad. Instead of feeling joy that day, he had to take that away, ruin this occasion for her, and make her feel like total shit. It was and still is horrible that Dennis CHOSE to do this ON PURPOSE to hurt his child. He tried to manipulate her by telling her she would build her credit score. He also made sure to mention that I was the reason why there wasn't any money, that he had saved $200,000 in the business, but when I left it all drained (that is a lie – I saved $200,000 in the business, and it was drained when he hired the two salaried salespeople) and I was $75,000 over budget last year (I love how he continued changing his numbers every time he brought it up – as much as I was always upset and stressed, it almost started to be comical – dare I say dark comedy?). Later, I ensured Harlow knew that if he made her get a student loan, I would pay it for her, as we knew I was leaving him within months. There was no way I would let her be afraid or more stressed than she was already. And speaking about money, he tried to continue controlling Harlow by telling her he was going to put her in the business as a consultant so she could put money in a 401k, and he would match it (very strategic and calculating to keep financial control of her, as well as an unethical business practice). So, when they went to open accounts for her, she took $5,000 from her savings to open one of the accounts, then they opened another account, and she put $2,750 in for him to match. He matched it all right, taking the $2,750 matching from her COLLEGE FUND! He didn't tell her or me (deceptive), and I didn't even have access to that account, and the only reason I knew what he did was from the receipt he carelessly left out. How disgusting that he told her he was matching it and stole it from her college account while trying to look like a hero! At the beginning of July 2018, he purchased that newer SUV that would cost an additional $500 per month. It was in 2017 that he bought his Mercedes at $680 per month. Remember how he kept telling me and everyone that I ruined our finances? If that were so, he not only wouldn't have purchased one vehicle but a second one for himself, especially just months before his only child went to college. Did anyone else notice this besides me? Luckily, Dennis decided not to go through with Harlow and the student loan. He changed his mind because he spoke with some friends about it, and they convinced him. I'm sure he felt shame and had to back down from his threat. Someday, I hope to find out who changed his mind and thank them.

I think it was a day or two after the "Are you texting" incident that his friend, who was mutual friends with Kip, was in town. Kip and her two boys came to our house, and we walked to dinner. Remember this – during the summer of 2018, we all went to dinner as families. The things that stood out to me that night were, at one point, she asked me about my job, to which I told her I didn't like talking about it because Dennis didn't like that I wasn't working for the company anymore and was working for someone else, and the fact I walked and talked with her around the lake, to and from dinner.

Dennis's birthday is in mid-July. In 2018, it was on a Thursday, and the three of us had dinner and dessert for him at home. My parents treated us to dinner on Friday at an authentic New York Italian restaurant. On Saturday, he had a guys' day with a few of his buddies at a golf entertainment complex, and then they all came to the house to party, watch sports, play pool, and have pizza (and day drink!). At around 6 p.m., he wasn't anywhere to be found, and his buddies asked me where he went. I looked for him and found him on the third floor, on the bench in the master bathroom, on the phone. When he got off, he told me he was on the phone with Stevie, who was supposed to be getting married on an island that weekend. He told me Stevie was on the way to a venue to take wedding photos before they left but that his fiancé was holding a surprise wedding for him. Dennis said he had known since Tuesday, but it was a secret. I was shocked that if he had known for five days that his best friend from childhood was getting married in a surprise wedding, why didn't he consider going, with or without me, or even mention it? Not only was I so happy for Stevie, but I was also profoundly disappointed at the lack of care from Dennis. He could have postponed dinner with my parents and his outing with his buddies, as the wedding was much more important. I would have encouraged him to go if I had known before then. I have a theory why he didn't go because he's so sneaky and manipulative. I believe it was because we had dinner plans that Saturday night with Otto, who was home for the weekend and was the President or CEO (it doesn't matter to me) at a company in another country that was being sold, and he was netting a considerable check for millions. He asked us to go to dinner to celebrate. Dennis was saying that Otto was keeping his new prospects a secret but was discussing it with Dennis in confidence because Otto trusted him and sought his advice (as he said, so many others trusted him and told him things in confidence – eye roll!). We all went to dinner, and the entire time at a table with 7 of us, Otto talked freely about his prospects and the proposed salaries (was it really a secret, and Dennis was his only confidant?). At the end of the meal, Dennis paid for the entire bill because Otto was so focused on himself that he didn't notice the check was on the table for quite a while. Of course, Dennis had no issue with the hundreds of dollars that cost our family and our budget! Another theory was that he told Stevie's fiancé earlier in the week when she invited us that we couldn't go because of me. I'm sure that's what he told Stevie as well. And by the way, he told Harlow and me annoyingly that he wanted a second birthday cake from us because we didn't sing happy birthday to him and that he wanted us all to watch The Minions with him, knowing that neither of us liked that movie.

I was glad I had been making notes on my phone with all of the times Dennis was out with friends golfing, partying, and Sunday Fundays, on guys' trips, lunches, dinners, taking time away from work, and going to the gym during work hours, etc. A few times I was on debate trips, he would be out until the middle of the night (like 2 or 3 a.m.), and he responded that since I wasn't around, he was able to be "a little bit of a night owl." He continued trying to be secretive about many of his plans, so I don't know everything. Still, it was a lot, considering he complained to me and everyone else that I was ruining our finances and spending all of Harlow's college money. He was going out with guys well over half his age, partying with them, and being their hero. He worked out twice daily and went to the gym with his friend, Sam. Also, this month, he committed to a friend he was in for a golf trip in Europe the following summer that would cost $5,000 per person.

At the beginning of August 2018, one month before we were supposed to leave to take Harlow to college out of the country, he still hadn't made arrangements for us to go, even though that's when he went on the fishing trip to the Bahamas, the golf trip to South Carolina, and the "business trip" to Las Vegas all that month. I also found a receipt from a wholesale club for two patio umbrellas at $700 and a slip for two paddleboards that also was several hundred dollars. He also went out with friends that month – boy, he was a busy bee! He contacted me at work one day and said JetBlue was having a sale, and he wanted me to make arrangements to visit my sisters, Taylor and Lisa, in New York for Thanksgiving, and the tickets needed to be purchased that day. I told him I wanted to look at the flights that night, and he was annoyed that I didn't let him buy them at that moment. That night, I looked at the flights and booked the trip (he wasn't home – I think it was when he was on one of his trips). At first, I thought it was nice that he wanted me to do that, but then I realized it was a scheme, and he was way too enthusiastic. I thought about it, and it hit me: he was going to make trip arrangements for himself for Thanksgiving, and if I were already going to New York, there would be nothing I could do about it. I was betting that he was going to visit Harlow and also going to see our friends in Switzerland to meet their baby. I pegged it! He told me a couple of months later, however, not only was he going to those two places, but he was also going to Ohio to a college football game with other friends. That was incredibly sneaky, manipulative, premeditative, and calculating (as well as expensive). Speaking of my sisters from New York, I reconnected with them in January 2016. My biological father had given me up when I was about eight years old to have a family with his second wife. I saw him and his family once when I was twenty, then he was killed in my latter twenties, and I didn't see any of them again until my sister Lisa contacted me that January, and then Taylor. I remember the first night Lisa called me. When I saw her name on the caller ID, I couldn't believe it and was ecstatic. At the same time, I felt fear that I would be in trouble if I answered the call because Dennis and I were watching a show that evening. Reconnecting with them was heartfelt, and we planned to see each other that Memorial Day weekend with their daughters at our house. Right before they came into town, Dennis confronted me and asked how dare I jeopardize our family by bringing those strangers into our home. Asshole! He wanted to ruin it for me and put me on edge while they were in town. Again, he didn't want me to be happy or have people in my life who made me happy. He wound up loving them, or probably at least pretending he did because they are incredible people (he wore his 'mask'). Taylor told me afterward that they all noticed how he was treating me, how stressed I seemed, and how he treated Harlow, which broke her heart. I felt so blessed that my sisters were back in my life, and it was disheartening that I had to hide how close we had gotten in such a short amount of time. Towards our relationship's last couple of years, I often talked to my mom. She was the main person left in my life that I could talk to, besides my friend Skye. I had to pretend that I was talking to her for her sake, instead of mine, and that we weren't that close so he wouldn't try and ruin it. He also discouraged my relationship with my other sister, Madison. He couldn't have me close to anyone.

Now, about the worst day of my life. It was August 11, 2018. Harlow was on her graduation gift trip in the Pacific Northwest, and my parents were on their annual vacation, so I was very vulnerable. It was a Saturday night, and we went out for dinner at one of my favorite places because they have a really good happy hour (and inexpensive). When we got home, I told Dennis I would take off my makeup before watching some shows. He sat at the dining room table while I was at the kitchen sink, saying we wouldn't watch shows and needed to talk. My heart sank because I knew he was about to attack me verbally, and

I could do nothing to stop it. He told me he didn't think he wanted to do this anymore. He didn't want to be with me anymore, he hated his life and started in on me (I believe he either realized he was losing control of my mind and heart, so it was his discard stage, or he could have thought by saying that it would make me afraid for him to gain back control). I asked what would happen with our trip taking Harlow to college if he didn't want to be with me anymore. He said he already canceled the trip, and I yelled out in disbelief, and then he said he hadn't canceled it yet, but I won't be able to go. He accused me of cheating on him again. He said someone following me on Instagram blocked me a few months ago (I had no idea, but why would he know that? Because he's been stalking my social media for years!). It coincided with the person who called to tell him I was starting a relationship with someone, that it wasn't sexual yet, but the beginning of a relationship. I told him I believed he was projecting (he was absolutely projecting, and I believe it was a confession about what he was doing). He denied it and kept interrogating me about who this person was, which I had no idea about, so I looked at my followers and whom I was following and couldn't see anything. Then he pulled up the name, and it was a private account. I told him it probably was someone from debate who, now after graduation, didn't want to follow me anymore. He kept attacking and accusing me, as always, and telling me by name who didn't like me and others to remain nameless. After a while, I started pouring myself wine as I stood at the kitchen sink and stood there for at least an hour and a half drinking. I was becoming intoxicated and would walk away to go to the bathroom or take care of the cats, and I started cursing him under my breath. He heard me, and I just denied it - oops. I finally reached my point with him, was completely intoxicated, and started crying hysterically. We went upstairs to our bedroom, and I remember being on the floor in a ball, just crying, screaming, and yelling about how much I hated him and was cursing at him. I don't remember much more than that. Then, in the middle of the night, we were both clearly awake, and he reached out to touch me, and I moved away from him because I was distraught. He got angry and said how cruel I was to him, and I knew, as with so many other times, that I needed to pretend it was all my fault. Out of fear of what he could do next when we woke up in the morning, I asked him to cuddle and told him I wanted to make sure we went to church. He started to tell me that not only do we need to participate in church, but we also need to start discussing the lessons at home to apply them to my life. Then he said he didn't believe that I was really cheating on him, but he did say something about me owning what I've done and admitting everything I've done wrong. He also said the night before that he felt sorry for our little girl and what I've done to her and also said again how she has said to him that I'm the most toxic part of her life. He mentioned Mary and how she told me how I am, that I need to own what I've done and to learn to admit when I'm wrong. So, I was so upset that he said I couldn't go to take Harlow to college. I felt so helpless, and that's exactly how he liked me to feel. Also, during the attack, Teresa's name came up. He asked how dare anyone tell him whom he could and couldn't be friends with and was going to continue being friends with her and continue doing business with her; he said again that he met her in parking lots to give her merchandise and pay on PayPal so it wouldn't be on the company's radar (so I guess he was talking about her when he accused me, although I'm sure there were at least a few others). He said Teresa had the right to sue her company, bashed Bette, and said she was ruining the company, and Mike had no idea that business was hurting and the stocks were going down. Then he accused Bette of being an abuser to her husband, which he had said for years, and that she was an alcoholic like her father.

What I asked myself over and over, year after year, was why he was hurting me so deeply. Obviously, he was doing it purposefully because he was so calculating and premeditated. What went through his mind when he planned his attacks? Did he carefully choose what he would attack me about and when? How did he come up with the lies he would accuse and blame both Harlow and me, and were they really about him and what he has done and was doing to project them onto us so he didn't have to take accountability or responsibility? What happened in his life that made him want to do this? As much as he would say to me that reasons were excuses and weren't allowed, I knew there were reasons why, but I still couldn't believe any human being would treat another like this, especially his spouse and child. After our house was robbed, we considered getting a gun and learning how to use it for protection. I felt vulnerable and unsafe and needed to take an extra step in protecting myself as a woman. I wanted a gun and to take lessons on how to shoot. I am so thankful we never went through with it because, looking back, I could see it would have been a real possibility that one of us could have used it on the other during any one of these attacks. Thinking about it now horrifies me and reminds me of so many stories I read about and have seen in the news, and it happens every day. It could have been us, and our story would have been just another one where family, friends, and neighbors expressed how we seemed to be such a happy family and they never expected this to happen. How many times have you seen stories like this?

The next day, we were at the grocery store and ran into my friend Jana's friend, Khloe. After we finished talking to her, Dennis turned to me and said it was nice to run into someone who thinks he's a piece of shit because I lie about him (no, I tell the truth, I'm not the liar). I stayed silent like many other times, but I knew he'd been blame-shifting for years to his friends and lying about me to make himself look good and like the victim. A couple of weeks later, he started in on me before I left for work about money and our budget. I started running out to my car, and he closely followed me. Then he went on his phone and started playing audio of me screaming, crying, and cursing from that night. So, he taped me, and I didn't realize he videotaped me. I know that because he showed someone, and that person told his wife, who told me. So, he was showing me in this video to people and telling them that this was his cruel, alcoholic, abusive wife, whom he's had to put up with for 20 years. I can't even express my disgust and anguish. I really hope that the people he has shown it to actually realize that something very traumatic had to have happened for me to get to that point (reactive abuse). It's the worst thing that anyone has ever done to me ever! Ever!! This is the reason why it was the worst night of my life, and this act alone was enough to leave him, but as you know, there was so, so, so much more. I would like to see that videotape and want to hear what he was saying to me to get me to react and hope that, at some point, I will be able to. Also, keep in mind that when you see or read stories about an abusive relationship, and people say they both were abusive, in most cases, one of them was abusive, and the other was reacting to the abuse, which could be considered self-defense. For the record and complete transparency, when I was with my physically abusive husband, there were times he physically attacked me, and I fought back. The times (plural) he was choking me (yes, he tried to choke me, and I sometimes wonder if he would have really killed me), I grabbed his neck and tried choking him back to get him to stop. Do you know that when I called the police on him, I could have also been arrested for violence, even though it was because I was defending myself? When I said to the police he was violent, my husband said I was violent too. If I had him arrested, he could have me arrested, so I'd have to back off. How is that justice and protection for my well-being? I still think about it over 30 years later. Also, when Dennis was baiting me to hit him, if I did, he could have called the police and had me arrested for domestic violence.

I think it was a day or two after the attack he videotaped; he verbally attacked me for about two hours while he was telling me he was going to the Bahamas that weekend, accused me again about the Instagram person I didn't recognize, and how cruel I was to him that other day. I said it was a reaction to him accusing me of cheating on him, and he responded that he didn't accuse me of anything, that he only calmly asked me a question (gaslighting), and that I was the one who was accusing him of cheating on me with Teresa. He reminded me that I've been mean our entire marriage. After that part of the attack, I was able to audiotape him. It was imperative to me before I left (escaped) that I got him on tape to prove to myself what he was doing to me. I listened to it and wrote down just about all of it. As I said, he was already verbally assaulting me, and I was able to catch some of it, which I believe was about an hour. Here it is:

I watched you destroy relationships, our marriage, harm our daughter, and our business. I don't like that's your reputation and that our daughter had to go to counseling because her mother is the worst influence ever. There's no joy in this and Harlow's pain. You are the only person who owns the keys to fix this and number 1 the ability to admit what you've done wrong, and that's not in your mental capacity. Everyone knows what you've done, and you don't know it. It doesn't change the truth, even though you ignore it or deny it. You drive everyone away. I don't lose friends, and I've lost my daughter. I'm sorry to have to bring it up, but I wouldn't be able to live with myself if I didn't try. I tell you out of love that you're so destructive. All the relationships you've destroyed, and you have a willing destruction. Counselors tried to help, but you reject self-awareness and accountability. Am I wasting my breath? You've been given the gift of many things, and you destroy them and need to stop repeating the behavior, but you don't want to. (Then I said, "I thought I'm nice"). *You have for a few months because you got caught with the apple. Society says there's consequences to our actions* (and then compared me to a murderer) *and you've murdered so many relationships and murdered other people's reputation based on lies and suddenly act nice. Everyone knows what you are and how you've acted for 19 years, and nobody buys it. The old Jeanelle shows back up with a conversation like this.....the cursing and screaming, the insults, the fuck yous. She's still in there; she's just putting up a front because she's afraid to be single, and she's afraid to pay her own way; it's finally caught up to her. It's easy to be nice when it's easy, but when things get difficult, what do you do? This list of what you've done wrong is so damn long, so much carnage, and you say you can just put it behind you but others can't because you beat the shit out of people, and they still feel the pain, and they can't heal until you help the healing. Harlow told Hailey* (her new counselor) *all these things that hurt her, and Hailey didn't sit you down to apologize because she's over it, and part of her healing is to admit what you've done. This isn't Dennis talking, but the person you sought out to hide from me and Mary. A million counselors would say the same thing. This poor child will never be whole until you own and apologize, and the child believes it, and the person who is apologizing is sincere from the heart. When I was getting my hair done, I read an article in Oprah's magazine* (he was reading the Anti-Christ's magazine???)

about an actor who said he was misogynistic to his wife and when you recognize what you've done, you never want to stop apologizing, and he said he would spend the rest of his life and will never stop. When the counselor forces you to apologize because you need to do this for your daughter, you're stuck on step one. You can't ever understand what you've done wrong to right your wrongs, and you probably won't ever, and you can't admit that Dennis is right and he doesn't deserve this. I have a tremendous reputation except to the people you've lied to and I am comfortable when I make mistakes and own them (used an example with one of his customers). *When Otto makes a mistake what does he say? He says, "Oh shit" how do we make this right, and you dig your heels in, "I'm fucking right because I have to be fucking right."* (Then he used the example about how I want to drink eight glasses of water a day but the person who started it never meant for anyone to actually drink eight glasses, that most of it are with fruit and vegetables and a couple of glasses of water a day), *and even though I tell you it's wrong, you still do it because you have to be right. I always admit when I'm wrong to my customers and blame myself, focus on the resolution and not the problem. But, no one can move forward with you, everyone throws you by the waste-side and it happened with Harlow and she learned from you to dig her heels in and not have grace or forgiveness and no one talks to her and even though her classmate made those gross videos, to say something about it wasn't worth losing 30 friends over it, not worth it* (Harlow is the type of person that when she sees someone getting hurt unfairly, she will put herself in harm's way to help them and is willing to give up mean, fake friends or anyone else to save a good person, which is incredibly admirable and shows her incredible character). *She learns from you and sees you do it and follows your lead. And let's make up a lie about my dad to the state department for children and families and make me out to be a monster* (yes he's the boogeyman) *and she made me into a villain and made me look like the bad guy so you look like the* *good guy and in the end it made you look like a piece of shit* *because now Harlow says "why did my mom lie to me". She's* *learned from you that when the chips are down, make up a lie.* (By the way, school administration is trained to identify if a child is being abused physically or emotionally, and it's not taken lightly to call the authorities, being such a serious allegation. He then brought up our previous marriages and how I told her, but she found out online and asked me about it. We were already keeping whatever we could from him, so of course, we wouldn't talk to him about anything openly. When he found out, he just explained it away). *And they all get proven wrong,* *that agent knew it was a lie, and interviewed all of these people* *and she knew it was a lie because when the call came in and I* *spoke about our history, there was a funny look on her face like* *she understood, but it doesn't make it better. Why am I even* *talking, I guess I'm just the never-ending optimist and I hope* *at some point she's going to grow up and not the emotional* *maturity of a 14-year-old that screams as she's going down the* *hall "I hate you, I hate you, why are you so mean". I told you* *how you hurt me when you got caught in all the lies and in* *counseling you said I was so mean and said how dare you.* (He was sighing through the entire thing when he paused for emphasis) *I'm invested in you and I love you and hate* *watching you have a self-destructive life in so many ways and* *I fought you on it and you destroy everything around you and* *you say "well fuck them, I don't need friends"* (I did say to him I no longer wanted friends because I was so sick and tired of him ruining all my friendships and it was better not to have friends at all, or pretend until I left him). *You need your daughter and you need when she's an* *adult to be your friend and sadly she's running away to Europe* *and she's never going to be back and my heart breaks for you* *babe because you absolutely shun any help and can't look in* *the mirror and maybe you should accept the help and you're going to lose the game* (started comparing me to a sports game) *and you don't want to, meanwhile everyone else in your life has thrown you by the waste-side except for one person and that person you don't want to help because you hate him and he hasn't done anything to deserve your hate other than to stand up for what's right.* (He sighs, and I say, "I'm sorry honey. I love you," with my fake smile) *I'm just sorry I can't make you happy and it feels like my mom right now because when she was on the phone. I have so much love to give and when I was sitting on the arm of the chair in your apartment and I was holding you and you said that I was so touchy* (that's when I broke up with him in 1998 because it was so uncomfortably intense, and now I wonder if my subconscious was picking up on his evil) *and I love loving and pouring out love and I have someone who is rejecting it and I don't know why we ended up together. I should have seen this person doesn't want my love. I have so much love to give and I just heard it from my mom. And, the one person I want to accept my love doesn't want my love and it's tragic and there's only so much I can do honey. I don't want you in a relationship where you hate me and you should find someone you like, why do you like this unless you just like pain, does that make sense?* (I say to him, "I don't hate you, I love you") *I can't count how many times you told me last night you hate me, those are your true feelings. It's hateful.* (I said, "I was angry because you were taking the trip away, you did say," then he cut me off as he usually did and said) *I told you immediately I didn't, so that was done.* (I said "At first you said that you did", and then he said) *you are correct, I just wanted to see what your reaction to it was, so I just said you're not going, so I cancelled it, so there, there, let's get off that subject, that had nothing to do about anything, so I said I didn't so that conversation would go away and this was an hour later when you were screaming at me so it had nothing to do with that, you were drunk and your true feelings come out when you're drunk.* (I said, "I was in a lot of pain because you were gonna punish me by taking that trip away.") *Then explain the other thousand times you said that to me, you've screamed that at me for 18 years Jeanelle, you either hate me or you're the meanest person in the world, so I think you hate me because you've been loud and clear that you do and your actions show it. Who goes around and makes up lies about somebody to try and give them a bad reputation if they love them* (projecting, except he was correct that I did hate him*)? Who lies to their own child about their father and doesn't consider the fact you're hurting your daughter to hurt their father with blatant lies by taking the exact things they say and saying the exact opposite, unless you hate that person. We weren't talking about a trip to Europe when you lied to her at 8 years old and it was funny and she said you told her you didn't want her to end up a fuck up like you were and I realized you said it. Wow, I defended you at first because no one in their right mind would do that, to make me look bad, but instead it made our daughter fragile, insecure and stole the most important relationship of her life.* (I told her that he told me he didn't want her to end up a fuck up like I was after she already had been questioning how he treated us for years, it is what he actually said to me, and she wasn't 8, she was around 13 after she said something to me about defending him. Also, he stole their relationship by the way he treated and judged her) *If you understand it or not, every psychiatrist will tell you the most important relationship of her life is the one with her father and you lied to her to steal it from her and she knows that and the older she gets and processes it and when she's in college and starts to know these relationships through her classes she takes and looks back and every time she and I get together one on one, she wants every minute I'll give her "can we go around the lake one more time dad, can we drive around a little longer" she's saying I want this relationship and I'll give her anything she wants because she's starving for it and the more she gets from it the more she realizes "hey, I know who this guy is now, I* *understand why Otto loves him like a brother and Reynir respects and loves him and I know why Mike says he's one of the smartest people he knows" because they see the truth in him, because no one came up to them and lied about him for years and a year and a half ago I said to you you're the only one who can help her and you said no, I won't do it, because that would involve you saying you were wrong, dad was right "dad I'm sorry I did these things to you and made up all these stories about you and each thing I made up comes to the surface is the exact opposite from what I said is the truth". You will never do that and she'll never be able to move on from it and she knows it, and I know it, but you don't own it, so you'll never move on from it. And, all I can say is it's tragic, it's the only word I can use and now you've set yourself up for this life. Four hours a day for nine months a year was bad, now 50 weeks a year and 8 ½ hours a day until your 70 years old and you complained about working until you're 60 and sadly there's a lot of people who are saying you're getting your comeuppance right now* (As we all know at this point the reason I said anything negative about working for the business is not only because I disliked being a bookkeeper and was forced into it, I really hated working with him and would have to make things up why I didn't want to be there, plus the most important part of my parenting was to be a stay at home mother. Also, when I was on vacation, he wouldn't allow anyone at the office to help me stay caught up with my work, so no matter how long I was gone, all of that work piled up, waiting for me when I returned, which he did on purpose). *You've gone after me so hard and tried to hurt the business and reputations and you've ended up with the life you thought was the worst possible because you represented four hours a day was intolerable and three months off a year was a shit life and it's sad that people are thinking "well, she's getting hers now". I'm sorry I just went on, I just needed to get it off my chest. At least I have a clean conscience about it.* (I said, "I love you, honey," and he said) *you have a funny way of showing it. I won't bring it up again, Good night.*

"If the person you love ever made you cry so hard it brought you to your knees in despair........

They are not worthy of you."

In part by Berkana.vuno

I wonder now if he ever rehearsed these long, attacking monologues. He certainly mastered his craft – I wish he could have used this talent for good instead of evil. It was so upsetting and stressful listening to this, and along with being tense, my heart was racing during the entire tape (triggering). I went right back to that night and re-lived it. I wanted to roll up in a ball and cry. To have someone over hours continually tell you that people don't like you, that your daughter doesn't like you, that everyone knows you are wrong, to the belittling, put-downs, lying, blame-shifting, manipulation, scapegoating, gaslighting, triangulation, character assassination, and everything else he would say to make me feel bad about myself and control my thoughts. This is only a portion of one of the hundreds of times he would verbally attack me, and a lot of them were much worse than this one. I had to sit there and take it, and I could do nothing to prevent them. That night, I was trying to go to sleep, and he kept me up half the night because I had to hear what he had to say and was not allowed to speak for him to stop. When I tried to tell him I loved him and other things, I hoped he would stop because I couldn't defend myself. I would pray the whole time for him to stop and I felt helpless, defeated, and heartbroken while he was doing it. Listening to it and typing it all out, my heart rate was still elevated, and my entire body tensed. I was only able to get a few other audio tapes of him verbally attacking me, but they mainly were continuing to speak negatively about Harlow and blaming me for it, along with complaining that I destroyed our finances; I've made so many bad choices, I'll only be marketable for a couple more years so I may as well stay with him, Sue Ellen and Dan, and Sarah and Mike, and everyone else doesn't like me, people question why he's with me, he always makes good choices and good decisions, and I need to trust him, or our marriage is over, he is a good Christian and just wants to help me, everything is his, and I can leave with nothing, stop playing the victim, etc., etc. just like every other verbal attack. I really wish I had started taping him much earlier. What I know now is that every time he would tell me that no one liked me, wanted to throw me away, that Harlow said I was the most toxic part of her life, and she would abandon me, and I wouldn't be marketable if I left him, not only was projecting but also is a form of brainwashing. He was conditioning me to believe it all to continue his power and control over me and to think that if I left him, I would have no one and nothing. He wanted to ensure I was damaged so I wouldn't be marketable and no one would want me. This also kept me completely dependent on him to reaffirm my isolation from others.

Not long after that, I noticed the person from Instagram was actually following Dennis on Instagram, so I googled the name. Nothing at all came up except the Instagram account. Because Dennis was such a liar and schemer, I believed he made him up to accuse me of something and try to get me to admit to something I was doing. I spoke to him about this, and he was so angry that I would accuse him of such a thing and requested to follow that person. We found out later that someone we knew changed his name to an alias so he could follow half-naked, trashy women without people knowing it was him. I believe Dennis is still following this person, and this person is still following him to this day (I actually couldn't believe it, but that person requested to follow my new Instagram 3+ years later, and I did not approve the request). One morning that week, he left to play golf with someone else's son, whom he was obsessed with, and I had a weird feeling that he left the garage door open. I looked out the garage door, and it was open. I'm so thankful I checked because I was about to shower. I wonder if he was planning something and intentionally left the garage door open. I didn't trust him and knew at this point that he was capable of anything! He had left the garage door open before, but I never got such an eerie feeling as that morning. It could have also been that I had been through so much psychologically, and paranoia was kicking in.

We finally arranged to take Harlow to college, and I was tremendously relieved. It was extremely tense while we were there with her, and I was filled with anxiety. For part of the week, we stayed with friends who live in another part of the country, Laura and Ned. The guys went golfing, and we girls went shopping. Laura sensed something was wrong because she saw I was terrified to spend money, and I told her what was happening. She had a similar prior marriage, so she understood completely. She started crying because she remembered what it was like, and I also felt her pain. She later told me that Dennis showed Ned the video and told him other things to make me look bad and him like the victim. One of the nights we were staying with them, Laura and I were dancing to 80's dance music in their kitchen (Again, Dennis hated me dancing for some reason – was it because I was laughing and filled with joy? You may be asking if I'm a good dancer – well, the answer is not really. I like to dance anyway, but I would love to take lessons at some point!). We had the absolute best time, and it was so much fun. Dennis had a scowl on his face and was on his phone the entire time. He seemed very annoyed that I was having fun. Laura has become a very good friend, and I appreciated her understanding of what I was going through.

Now Harlow was at college, just what I always wanted, but I was also filled with the pain of knowing she had to go far away to be free. I was always happy for her when she was out of the house, especially when she traveled with school or friends, but at the same time, it terrified me to be at home with Dennis alone. Harlow being in another country for college was such a blessing for her and scary for me. I was going through so many different emotions during that trip. I felt relief that she could finally relax, be herself, and start her new life. She could have independence and relationships and live her life as an adult. I also already missed her dearly and tried to be happier for her than sad for me while my heart was really broken thinking about her entire childhood and what she had to endure for so many years.

When we drove away from her that last day, I silently cried to myself and hid it from Dennis. Like many other memories, my heart still aches as I relive those moments and feelings. Now, the next thing I knew I needed to do was to start planning my escape with a new fear of the unknown future.

By this time in my marriage, and for a long time, my health started to be affected by how I was being treated. I couldn't sleep and would wake up in the middle of the night, and everything he was doing and saying would rush into my thoughts. I felt like I was never at rest and was exhausted every hour of every day. I felt like, at any moment, I could burst into tears, have a breakdown, or hyperventilate. I wanted to crawl into a corner and hide. I had to keep going and just take each moment as it came. Because I couldn't show any negative emotions, I had so much bottled up inside me, about to explode. Also, for years, I slumped over, like I was physically defeated, and Dennis would constantly take his hands and try to make me stand up straight. Did he know it was because of him? I was paranoid and terrified every moment of the day, not knowing when I was in trouble, the next attack would come, or even a nasty remark. When you're in this type of relationship, the verbal attacks are like having a grenade thrown at you or walking through a land mine. His words were his weapons, and having to sit quietly and listen to him attack my character and everything else about me was psychological torture and terrorism. I became afraid every moment of every day. The only thing that kept me going was Harlow. I had to get through this for her sake; we had a goal, and I didn't want anything to get in the way. I had hives and rashes, was itchy from head to toe, had a tightness in my jaw and twitching in my eyes for years from the stress, and had stomach issues. At one point, when I turned 40, I briefly went on anti-anxiety medication and hid it from Dennis, but I stopped taking it because I didn't like being on prescription medicine and was afraid of what he would say to me. In the months leading up to my leaving, I felt like a shell of a person, and my spirit was gone entirely. Behind my eyes and in my heart, I was numb, and it took every breath and ounce of strength I had to get through each day. I didn't know it then, but studies prove mental stress is worse for your heart than physical stress, and our bodies process emotional pain just like we process physical pain.

"I spent so many years walking on eggshells….. never doing or saying the right thing. One day I decided I'd had enough and stomped all over them. Those broken eggshells cut me deeply as I walked away…. But this…. Was the most beautiful pain I had ever felt."

S. L. Heaton

MY ESCAPE

When you leave an abuser, you can't just tell them, you need to secretly escape

I CAN'T COUNT HOW MANY TIMES THROUGHOUT OUR MARRIAGE I WOULD think or say "I'm not allowed," or "I'm going to get in trouble," and people would question why. Dennis had me living in a constant state of anxiety and panic, which should never be normal in a relationship. So many times through the years, people would ask me why I stayed, or why I couldn't walk away when he said horrible and untrue things to and about me, or why I couldn't sleep in another room or go somewhere else when he was like that. It was and still is very difficult for people to understand why I stayed and took it. Besides all of the threats to have a judge take our child away from me, he had me financially helpless and continued to threaten that nothing was mine and I would need to walk out the door with nothing. I wanted to ensure that Harlow got the best education possible so she would always have a way out, be able to take care of herself, and never be in the position I was in. That didn't stop me from continually questioning myself and my decisions. I believed that because he would do and say what he did to Harlow, I was glad that I was at least there to bring her back up afterward. And I would try to change the subject and say she had homework or it was time for bed (anything for him to stop). I was afraid to leave him and share custody or tragically lose custody like he threatened because I couldn't be there when she was with him. I knew in my heart he would continue being that way to her and worse if I wasn't there. I would have been able to escape, but she wouldn't. All I would think about was her and that I had no choice but to suck it up and take it for as long as it took to get her through. Those thoughts are what kept me going and gave me daily strength. I also prayed all of the time, several times a day. I would do it all over again if needed. I don't feel sorry for myself at all. This was my purpose and my choice. Even so, I will always feel pain because Harlow wasn't able to grow up in a happy household with loving parents and a brother or sister.

The other way I tried to cope with everything and being controlled in so many ways was to do little things I could control. I volunteered at school when I could and spent as much time with Harlow as possible. I made sure to make a weekly menu for dinner. I enjoyed cooking, so it occupied my time and gave me some joy. I also took my physical fitness very seriously. I worked out an hour a day, six days a week. He would often comment on me doing something for him instead of working out, but that was one thing I wouldn't let him take away from me. With that, I could stand my ground and have a little control over my life. It upset me when he wanted to go to the gym with me because that was such a sacred, quiet time. I used to enjoy running errands, even just to the grocery store, but he started coming with me towards the end, which made it incredibly stressful. There were certain things I regularly did that, over time, became very scheduled, overly so, presumably also because I needed that control when so much of my life was out of my control. I see it so clearly looking back now.

I started planning my escape when we got home from taking Harlow to college. I looked at places to live on my lunch hour, using my work computer and phone because I was afraid to do any of it at home or on my cell phone. My mom also helped me obtain a 'burner' phone so he couldn't track my calls if I needed to use a cell. It took almost a month to identify the right place. I wanted to be somewhere I felt safe, that he couldn't drive or walk up to me in the parking lot or to my door. I also wanted to ensure they allowed cats because I planned to take our two kitties. I'm the one who cared for and loved them, and there was no way I would leave them behind. He also checked my emails, so I had a secret email to use with my attorney and the apartment complex. The apartment I chose had a parking garage, a security guard, and cameras, and you had to buzz someone in, which took away some of my fear. I even went so far as to make sure my apartment was in the interior of the buildings so no one could watch me or climb up to my porch. I couldn't afford it with my salary but was assured by my attorney that I'd get temporary alimony during the divorce process. I was terrified of Dennis finding out I was leaving him because of all the threats, and my anxiety was at its highest point. I didn't know what he was truly capable of and had to expect the worst. I had no idea how I would leave because of all the times he told me that if I wanted to leave him, I had to leave with nothing. I didn't even know if I could take my personal belongings, like my clothes, car, and other items. I was a nervous wreck. Our house was filled with cameras inside and out, and at every point of entry, we would get a text when they sensed motion. I didn't know what I was going to do. I wanted to leave secretly and wondered if I had to pass things out the window.

I also had no money at all. All the money in our monthly checking account went directly towards monthly bills. I had no access to anything else. I had to borrow $10,000 from my parents to retain my attorney, obtain my apartment, and buy a bed. I knew there was no way to take any of the furniture from our home because I didn't have a way to take it. I couldn't afford to hire a moving company and still didn't know how I was going to move out. I kept praying for a way. My boss at the time was nice enough to let me bring some things to keep at the office. I wanted to make sure I at least had a change of clothes and pajamas, toiletries, some toilet paper, and a few other paper products, soap, etc., just in case. Dennis kept having people stay at our house for at least three weeks and weekends in a row. When Stevie stayed at our home, my prayers were answered on how I could leave. Our security system cameras went out, and during that time, I had to reset everything, and nothing was videotaped. To get it back online, I had to unplug the entire system. It happened a few times that week, and it was my answer. I was going to be able to unplug the whole system, and it would be like the system went out again. Times before that, when it went out, as soon as it was back online, all of the videos showed up, but when the system was unplugged, nothing was taped. It was a miracle that happened precisely when I needed it.

Finally, I had a date in mind, November 10, 2018. I didn't mean for it to be the day before our anniversary; it just worked out that way. It was a Saturday, and I knew he was golfing with my stepdad at a course at least an hour away. That would give me six hours to move. I was also in contact with my attorney. We planned on filing for the divorce mid-week when I planned on leaving, so if he watched the court website, there was less chance for him to see it. My attorney also arranged for Dennis to be served with the divorce papers as soon as he got home from golf, so he couldn't change anything financially because a court order would be in place. If we didn't do it this way, he really could take my car away, cancel my medical and auto insurance, etc., because everything was in his name. My mother, sister, and nephew were going to help me move, along with a couple of their friends. We had a couple of SUVs to load up. In the preceding weeks, I went around the house and identified little things I could take, and besides my car, I wound up taking the following:

- All of my clothing and personal belongings
- About 10% of the Christmas decorations (which was still a lot)
- About 5% of the kitchen items
- A couple of wine holders and about 16 bottles of wine (out of about 600)
- 2 out of 12 TVs (yes, we excessively had 12 TVs)
- My spinning bike, dumbbells, etc.
- My jewelry box and lingerie chest
- A small outdoor chair set
- A handful of household decorations
- The photo albums (the reason I took them is because I knew the negatives were in the safe)
- Our two cats, as there was no way I was leaving them with him

That's about it. That's all I could take from our 5-bedroom, 5-bathroom, 4,300 square-foot house. I also felt some guilt in leaving (I have no idea why), so I didn't want to take any more than that. I also figured that, at some point, I could get at least a little more. It made me sad because I had saved so many things from Harlow's childhood that I couldn't take but hoped to get at some point. I left all her baby clothes, Christening dress, dolls, stuffed animals, ballet recital outfits, every video of her ever, and so many other special things. I didn't have much of a choice, and many of those items were stored at the business's warehouse.

Leading up to the day I left was highly stressful. I was terrified he was going to find out. I feared his reaction and what he was capable of. I still can't believe I held it together. The night before my escape, we went out with another couple, which was a good distraction. The next morning, I pretended I was going to the gym as usual, and it was my cleaning day, so he knew I'd be busy. I had made reservations for that night to go out for our anniversary. I had a plastic smile on my face, like always. I even went to the gym briefly, so if he had me watched, I was there (because he did have someone watching me at the gym). When I got home, I unplugged the security system, and we started packing everything. I did have a lot of clothing, shoes, toiletries, and other personal items. Towards the afternoon, we identified that a couple of SUVs would not be enough room, so a last-minute person who came to help suggested I rent a small U-Haul box truck; she called around and found the last one left in the area. I went to rent it, and we loaded up everything else, which was a mess because most of it was in giant trash bags. I reset the security system before I left. I was so nervous that a neighbor would see me, so we loaded the SUVs in the garage and the U-Haul in the driveway as quickly as possible. We went to my new apartment and unloaded. I was happy to have a bed, and my mom lent me some sheets, a few lamps, small tables, and a couple of chairs. I am so thankful to my family for their help leading up to that day. Their support was priceless. Already, I felt like a piece of my spirit was restored with my leaving and the beginning of my freedom. For all the years, Dennis slowly and methodically extinguished my light, and a glimmer of it showed up that night. I had so many emotions that ran through my head in the weeks leading up to my leaving and the day I packed up and left. I felt like I could have fallen apart at any moment; I was terrified and nervous, but I knew I had to do this and had to move forward. I pretended to be strong because I had to. I didn't have a choice and was ready to put this relationship behind me. It wasn't even really a relationship – I don't even know what to call it. I was glad it was over, unaware of what would happen next with the divorce. I was free from his psychological torture and emotional prison. But it wasn't the end of the abuse. After leaving him, I had no idea what he was capable of and was extremely naïve thinking I was done with the monster. I wasn't.

My apartment with garbage bags

I was so thankful I texted Whitney when I was alone at my apartment, and she came over for a little while, and we sat on the floor. I had to walk over to the grocery store for a piece of fried chicken for dinner because I didn't have any food, and since the towel I took was at the office, I bought a towel to shower. I was exhausted but also relieved. The next day, Whitney and I went to brunch, and it was so nice being free with a friend and not worrying she would be taken away from me and I wouldn't get in trouble for seeing her. I apologized for what happened to my friendship with her and was so happy that I could authentically be her friend and not have to pretend we weren't anymore. She understood and said she didn't think we would ever be friends again. This was the first of many reconciliations, each one restoring pieces of my spirit.

That week, miraculously, there was extra money left over in our checking account, and my attorney said I was allowed to take half of it, $2,500, which was so valuable in starting over and being able to purchase so many things for my apartment. Because I made such a small salary, I almost didn't qualify for an apartment alone. The only thing that saved me was our previous year's tax return because we filed together, and he has a high income. I felt like I had to jump through so many hoops just to leave him and was so sad it all had to happen this way. I was so blessed that things fell into place, and I could borrow money from my parents. If I hadn't been able to, there wasn't another way to leave because I had no money otherwise. At that point, I realized I would have had to stay, like many others in my position. I have no idea how someone being nonviolently abused can turn to for help, and there aren't laws that would have protected me or anyone else. By the grace of God, I found a way to leave, and every obstacle was moved aside for me.

When Dennis got home from golfing, he was served with divorce papers. He tried to call me, but I didn't answer. I knew I couldn't talk to him because he would try to confuse and blame me. I never wanted to speak to him again, either in person or on the phone. I never wanted him to be in a position again to verbally assault, gaslight, or experience any other horrible things he said or did to me. I knew to get everything in writing from this moment forward, so there was proof of what he said.

Then he texted me:

Dennis: Are you coming back tonight or not?

Me: I am not

Dennis: You don't need to be unreasonable like this, would you please come to at least we can be civil to each other. Please at least call me, you're my wife and I love you and care for you and want to at least know you're safe and I think it's fair that we at least talk. Jeanelle please at least call me so I know you're safe and we can discuss how this affects Harlow cuz I'm sure you've probably told her but she's our daughter and that's been the most important thing through this whole process. This also has huge financial implications on Harlow's school so we've really got to talk about this. Jeanelle please be kind and at least call me we talked about going to counseling and I've asked you to set it up I think that a lot of good could come of this if we work together and nothing good is going to come of this for anybody in this situation I love you very much.

Me: I'm fine. I prefer not to talk on the phone and only communicate in writing.

Dennis: Jeanelle please talk to me, you did this last time too this is not a solution please talk to me you know I love you very much and I know you and I are both hurting but we can fix this together through counseling, forgiveness and trust. This is not where we are in life and how we treat each other as Christians. It's funny when you said that you didn't feel the love for my hugs and I went out of my way to make sure you knew how much I loved you and showed you that and thought that that was going to be a great starting point not that you were working on getting divorced.

He texts me a picture of flowers and a card for our anniversary.

Me: I really don't see our relationship ever being happy. I'm sorry but that's the truth and I'm sure that you know that in your heart and in your mind. I know that you don't love me. And it's okay. I think ultimately we will be happier without each other.

Dennis: Honey I've asked you not to speak for me, I do love you I wouldn't be going through this right now if I didn't I've asked that we go to counseling because I believe that we're close we're going to church together we're hanging out together and I know you love me honey this is not a solution we're a family and I married you For Better or For Worse and I know that if we go in and have guidance that were both willing to listen to We will have a happy forever. I know neither of us will be happier without each other because we've had some great times things got off the rails and with guidance they can be put back on but running and hiding from the problems is not the solution it just becomes another problem I love you.

Me: I am sorry, but I don't want to go to counseling and listen to all the negative things that you say about me. I am over the blame, accusations, and negativity.

Dennis: Jeanelle there aren't negative things to say about you there are things that we've done to hurt each other that need to be admitted and forgiving I forgave you when we first were married for something that was very traumatic in my life and prove to you I know how to forgive but you apologized for it and you owned it and that's how I was able to forgive you if you can't face the things you've done then you're correct we won't ever be happy but if you can face them own them then we both can bury them but they don't go away just because they're out in the open that makes them hurt and you are the person as I told you for 2 years that holds the key to our happiness.

Me: I am not happy with you. If it wasn't today it would be one day down the road. So it's today.

Dennis: What are you not happy with me about.

Me: How are relationship is miserable – and has been miserable for a very long time. Believe me when I tell you that you will be happier without me. You just don't know what yet.

Dennis: Our relationship has been miserable for the last 2 years and I do not deny that for a second when I found out all the things you have done to try and turn Harlow against me that were based on lies that was horrible Hailey understood that and talk to Harlow about it too so it's not my opinion it's a fact of what happened but it doesn't mean that it can't be forgiven I was very happy prior to this when we bought this house I was very excited about what we were going to do and how we were going to turn this into the next great house and how great parties and have friends over and enjoy the rest of our lives in this great location together.

Me: I am sorry. But, my decision is final. Absolutely I will not change my mind.

Dennis: We had a lot of very happy times but yes you do know when you started in counseling that you have some deep-seated issues that have manifested themselves in beating me up over them that's no secret either you know that and yet I have stuck with you because I believe if you get into counseling and instead of have the position of everything bad in my life is Dennis's fault saying the bad in my life I put behind me because of the circumstances of my childhood and I Now understand as you were starting to that I've carried these things forward and I've penalized somebody for them who didn't deserve it and he loves me very much and he understands it and hasn't turned his back on me because of it but has encouraged me to get through it. I want to love you and trust you but I think you understand that when I found out the level of things you've done behind my back even like today it didn't need to be done this way it tears me apart and it steals that trust

Me: If I did not do it like I did it today, you wouldn't have allowed me to leave you. That is what I want, and I didn't want you to force me to stay with you.

146

Dennis: But I know as we've gone to church and you started to hear but it's not my opinion that we own our mistakes and you hear the preacher talked about his mistakes and his wife's mistakes and owns them that our God forgives them and again I've shown my ability to forgive but it can't be forgiven until it's admitted and that's what the counseling is because it's not judgmental what's happened has happened it's acknowledging it and forgiving it and bearing it together. Honey I don't want you to stay with me unless you want to stay with me and I would never force you to do anything I want you to be happy but I know this solution doesn't make you happy I know this is a temporary reaction just like when you scream at me and tell me you don't love me that it's a reaction

Me: I agree – it's a reaction. But it's a reaction to something that makes me feel the way I do. I want to be at peace – and I am not at peace in our relationship.

Dennis: But you have not tried to work this out professionally you went to three counseling sessions and came out of it claiming the counselor told you to get divorced and you're using the word Force again which I've never done anything to force you to do and that is the daddy issue manifesting itself that you've got to recognize who I really am because there's no way you can move forward if you don't know who I am and there's no way we can move forward if we don't acknowledge who you are and then we bury things together. You're not at peace in our relationship because you know that I'm still unhappy and asking you to own your mistakes so I can forgive you and just like you said earlier you don't want to go to a counselor to have to go through that process which means you can't get peace and we can't move forward like I said you own the key to our happiness and the roadmap has been given to you this isn't a secret it's not like we've got to go to Mexico and get some miracle formula the formula is there in front of us we know what it is and it's very simple to do but it takes both of us.

147

Me: No, my answer is no

Dennis: So your answer is no you don't want peace because you understand peace involves you owning your mistakes and me forgiving you we've been talking about this for 2 years that that's all it takes and you are refusing peace because it means that you have to own your portion of the problem? Again I've proven the ability to forgive you and never bring it up again I had long since forgot the lies that started our marriage because I forgave you I've never brought it up or put it in your face and the only time it was mentioned was when you brought it up to Mary and I was like oh yeah I forgot that happened because you were my wife and I was deep in love with you and trying to build our family and our future. Jeanelle what I would at least like you to consider is that we go to counseling and if this ends up being the right decision then that's fine but I don't believe that this is the right decision for either .... Do you think I would be going through all of this if I didn't love you?....If I didn't love you and was looking for a way out then I would see this is an opportunity but I don't I love you with such deep passion and want you to be happy and understand what's missing from your life to make you happy it's not a secret everybody knows it and everybody wants you to be happy but I'm the only one that's putting up a fight to get you there. It makes no sense to me that you'd want to abandon the one person who's never left your side. It's funny Bill talk to me today about our loss of friendship and how my defending you so strongly was apart of it and I laughed and said she was in the right I'll always defend her when she's in the right and yet it was worth losing friendships over versus my wife called a b★★★★ and not taking the time to understand the circumstance before they judged her.

I guess he forgot that he said Sue Ellen called me "shitty" and not a "bitch." I'm also sure he didn't defend me and most likely bashed me to Bill. Dennis asked me a question about the combination to our safe so he could get his passport. Gee, what time to ask about that? In transcribing all of these texts, I noticed his lack of punctuation and corrected it at first, but then felt it was important to note his lack of care, except his dot, dot, dots for emphasis. He rambled in his texts, just like in person (gaslighting, blame-shifting, and word salad).

> *Dennis: I hope you recognize that we have not made the true effort 2 to work together to get this done and that you will consider putting forth that full effort before making a permanent decision that is so destructive for everybody involved. I said a lot tonight because a lot needed to be said but I want to make sure that you for the one message that's been consistent throughout this....I love you very much and I'm fighting for your happiness my happiness Harlow's happiness and a happy future together. We are a family and I have never turned my back on you and I've only wanted to help you with the burdens that have saddled your happiness for 52 years it's unfair for how your childhood was but that doesn't mean your adulthood has to suffer for it not when you have somebody who understands and is willing to work with you to get over it and not walk away from you. Tell the kitties good night...I missed boy time!*

He asked me about the security system password. Again, interesting question.

> *Dennis: what did you do when you hid all the cameras today so I wouldn't know you were leaving. Good night – 'kiss face emoji' I love you.*

All that on that first night. Boy time was when he watched sports, and our male cat would hang out with him. I found it interesting that he already thought about how I left with the cameras. I wonder if that had given him a sense of security that I wouldn't secretly leave. Oh my goodness, I just looked at the texts from the next day – our anniversary – it was quite a lot. He was trying so hard to manipulate me into believing everything was my fault and nothing was his, along with all the gaslighting. He immediately threw in about Harlow's school and finances to use that as ammunition and a threat to get me to come home. I may have had an abnormal childhood, but I was way past it when we started our relationship. He was the one who, time and time again, brought it up to use against me and brought up old wounds. He continually reminded me to keep those wounds open to make me weak, vulnerable, and negative. He also tried to confuse me into thinking that our marriage was good except for the last couple of years, and of course, it was all my fault. That's what an abuser does; he continued to bring up old wounds to make me feel bad about myself so he could bring more blame and shame to me. It was also to gaslight me, so I didn't realize how many new wounds he gave me. I had enough and knew what he was trying to do. Our marriage was never good before we walked down the aisle, and it only got worse as time went by, year after year. Only good times were scattered in with all the bad to invalidate reality. The good times were there as shiny new objects to focus on in a pile of garbage.

November 11, 2018

Dennis: Good morning...I figure the cats have got you stirring by now...It is our anniversary and I would appreciate being able to get together...I know that you know I love you and I know that you love me...I know you're saying I don't love you this way for you to help accept us being apart and is necessary for you to tell yourself but know that's not true...Honey we are right on the edge and if we could work together as a team which went away a few years ago and we used to be so good at it we can conquer anything together...Please let me know when we can get together it's not healthy for us to suddenly go from 19 years together everyday to I refuse to see this person I don't deserve that and you don't deserve that.

As I've said and fought with many people over the years you are not disposable and neither am I and neither is this relationship it deserves the care that it needs we have such a depth and the tough part is over of identifying how we got to where we are now we just need to work together and go to that great place that we used to be.

Interestingly, his choice of words changed from all the verbal attacks when he told me people wanted to throw me away as part of his attacking me to feel horrible about myself and think no one liked me to now defending and fighting that I'm not disposable. Gaslighting at its finest!

Me: I am sorry but I really don't want to see you. Being around you stresses me out and I just want to be at peace.

Dennis: Jeanelle if you have the belief that you've apologized and all I'm asking for you to do is apologize so that we can put this behind us then if I'm saying I have not heard it from you and you really did apologize then that means you are sorry and if that is the case I don't understand why you can't clear that I have not felt this and I have repeated myself that this is all it's going to take for me to gain the respect in you that you want and I want to have for you and to be able to put this in our past and then map out a great future because I know where you are in life right now is not what you want and it's not what I want for you or for us but running and hiding is not a solution zero effort has been made to hear that I also have feelings in this and instead you take that I tell you of my feelings and say it's an attack on you and it's not I don't want to talk about what has happened I want you to be able to so as they say the truth can set you free and we can end this I know you understand what has happened and I believe you're willing to own it but until that happens we can't go forward and all I want to do is bury this thing like I have the past mistakes and love you and hold you in my arms and kiss you and look in your eyes and tell you how much I love you and happy anniversary.

And if you don't want to do that then it's crystal clear to me you aren't sorry because something as simple as acknowledging your husband's feelings and apologizing for doing things that you realize were very hurtful is too much then you don't love me and you're just transferring that feeling by blaming me cuz you want to blame me and it's actually you because I know this if there were one thing I had to do to make our marriage work and it was told to me by you crystal clear I would be able to do it but if I couldn't then that would mean I wouldn't want this really so you're transferring this to me is my blame is just avoiding the real issue and if you really are sorry as you said you are and you really want to reconcile and put this in our past you own that and it can be done as it's been done before so if you refuse to then I understand this is all about you and not about me.

And that breaks my heart because I've never stop loving you and I can never quit on you and I've never wanted to get rid of you because I have true love for you but part of true love is that I have to be able to trust you and part of true love back from you is building that trust.

When you told me what Bette told you about Teresa it broke my heart that you carried that burden for 5 months and I thought that was so cruel to do to somebody and I didn't get defensive because I would never do anything against your honor and I understood how much pain you were in and I made sure that you knew how much I loved you and I've been begging you to let me know how much you love me because what happened going back to Chicago all the way through French (other situations) for was nothing to do with loving me and that hasn't been reconciled and it's right there honey if you really are sorry I don't understand why you can't express it so we can get rid of it because just like the first time I don't bring things back up because I'm always moving forward but I'm stuck right now because how do I move forward with those things that have happened and you are in control of that and this is something that can be fixed today and we can start this great future for the next 19 years of wonderlust so please don't blame me and say that I don't bring you peace I can bring you great peace but it's a two-way street and certainly I haven't had peace from what I've learned has been done behind my back.

It's up to you if you really want peace with us then you can make that right now I'm here to welcome you with open arms and I'm here to hear your story and put this in our past but it takes two baby.

Me: Please leave me alone.

Dennis: Okay I just wanted to make sure you knew that I'm not quitting and I understand that this is what you want and you don't love me and that's okay but I didn't want you speaking on my behalf I'm things that aren't true so I was going to drop off your flowers and card but I guess I won't do that.

It definitely hurts that you're sitting there with the keys to success and you refused to use them because it involves you taking ownership and it kills me where not only this is going to end but other relationships in your life and I'm trying desperately to stop that from happening to you because I know how traumatic it will be.

11:11 on 11/11….sorry but you can't stop me from loving you.

Boy, did he lay it on thick? He went back and forth with the I love yous; we were great together and just have a few issues which I had to own and apologize for, and he would take me back and blaming others like Bette for burdening me and our love was amazing, and he had flowers and a card and wanted to see me for our anniversary, and I held the keys to our happiness. I also like how he was dangling our future together as a wonderlust! He also mentioned his feelings, and I guess he didn't remember that emotions didn't matter because it wasn't the truth. Reading and writing all of this, after my healing process and education, really helped me see what he was doing so clearly.

153

This is an email that he sent on November 12, 2018, at 11:11 a.m. – strategic time, I'm guessing:

Jeanelle,

I love you very much, and I know that you love me!

This is not about changing your mind, this is about changing your perspective, which will change your life for the better, forever.

I know you like her so I thought you would appreciate this:
"The smallest change in perspective can transform a life. What tiny attitude adjustment might <u>turn your world around?</u>"

— Oprah Winfrey (he had this printed in red)

Please read this all the way through, it will take about 5 minutes, and it will be well worth it.

Please know that I come to you in Peace and Love and that all I want is happiness for all of us.

I beg you to allow us to go to counseling to be able to conquer the one thing that keeps hindering our happiness, and that is the 'daddy issues' that have been identified which causes things to be seen from a different perspective than other people. There is no denying it, life has followed the pattern to a T, and there is nothing wrong with that, it is a simple truth, but what is wrong is if we allow it to rule and ruin our lives and do nothing to change it.

Certainly your father abandoning you, your second father abusing you and your stepdad being absent (your descriptions of them countless times) caused this and makes it that anyone perceived in this role can harm you. The perspective anticipates harm and sits around waiting for it to happen. Even though the harm does not happen, the truth about this person cannot be seen because the guard is always up.

Due to this I am not seen as your partner, but instead as an authority figure, and there is rebellion against this. In our case, this causes my true character to never be seen and it becomes a downward spiral. I get upset because I don't understand how the real me is unknown, I tell you how it hurts, your perspective sees this as an attack and that causes you harm and then it is just a vicious circle.

This is why the perspective wasn't as a partner at our company, but as Forced, buying a great house was Forced, driving a Mercedes was Forced, going to Europe for a month was Forced, etc. None of these were actually Forced, these are things a successful couple gets to enjoy due to the fruits of their labor, <u>but the perspective had them viewed as Forced, so they could never be appreciated for what they were.</u>

It makes people hear things about me from a perspective that they do not have, and people who know me can't understand why things like this are said, and this is where issues arise. I then feel rumors are being told about me that are not true. Harlow hears these things that makes her potentially not have a good relationship with me, due to the things she fears. This perspective has become hard-wired as a protection mechanism from these unfortunate childhood occurrences. <u>This is what this condition does without anyone ever realizing it.</u>

I KNOW that WE can learn how to manage this TOGETHER with proper professional help. Once it is understood that I am not an authority, but a partner, we will then be able to have that Peace and Happiness we seek.

This will allow us to focus on finding a way to live TOGETHER as EQUAL PARTNERS and have Peace and Happiness. If you wanted to come back to our company, in a role that YOU want, where you are able to help contribute to our success, but be able to have the freedom of schedule that you always had so that WE can enjoy life together, I would welcome that If you wanted some other type of job somewhere else that is 100% fine, that is your call.

Honey, I HATE that I am going to see Harlow and Reynir, Eva and their baby without you. I always have loved watching you map out our trips and see the joy and excitement you have researching what we are going to do and more importantly, where we are going to EAT (it is truly one

155

of my favorite things ever, I love your spirit of anticipation!) but we are at a point where perspective has refused our partnership and I felt I could not just stop living because of this, so I am having to go alone. I will book your tickets right now if you tell me you can come!

I beg you, please, please, please have the perspective to know that this is 100% from a LOVING position. There is no blame here, there are no accusations here, there is no negativity here, this is 100% LOVE. We both have done things to get us here and we both can do things to get us to where we need to be. LOVE WILL CONQUER ALL (and good counseling will help)!

We started down this road two years ago but so many obstacles were put in our way that we lost focus on this critically important solution, but we made it through those tough times TOGETHER. It is funny, we both put ourselves to the backburner for Harlow's sake – and I think that is a great reflection of US, but now it is time to focus on US. Harlow is doing GREAT and is on her way to an INCREDIBLE LIFE. We were in such a worse place then and we are so close to greatness now!

As we have learned in Church TOGETHER it is OK to not be perfect, none of us are, it is the norm, but it is not OK to ignore the issue, we ALL need to grow, and this issue is at the center of the problems our life has had, so it cannot be ignored any longer, it ruins us if we do.

It is so unfair that you have been saddled with this by other people's actions, but it is even more unfair to have the ability to find this Peace we all seek and not take the actions to gain it. <u>Getting divorced does not make this issue go away, it just moves the problem to a new set of circumstances, but you will be alone.</u> The problem will NEVER go away without help, we have proven that, we only will go away from each other, and that is not a solution.

NO ONE in this family is in a better position if this family is destroyed, not even the cats! Lol

I miss you with ALL of my heart. I would welcome you back home whenever you want, this is OUR home. I have no anger over this situation, I understand how we got to this place. I just wish we could have started counseling long ago to never have to be where we are today. It is funny, when Harlow and I spoke this weekend, she talked about herself and said she wished that she had started with a counselor earlier in her life. I took that as a HUGE sign that she knows how valuable this process is (and perhaps subtle encouragement). She has grown so much and really impressed me in our conversation! And, she does want us BOTH to be happy – that I am sure of!

I have only ever wanted to give you everything within my power to make you the happiest girl in the world. But when I felt things were being done against me, I put up my protection, which I hope you can understand. And I will learn how to not do this.

Please, go to counseling with me, we can conquer this TOGETHER. Identifying the problem is the hardest part, that is DONE. Your attitude has been so wonderful, but hiding from the problem will not fix it, and getting divorced is the ultimate way to hide, it does not help you find Peace, but just the opposite, it creates turmoil for everyone. We just have to learn how to trust each other with no fear.

I will support you 100% in this, as I think you already know, but I want to make sure you hear it loud and clear from me. This is ALL about POSITIVITY and gaining the perspective to get the Peace and Happiness we deserve.

I want nothing more than that and for US to have a great rest of our lives as PARTNERS in ALL things.

I hope you can believe in US as much as I do. I know we love each other deeply and KNOW WE can conquer this. We made it through 19 years and some really tough times TOGETHER, now is not the time to quit, we can do this if we are committed to each other, and I am committed to you with all of my everything, and I believe you are to me too!

157

I LOVE YOU WITH <u>ALL</u> OF MY HEART!
(Printed in red)

With only Peace and Love, Your HUSBAND and PARTNER,
Dennis

So he blamed all of this on my father figures? For the record, my stepdad is wonderful. I love how he tried to scare me by saying I'll be alone if I don't reconcile with him. Did he not remember how he completely trashed both my character and Harlow's time and time again? Did he think I forgot, or did he think all of his gaslighting worked? Or does he really believe all of his shit? Didn't he remember calling Oprah the anti-Christ so many times, and now he's quoting her? I guess he also isn't aware that I knew he schemed me not being able to go on that trip, and now he's dangling it as another shiny object. He's also dangling counseling as the answer to our problems. I guess he doesn't remember all of the times he said I didn't want to go to counseling because of what a counselor would tell me about myself. He remembered all these things, so he was now talking about it. He just doesn't realize that I remembered, too, or he was just trying to confuse reality. And all of the other shiny things in our lives he provided were just another part of the cycle of abuse to confuse me further and for me to want to work harder to please him and for his control.

November 13, 2018 – Texts:

> *Dennis: Good morning...Give the kitties kisses for me...I'm trying to not contact you as per your wish but I did sent that email yesterday because I hope you were able to read it a few times though I doubt it will do anything I really want to figure a way to make this work because I love you.*

Then he asks about his passport. When I took my passport, I accidentally took his as well.

> *Dennis: Can we talk?*

> *Me: I'm sorry but I want everything in writing.*

Dennis: But when I texted you you told me to stop texting you so I can't put it in writing lol

Then we discussed my dropping the passport in the garage, and he said to pick up the flowers and card.

Me: Are you already gone:

Dennis: Yes. Honey I'm not the boogeyman. Can you tell me how Harlow was when you talked to her about this.

Yes – he absolutely is the boogeyman. Who tries to fool you into thinking they're not a monster or the boogeyman? A monster or the boogeyman!

I asked if he wanted the garage door opener back, and he said to keep it in case there were other things. I'm still welcome to come and go from there because he hasn't shut me out of his life (however, I was terrified to be anywhere near the house). Then he asked if I forwarded my mail, and I said yes. He asks again how Harlow was when I talked to her, and I tell him she seemed fine. We also discussed the house alarm.

Dennis: I hope you are doing well I know I shouldn't tell you but I do miss you and I do love you I'm sorry we are at this position and I wish that you would consider counseling and not rush to a divorce because it's going to be painful for everybody and I don't think it's necessary I think we're too very good people who deserve greatness from each other.

If counseling doesn't work then we both would want a divorce so that's why I don't understand why we wouldn't at least make the effort we saw how positively it is effective Harlow and she is an advocate for it.

Me: I want to be happy. And I'm sorry but I'm not happy with you.

Dennis: Do you really believe that we couldn't work a way out to be happy with trust

Me: I am sorry but I am not happy when I'm with you. Please let me get ready so that I can have time

(to drop off and pick up)

Dennis: I know that and I wasn't happy when I was with you we both were showing that but it was because we both had our defenses up at full throttle. And that's where the trust comes in. Okay I do love you and I do ask you to reread the e-mail and please consider giving the full effort that this marriage deserves before quitting...I think that is the least we could do for each other and for Harlow.

Then he asked about dry cleaning, which was a strategy that he needed my help. And I no longer have time before work and will stop by at some point that day.

Dennis: I do want you to think about one thing because we've never had this level of unhappiness at home when you get in after a long day of work at a job that you don't truly want and all you do is end u....and if u enjoyed the job and success then that makes it fun and our time together is positive all the time.

I know there are solutions that are available to us so that we both can have a happy life together...5am-7pm straight trudging and not enjoying what u r doing is not the formula... whether we are together or apart.

As I told you that is why I had to start to do things other than work like we used to...I was miserable going 6-7 everyday.

Me: Please stop – I'm at work and you are stressing me

Dennis: Okay…did u drop off my passport

I told him I didn't have time (I guess he was too busy writing that he didn't notice I already said that). Later, I texted him that I dropped off and picked up. He asked me about the bills and logins.

Dennis: Hope u were typing your resignation letter so we can start happy life again. 'heart eyes emoji'

Now, he was also dangling me resigning from my job, thinking that was a reason for our troubles. At this time, I was still so afraid of his words. I also wanted to ensure he wouldn't do or say something to make me come home. I needed to stand my ground and also say as little as possible. Since I had revisited this for the first time almost a year and a half after I left him, I had time to put it in perspective. His twisted, manipulative, and gaslighting words did not affect me now. I saw right through it.

An email from November 13, 2018, at 3:32 pm

Jeanelle,

Sorry I keep buggin' you, but you are my wife, I love you so much, and I know there is a solution to keep us together as a family and make us all have peace and happiness.

You certainly caught me by surprise. I had no idea you were so miserable. I also did not know I was. I would have preferred we talked as we may have been able to lovingly work out a solution, but I do not think you felt that was an option. Now that this move has been made it forces me to try to see this from all angles (as you can tell) and through other people's eyes.

This is all about me changing my perspective. If I can ask you to try to do this, then I have to be able to also.

You stated in counseling that you would not have married me if you knew you had to work, and I believe that to be true still, that you do not want to work. It hurt when you said it, but I have decided to see it as a positive, that you believe in me enough to think I can provide for you financially…change of perspective.

I think the following is true of our history as I have been looking through old photos and watching your expressions. Up until you started working you were very happy. But in late 2004, when you started working, that is when things started to change. You continued working and continued getting more and more miserable as the business expanded.

You were very clear for some time that you wanted to quit, and I was so afraid of what would happen if you did, because we needed someone we could trust running the money. So we fought about you staying, and that made you perceive me as MEAN and controlling while my intention was for our families security….and this made you even more miserable. But my fear has been conquered and we have that person who we both trust immensely running the money. MASSIVE problem solved.

When you left work and had the summer of 17 off, you were happy again, I definitely could tell. But, you did not stay within the budget we agreed on and for that, it caused panic. I discussed it with you and since the only solution either of us came up with was for you to get a job, you again saw me as MEAN. We had an obligation to Harlow to pay for her school and we had no idea how much that was going to be ($70K plus??), we were over budget and we were not going to fail her. So you took the only job you were offered. And I thank you for that!

I began resenting that you would work so hard for someone else's family for 8.5 hours a day and no time off with so much control, but you would not do that for our family had I asked you to at our company. But you did not do that for their family, you did it for ours and you did that for Harlow. I had to change my perspective to understand that.

Unfortunately, the result of getting a job was that you had to be up from 5AM and go non-stop until 8 PM, with one hour to relax and watch TV before passing out for the night. And if 4 hours a day made you exhausted as you represented at our company, then this was killing you. So you became more miserable because you associated the need for a job back to me as MEAN as you have said I made you. The reality is that I did not make you, the going over budget did. I believe had we sat and gone over the budget <u>TOGETHER </u> *and created a real solution, we would not be where we are today.*

If this is correct, and I do believe it is, this allows me to finally understand how you can represent me as mean. I am anything but mean as so many people have attested to and are confused by why you would say such a thing. It was not the issues I feared that made you say this, it was your perspective. I believe if you take the perspective so many others have about me and do not have this issue blurring your vision, you will be able to see me for who I really am, and accept that I am compassionate and loving. You have told me this as recently as when you were not working in 17, but again, when you started working, I became a different person in your eyes.

We get along great, we don't fight, except about you are telling people things about me that I think are mischaracterizations. I am not even sure you knew why you were because when people would say, "what does he do that is mean?", and you could not give a specific, just that "he is, trust me". There has been so little dialogue and US time because I have set you up for a horrible life in your eyes and I have now reached EPIC MEAN status because you are miserable, exhausted and not happy. You feel that I am attacking you because I want to understand how you can say such things about me and want apologies. But you see me this way do to the circumstance and can't apologize. Again, changing my perspective and seeing it through your eyes. Which I hope you can do back for me to realize I was not trying to be MEAN I was trying to make sure we could pay our bills.

We enjoy spending time together, we have so much fun together, we are a great couple. We throw awesome parties and have great times with our friends, but beneath the surface there is a huge resentment due to this issue I could never understand, so we lashed out at each other, both feeling we were right, and I think from each perspective, we were.

When we are together it is great, watching shows, going to church, shopping (I love for you to model in the dressing room, as you know) eating, traveling etc. But you cannot lose that view of me as MEAN because 5AM rolls around again and again.

I make the mistake trying to understand this and see it from the WHAT you do with relation to my reputation and discuss things like daddy issues to try to understand, but I needed to change my perspective and see it from the WHY you do it. I am not providing you the life you expected and you resent that.

But if we remove the reason WHY you do that, and make it so you do not work anymore, then I believe you can see the real me as I am delivering what you expected to make you happy.

The solution I believe is to figure out how to live within our budget so you can stop working right away. I want you to be able to spend the whole time Harlow is home with her.

We would just HAVE to set a budget and live within it. Harlow is the most important thing financially for the next 9 years. We do not have to have a HUGE house, we can have what we NEED. We don't need 3 cars, MB, etc. if we can afford it great, but we do not NEED it. What we NEED is for all of us to have peace and happiness, and that will only come when you are not having to work, you have gone on record it is not for you. I do not think moving to a new place and still working these exhausting hours will make you any happier, you just were able to get away from the person you thought was mean.

Your running our house and making the incredible meals you do and keeping our home the way you do should be your 'job' as that is what fulfills you. If you get to do some volunteer work then I think it will even more, we were here 2 years ago, but a simple mistake of not setting a realistic budget together stole that all away from you. Instead of me just asking you for the number, we should sit down together and make sure all costs are accounted for and we make decisions together.

If you would like to explore this option I am 100% open to it. There is no reason we could not live a very nice life off of my efforts at work and your efforts at home, as true partners, each using our strengths and talents.

I do believe you know I am gentle and loving. I am full of compassion and understanding. But changing my perspective has finally allowed me to understand how you cannot see the same thing I and others do.

I know your attorneys say not to talk to me, but this is a real solution and something I wish we could have just talked about earlier. I hope you think it is too. Leaving each other is not the answer, understanding each other and creating a solution is. The other thing we would need to do in my opinion is going to counseling to learn how to communicate better, so that we can create solutions before things get off the rails.

I love you very much and am trying to figure out how to bring you happiness and peace. I do believe I have been enlightened and have discovered it. I believe you love me as you have said.

I hope to hear from you on this, we are not enemies, and we have a common goal, peace and happiness, and raising Harlow to have the incredible life we know she will.

Of course being the hopeless romantic, I am I can only dream you will run into my arms and say, yes, yes, yes you big idiot, you finally get it – I love you!!...roll credits.

I Love you!

XOXO
Dennis

He pulled out the big guns for that letter! HE'S A HOPELESS ROMANTIC! (Hahahahahahahaha).......Gentle and loving, full of compassion and understanding???? Ultimate bullshit! I don't have to work anymore, and we don't need a big house and three cars, but it would be nice if we could afford it, as long as I stay within budget. It's not MY budget, it's OUR budget. He has Harlow going to college for nine years! He uses the 'perspective' thing as another way to gaslight and manipulate me into believing he really wasn't mean (or abusive), and I need to see his perspective as well. WE DIDN'T FIGHT BECAUSE I WASN'T ALLOWED TO ARGUE BACK WHEN HE WAS VERBALLY ATTACKING ME. Then he dangles volunteering because he knew I always wanted to do something to help others. And, of course, he lays on thick how much he loves me. He also believes I'm not physically talking to him because my attorney advised it. No, I know his manipulation tactics; that's why I'm not talking to him. This is called going 'no contact' with your abuser.

On November 15, 2018, I asked if I could bring him a couple of things for Harlow since he would see her for Thanksgiving and if I could drop them in the garage. I didn't realize that he was home getting ready to leave for the trip, and when I pulled up, I saw his SUV and realized he was home. He immediately opened the garage and walked towards my car, catching me in person. I was completely caught off guard and terrified. My heart dropped to the ground, but I got out of the car and handed him what I had for Harlow. He immediately held my hands in front of us and noticed I was still wearing my ring, and he was wearing his. He said he knew I still loved him and kept kissing me. I kept telling him I needed to return to work, and he continued holding my hands and talking to me. He told me that if I apologized to him (APOLOGIZE TO HIM!!!), I could quit my job then, and he would spend $3,000 so I could go on the trip with him. Finally, I told him I had to go and left. That was extremely stressful and was the only time I had to be alone with him in a conversation. Regarding my wedding ring, right after he made me give it to him that one day, my ring finger swelled, and I couldn't take it off at all. Not long after I left him, the swelling decreased, and I was able to remove it. I believe it prevented him from taking it away again.

"Imagine another year of not being considered, of not being heard, of not being seen. Imagine five more, ten more, twenty more spirit shattering, soul crushing years.

That goodbye was a blessing."

Kalen Dion

Email from November 18, 2018 at 6:54am. This email I was told that while he was typing this in Switzerland, he was hitting the keys hard with his angry demeaner, huffing and puffing. He wouldn't talk to anyone.

Hello Beautiful!

It's me again...lol. I love you with all of my heart and will never stop, so I am doing everything I know to in order to help make our relationship what it deserves to be. I would rather err on the side of expressing my love for you, than to wait and hope it comes to you. How could it be understood if I am not expressing it?

I hope you are having a great weekend and are excited about seeing your sisters next week! Please send them all my best and tell them that I look forward to seeing everyone again soon.

As you know, I am taking the time to understand your perspective and I am so glad to as I believe it is really helping. I hope you are doing the same. I do believe if we look at this from all sides, and fairly, we will see that miscommunication has hurt us tremendously, but not beyond repair.

I know we BOTH LOVE each other very much and are BOTH hurt. We need to LOVE each other back to the healthy relationship I KNOW we can have for the rest of our lives.

I want to put this in writing so we are clear in communication.

I would welcome you to share this, and anything else I have sent, with whomever you are leaning on for support because I would assume that they have not seen another side of this. I think that your move out has given us the needed space to do so and I think it will prove to be the conduit that brings us back together. I think if there is a clear understanding of how we got here they will encourage us to BOTH do our parts to mend this. I would hope that a true friend would want this marriage to survive if there is good reason, and I do believe there are so many great reasons.

Anyone telling us not to communicate is not interested in helping our marriage, they are only interested in helping our divorce. Since breakdowns in communication helped get us here, I think to repeat that behavior is not a good way to handle things, we have proven that already!

Below is based only on the facts of what happened, there is no blame, accusation or negativity, this is just to be factual and is supported by 100% LOVE to help get both of our hearts fixed and keep us together.

We have come to discover together that people hear something other than was intended, and that it is interpreted as disparaging of my character. These things hurt me tremendously because nothing is done to fix the misunderstanding. Below is one of the times this happened and I only want to look at this one as we DO NOT have to EVER rehash all of our mistakes. I am hoping WE can put these occurrences behind US to allow us to move forward with trust.

1. *Together, we read how Harlow said that "Mom told her Dad thought she was a failure if she did not make 100% on everything"*
2. *I knew this was not something I ever said and together we looked at emails that stated the exact opposite*
3. *I asked for this to be straightened out as this was hurting me, as well, and more importantly, hurting Harlow, in so many ways, including her self-confidence, as well as causing a divide between Harlow and I that was unhealthy for a father and daughter's relationship...*

this certainly explained why she had such hate for me that I now could understand

4. *Unfortunately this was never done and she and I each continued to hurt and our relationship suffered*

5. *On Thursday I illustrated this and asked why it was never fixed. I was told because it was never really said. This was the first time I was told this in almost 2 years of having this effect all of us*

6. *What I try to understand is why, if it was known it was hurting each of us, it was not fixed. If this was not said and was simply misunderstood, this was all Harlow needed to understand to fix the situation for all of us.*

7. *So this continued to be a source of severe pain and kept driving a wedge between us as nothing was being done to right the situation*

8. *At this point, thankfully, through much conversation, I have learned this is beyond her and she has moved on in life and knows that I would never think such a thing of her, now, if it can be cleared up with me too, I can do the same.*

I think it needs to be said that NO ONE thinks anything was done on purpose to hurt anyone. I would hope you know this, but feel it is necessary to say as it is critically important.

<u>What I am asking for is</u> ownership of these type of situations, so we can learn to not repeat them then WE are able to put them in the past and move forward with trust. That is what I am referring to when I say you own the keys to this. <u>And, I will own anything that I am unaware of that has hurt you. Please let me know as I am here to give the same back to you and I will use my keys too!</u> This is a two way street and a partnership, just like seeing things from others' perspectives, we cannot ask something of one that we would not willingly do back. This is not only for the other person, but it is for ourselves too, so that we can forgive not only each other, but also, and so

importantly, we can forgive ourselves, so that there is no guilt carried forward.

I do believe that once we can have trust, we will no longer have to have our guards up and we will no longer have to go on and on about these things as they will be behind us and will not happen again moving forward. As you have experienced, I do know how to forgive and put something behind us, and I believe in you that you will be able to do the same.

I have come to you about this whole situation in a few emails and have tried to focus on one specific topic at a time to keep the waters from being muddied. I thank you for taking the time to read these, I hope you have re-read them as I know they tend to be long, there are a lot of thoughts here, but there is a lifetime of history and it deserves to be treated with the utmost of importance to get it back to the point it should be, and on a path to even greater things!

I have sent three emails, and I feel this is a pretty good outline of them and what I believe, if we do TOGETHER, will lead us on the path to TRUE HAPPINESS, PEACE AND LOVE:

1. *I believe your needs were not being met with regard to employment and lifestyle and this made you see me in a negative light and mean for not supporting your needs. I hope that you are able to see that I consider your needs as important as mine and want you to be able to stop working immediately so that you can focus on coming home with OUR FULL FAMILY (yes, I am including the kitties in our family, they miss it here too!) and preparing OUR home to be able to welcome OUR INCREDIBLE and beautiful daughter for the holidays. I know you need to give 2 weeks' notice, so I hope you do that right away so you have all the time you need at HOME to prepare for the holidays. If you are thinking about a bonus and waiting for it, please do not, OUR happiness is more valuable than*

any money can bring. If you are my cheerleader and I have your support, the sky is the limit for financial success. I will certainly be your cheerleader in making our life away from work spectacular!

2. *I believe if we can own our portions of this we can put anything that has hurt us behind us once and for all. I know we are BOTH kind and loving people and want to be able to express that to each other with no fear.*

3. *Get to know and appreciate each other. I believe each of us brings great things to this relationship. But with all the things that happened neither of us was seeing each other for who we really are. The rest of the world can't be wrong, we are two good people who want happiness for ourselves and those around us.*

4. *Have open, honest and LOVING dialogue, we can help each other grow together as we know the only thing the other wants for us is peace, love and happiness and that our partner would never do anything but help us.*

We do not have wait until we are back together to talk. I believe lack of communication is NEVER the key to any successful relationship. if you want to speak at any time, I am here for you 24/7. I hate that you could ever come to the conclusion that I have anything but love for you and I do believe that you know for certain that I do love you, you are just hurting and this is a reaction as you have said. Let me know if you would like to talk about anything, not just this topic, even to just say hi and see each other's faces, hear each other's voices and feel each other's love. You can reach me here or on WhatsApp and let me know a time. I would love to see your beautiful smile and for you to see all of us, as this is a trip we should ALL be together on! You are greatly missed by all!!!

I miss you and love you with every ounce of my being, I am sorry we have gone through any pain.

I look forward to continuing to LOVE YOU forever…as
I have said before, you can't stop me from loving you!

All of my love,
Your husband, partner, lover and friend,
Dennis

XOXO

Well, I at least can say he's a good writer. I wonder how long it took for him to draft and revise all of this crap? Dennis still doesn't realize that I know him going on this trip was a scheme, to begin with, and had me make arrangements to go to New York so I couldn't go with him. All of these words are for his love-bombing. I wish these words were real, but I knew him and his evilness. All of this was a lie, just to get back together. He was desperate. And all I had to do was apologize for everything I've done! He also uses our daughter as part of his scheme, accusing me of ruining their relationship, but we needed to be a family over the holidays. He ruined their relationship. The only times I misrepresented him were when Harlow was young, and I defended how he treated us. He never put forth the effort to have a good relationship with his daughter. I did not respond to any of his emails.

Throughout our marriage, I always questioned my decision to stay with him until Harlow went to college. I recognized it was difficult for both her and me, but in my heart and mind, I always felt that if I left, things would have been worse for her. I got my validation on Thanksgiving Day while he was alone with Harlow at her college (I am leaving these parts about Harlow because this sets up the tone of the entire divorce). She started texting me (with WhatsApp so he wouldn't know) that her dad was reminding her of everything she had ever done, and she was crying, locked in her bathroom, with him yelling at her from the other side of the door. She said that he was making her feel so bad about herself. I felt so helpless at that moment that I wasn't there to protect her. He attacked her since he couldn't punish or attack me for leaving. Also, considering he had to be on his best behavior with everything being in writing with me, he had to take it out on her because there was no written proof and strategically waited until they were in there and alone so there were no witnesses. I was so angry and hurt that he could do that to her on Thanksgiving. He held the "keys" to their relationship, not me. This is how he chose to continue with her. He also extorted her. He told her that she needed to get me to go to counseling with him, or he wouldn't pay for her second semester of college! I was shocked that he would use that against his daughter and threaten her directly. Of course, I agreed to go, but this was only until he paid her second semester; then, I would proceed with the divorce. I again ensured Harlow knew that if Dennis wound up not paying for her college, I would ensure it was covered. I was at least thankful that I was aware of his scheming and would not let him manipulate us anymore. MONSTER!!!!! DENNIS, YOU WERE A MONSTER WITH ME AND A MONSTER WITH HARLOW!!!!! SHE DID NOT DESERVE ANY OF THIS!!!!! My heart was broken for her.

Texts from November 25, 2018:

Dennis: Hey baby…I hope u had a great thanksgiving…. can we please get together tomorrow after work…I have some things to give you from the trip and would LOVE to see your beautiful face! 'heart eyes emoji'.

Me: Tomorrow is not good for me and if we see each other in person I would prefer someone else with us too. Let me know what other days work for you and I can let you know.

Dennis: Can I call you please

Me: I prefer everything in writing so there's no mistaking

Dennis: I know Harlow has encouraged us each to go to counseling as she knows how much it has helped her…I know Skye has too..r u willing to go independently first to the same person and have them help us 1 on 1 so that they can help bring us together?

(It disgusted me that he was pleased with himself and called me baby. He doesn't know that I know what he has done to her, that he verbally attacked her, and that he is extorting her. He also doesn't know that I know Skye didn't say that either.)

Me: I am open to seeing a counselor one on one for now

Dennis: ok...would u be going in with the purpose of us working this out?

Me: That I would have to decide after I go a few times and see what takes shape

Dennis: But is your attitude that u want to work it out if the counselor sees a path for us

Me: I can't make any decisions right now, but would be open to talking to someone

Dennis: If we go in w attitude to succeed, we will succeed!

Me: I will just of course need some time to process everything and come to a good decision

Dennis: ok...I believe this is the most important step and I thank you for being open minded.

Me: Ok

Dennis: but...we have a HUGE issue financially

Me: I am sorry, but that's the least of my worries

Dennis: That is why I did not mention it first...I did not want that to motivate u...I want us to be together because we love each other and that's why I didn't mention it until after I knew that you were willing to get counseling because I believe it is 100% believe it is the solution and I believe in us

Though money is the least of your worried. It is real and we have commitments that we cannot honor if we do not make adjustments to this process.

Me: I understand

Dennis: what is it u understand

Me: That money would be an issue

Dennis: there is specific issues with regard to timing and Harlow's school

(Of course, there's the issue with timing because he extorted her!)

Me: Well I know there's enough to cover her second semester in that account right now before anything else.

Dennis: No, unfortunately there is not...you have told Harlow not to worry about money but if I have to go through with the reply to your attorney then our savings for her is wiped out, plus I need to sell her car as there is not even enough now for the initial retainer...if we start counseling right away, and postpone the reply to your attorney, then this money issue goes away for the time being...and permanently once we r back together and committed to happiness...u r able to tell him we r going to try counseling and he can notify the court.

Me: I cannot promise anything, but to at least start counseling.

Dennis: I am not asking you to promise anything what I'm asking you to do is tell your attorney that we are going to try counseling and to postpone the reply if not the law states that I have to reply to you which means I have to pay the retainer which means we are taking the money for Harlow and giving it to an attorney...If we are going to make it then that money will never need to be spent...If we don't make it then we can

*pick back up where we left off...But if we do not postpone it
then I have no other option but what I said above which that
means there's no money to pay for Harlow school unless we sell
your car urgently. There is no harm in postponing.*

(So here, he threatens college, Harlow's car, and then my car, and lies
that Skye and Harlow both want us to go to counseling and then threatens
while calling me "baby" and dangling gifts – I wonder what they were?)

Me: I will talk to my attorney about it this week.

*Dennis: Jeanelle it needs to be done tomorrow. Otherwise I
have to go through with it because you forced the hand.*

Me: Ok I will email him tomorrow.

*Dennis: Why don't you call him? Honey I know we're going
to make this work.*

Me: Ok then, I will call him tomorrow

*Dennis: Okay...I'm very excited because I know that we will
conquer this and in the end will be so strong together.*

He's trying very hard to control me and the situation. We then
discuss counselors, and his only priority is finding one. Towards the
middle of our texts, he asks to call me, and I remind him in writing for
now. Then he texts:

*Dennis: Since we r putting things in writing I want to confirm we
r not seeing other people in any way so that neither has that worry.*

Me: I have absolutely no desire to see anyone else.

*Dennis: ok...so that is a confirm?? If so, me either!!!!! I love
UUU...but I NEVER want u to EVER carry that weight
that u did b4...so I am not afraid to say it.*

Me: Again, I have absolutely no desire to see anyone else.

Dennis: so u have not either?

Me: Not either what?

Dennis: seen anyone else?

Me: I have not seen anyone since before we were dating in 1999, nor have I thought about it

Dennis: Thank you...me too...

Me: Ok, good night

Dennis: I will send u info on what Harlow talked to me about concerning counseling...she was very insightful.

He then says *"good night sweetie...I love very much and look forward to the beginning of the rest of our lives together as a happy family"*, and to kiss the kitties.

So not only does he need to sell Harlow's car, but he also says we need to sell my car – urgently! He also needs to ensure I'm not seeing anyone already (and LIES that he wasn't). He carefully includes the kitties in our happy family as another illusion to gaslight me into believing we were and will be again.

Here is the email he sent about Harlow and counseling from November 26, 2018:

Baby,

When Harlow and I discussed counseling I took notes as she told me that it was the best thing that has ever happened to her and she wished she would have gone years before. This meant a lot to me as she discussed how much she has grown and changed. I certainly have seen it myself. I will share some of these things in person someday as they are too special to just put here.

We discussed if we should go to Hailey, since she had a baseline on things, and even though Harlow knew that Hailey would not tell us things about Harlow and vice versa, she thought it was best we got to our own person. I would be fine with either, but since this focus is on us, I think a starting point of freshness is probably a good thing.

You said something last night in the texts about your commitment to this...

I asked "would you be going in with the purpose of us working this out?"...

you replied "That I would have to decide after I go a few times and see what takes shape."

This worried me because we cannot go in hoping to hear what we want to hear, that will definitely not happen for either of us. We are going to go in and hear the things we are doing wrong, and we cannot then decide, "this is not worth it", we both need to get the help we need. The purpose of this is to identify the issues and make the necessary changes for success.

Harlow said that the counselor is going to tell us things that are <u>very hard to hear</u>, but that they need to be heard because we are doing things wrong. To get better, we have to be willing to hear what is wrong to learn new behavior and not repeat the old. She said the <u>Hailey told her things that made her very angry</u> but ultimately, she learned that <u>this was necessary because it helped her.</u> So I ask you to please go in with the proper frame of mind to be successful, that we are there to make this work, and be open to what is being taught, not judging it and deciding whether it is good or not, it will be good in the long run. We have proven we know how to do it wrong, so we need to listen to the advice. After a few times, I am sure each of us is not going to be thrilled with what we have heard we have done wrong, but that is necessary to learn to stop and how to do things right.

What I most took from it is to <u>not give up</u> when we are not hearing what we want, if that were the case, and they were telling us what we want to hear, we would not need to go in the first place. We have both made mistakes and need to learn to not repeat them and how to communicate better.

I think she was prepping us for success as she did not have to go into such detail, but I am telling you, she is a remarkable girl and loves us very much!

I love you and look forward to the day we can feel it from each other 24/7 with no fear!

XOXO,
Dennis

What I say to all of this – total bullshit! I knew his manipulation so much clearer at that point. He wanted to make sure I realized the counselor was going to say things that would make me angry because he absolutely would try to manipulate the situation and blame everything on me, and then he believed I was going to have to admit I'd been wrong and he'd been right. We went back and forth about a counselor, and I decided on a Christian counselor, Ross. I was thankful that when we almost broke up and were seeing Mary, I already knew counseling with him would be an absolute waste of time, so it was a valuable lesson and blessing in disguise. I knew ahead of time that if he changed his behavior towards me, it was only temporary and would wind up just as bad as always and most likely worse. It was traumatic and sickening that I had to play this game and communicate with him because he was extorting his child. I also needed to be careful what I said to him because he still believed we were reconciling, and any time he wanted to see me, I had to pretend I wasn't ready.

"*It's never the perpetrators that are in therapy, it's always their victims.*

Abusive people believe they do no wrong, victims suffer for years trying to understand it all."

Sondra Haley, LPC-MHSP

5

MY HEALING

Deprograming

Counseling was priceless

I STARTED SEEING ROSS ON DECEMBER 5, 2018. DURING MY FIRST appointment, I let him know in a non-educated way what was going on with Dennis throughout the entire marriage and that I did need counseling but not to reconcile. I was there to heal and recover from being in an emotionally and verbally abusive relationship (not realizing there was so much more and it wouldn't be my only time having to heal). I prepared a list of some things that had gone on and why I needed counseling. I also told him that I had no desire to reconcile with Dennis and was leading him to believe otherwise until Harlow's second-semester tuition was paid, then I would proceed with the divorce. I told Ross I was telling Dennis I needed to work on myself before we went as a couple. Dennis was in complete agreement, considering he believed everything was my fault. Ross totally supported my wishes and plan. I told Ross that if I had to couple's counsel with Dennis, I would for Harlow's sake, but that I didn't ever want to see him again, ever! Dennis decided to see Ross as well, and I am so thankful because he was able to see Dennis's personality and what he said about me. Ross said something to Dennis, for him to completely back off from me through the holidays and Harlow's trip home until she went back to college. I was also thankful that Harlow went to see Ross once to give her account of what went on behind closed doors. This information from both Dennis and Harlow gave Ross a much more complete picture. Going to see a counselor brought back a huge piece of my spirit and was the beginning of my long road to healing.

Dennis and I had some tense moments at the beginning of December because he was going to a couple of holiday events that I had planned on going to, so because of never wanting to see him ever again and still being very afraid of him, I bowed out of the events, which he called me a victim and I was victimizing myself several times. He also reminds me that he's not the boogeyman. YES, YOU ARE THE BOOGEYMAN! I still have all of the texts and emails. We discussed going to the gym, and I made sure he knew I was only going on Saturdays and Sundays at 8 a.m., and he had all other times of the week. He told people he couldn't go to the gym because of me, but that was a lie. He said at one point that Harlow ran away from both of us to another country, and we didn't need to give her more reasons to run from us. He also thought I ran away to Jenie's house. He wanted me to tell Jenie I couldn't pay her rent because I had to use my money for Harlow's college (still trying to control me financially!). I told him I rented an apartment. I found out he asked one of his friends to follow me home to see where I lived, but that friend declined and also asked him to pass me at the gym to see if I was still wearing my wedding ring.

December 12, 2018

Dennis: Hi beautiful…Ross was fantastic…as you know he can't tell me anything you all talked about unless you approve it…I've given him carte blanche to say anything he wants about what I've said cuz I have nothing to hide…I will ask you to consider letting him tell me some of the things, especially with anything you identify that I've done wrong…if you do not know what it is there is no way I can work on it…I hope that makes sense because it seems pointless to go talk about the issues but hide them from me.….xoxo…I love u!

Me: Ok thanks

My goodness, trying to manipulate and control me into making sure he knows what I'm saying in my counseling sessions!

181

My last communication to 'reconcile' with Dennis was on December 14, 2018. Here is our last text trail:

Dennis: Do you have a few minutes?

Me: Can I text you after work?

Dennis: Yes or would you be willing to get together

Me: I would rather do everything in writing

Dennis: That is speaking as if it's focused on divorce instead of on getting you better and understanding what's going on can we please have some dialogue this is so impersonal and so cold.

(Getting ME better!? He was right because I needed to get better from being in an abusive marriage.)

Me: Please do not pressure me into seeing you when I am not ready

Dennis: I'm not putting pressure on you I'm asking the questions you realize that there are two people involved in this correct and I also do have an opinion and in counseling I've certainly learned that this is not the way to treat each other. If we're going to ever be healthy you can't continue to inflict pain. And I've never been anything but loving towards you when we're together so it's not as if you have something to fear other than realizing your love for me that's nothing to fear.

Me: Again, please do not pressure me into seeing you when I am not ready

Dennis: Again I'm not putting pressure please don't make yourself into a victim I'm asking the question and stating why I would like to see you if this is unhealthy for both of us please don't turn it into something it's not. You said you were going to be working on yourself and you've been gone for over a month we've had some dialogue in emails you've had counseling it seems it's fair to start to talk husband and wife about what's going on. I care immensely for you and want you to conquer everything but being an island is so unhealthy for both of us and I would wish that you would consider that I also have feelings in this and that you're not just the only person in this and that you have to control everything. And you know there's no one in the world who cares more about you or a sacrifice more for you and I think it's time to treat me fairly and not as if I'm some enemy.

Me: I have only been to two counseling sessions, and I am not ready to see you in person. If you need something please email or text me your question.

Dennis: And with Harlow coming home we have to be civil to each other which there's no concern on my end to be civil toward you and the longer you wait to see me the more awkward you make it so we need to remove the awkwardness and recognize that we are friends and we do love each other and that I'm here to support you in your journey to find happiness.

Me: I will not let you pressure me into seeing you before I am ready.

Dennis: Jeanelle, I'm not pressuring you I'm asking you because if I don't ask you then you don't know I'm ready because I don't want to have you think this is going to be awkward it's not going to be. But I think that you should consider my feelings too and not just make this all about you.

Me: Please respect my decision!

Dennis: I don't respect the decision because I think it's poor and respect you but differ with your decision

Me: Then the answer is no. I will not see you right now

Dennis: And that's the whole point it's your decision and that's very unfair in life and more so with Harlow coming home we have got to address this now and not later because she can not suffer anymore from watching poor behavior between the two of us. Well unfortunately you're going against the wisdom of people who say this is bad and I don't know why you won't listen to people who know more than you and I and realize that this is unhealthy if you're trying to get healthy I would hope you would take that advice.

Me: Now I would like to ask you to leave me alone, if you were not going to respect me and continue to pressure me

Dennis: And I'd love to hear what you've learned in the past month if you've really just been focused on yourself and introspective I would love to hear there has to be some movement toward realization of who you are after 5 weeks of being alone. Again I can respect you and differ from the opinion please don't label me something I'm not but I'm also letting you know that I have feelings and I have opinions too and you're being disrespectful to me by simply dismissing them and not having any movement forward in any kind of dialogue so please don't be so disrespectful to me. We have a little girl to protect who has been through so much and we need to be adults in this and show her what compassion and love is.

Me: I am not planning to see you over the holidays. Please do not get me anything for Christmas, and I am not planning on getting you anything for Christmas. I need this time for myself, and I will not be bullied into seeing you.

Dennis: She certainly has seen compassion from me and how I'm not angry about anything and we've talked at length about this but she needs to see compassion from her mother also it's very important

Me: Ok stop it – leave me alone.

Dennis: You're not being bullied into seeing me and no I'm not getting you anything for Christmas but it would be ridiculously unhealthy for me to be driving over to your apartment to pick up Harlow and not see you she has told me she's going to split time. So I'm trying to be proactive that we don't have you being this angry at me when she's here and you recognize when you see me that I'm not the big bad wolf but not make it so that she has to experience that that's what I'm trying to do. I just wish you could consider that there are two other people involved in this that are greatly affected by it and realize that your opinion is not the only one and that compromise and compassion are good things. Other than that I really don't need to talk to you about anything other than trying to be supportive of you and instead when I show you support you just shut me out and I'll never try to stop trying to support you and making sure that you know that I love you because you've accused me of not and I have to defend myself because that's an accusation that I can't live with so don't be mad at me for addressing what you said about me and making sure that the air is very clear. I find it funny on December 14th you can already know what's going to happen through the holidays and it doesn't feel like you're looking at counseling to guide you to do the right thing as you've already made up your mind about the future and that's troubling because you should be going to counseling with the intent to discover what's wrong and you should have been on your own with the intent to grow and to already know the future is saying that you're not actually considering what's happening I'm sorry I'm going on I'm going to leave you alone now but please realize that you knowing these things ahead of time doesn't show that you're actually doing what you claim needs to be done as you already have decisions made and aren't being open…..Again this is to make sure you know that I have not turned my back on you and I'm not angry with you and I am trying to make sure you know the door is always open and please don't be angry at me for showing you love that's very unfair.

So, this entire text trail was after I asked him to text after work, and he did not even respect my asking that. He could only be nice for a certain amount of time, and his anger was definitely coming out because he lost control over me while blame-shifting that I was the angry one. And yes, he is the big bad wolf! That was it, our last communication for quite a while. I think about how strategically he used his words very carefully since it was all in writing. However, simultaneously, he was trying to manipulate me into still believing everything was my fault. He continued lying about his conversations with Harlow and what she said, which was disgusting. He just couldn't not be narcissistic. Sometimes, I wonder what his words would have been if I actually had conversations with him that weren't in writing.

After I left him, I felt so lonely because so many people had been eliminated from my life, and I was so happy to have the kitties with me to keep me company and to love. I even postponed my Thanksgiving trip to see my sisters in New York because I was newly on my own, and it was best not to go. The kitties just moved to a new place, and it would also be unfair for me to leave them. It did keep me busy starting my new life and needing almost everything for my new apartment. I used my money wisely and researched everything to buy the best item at the lowest price. It was embarrassing, to say the least when I walked into a furniture store and asked to see the least expensive couch and dresser and was thankful I could afford both. Even so, it was therapeutic and comforting because, for most of the things purchased for our home, Dennis had to have input because he couldn't give up control. This was my apartment, and I got to pick out a lot on my own. I did get Harlow's opinion on many things, as she has such wonderful taste. I appreciated her input and loved her suggestions, and she also felt proud for helping my apartment look pretty and like a home. Each item chosen was special and had a story, and they brought more tiny pieces of my spirit back to me. My mom and stepdad gave me Harlow's bed, shelves, a TV for her room, and a couple of kitchen chairs. Whitney gave me a few end tables, which are also in Harlow's room. Carlton even gave me a couple of things from his room after he went to college. I felt so blessed to have this safe home to live in. It's not the 5-bedroom, 5-bathroom house I used to live in. It's better because it's mine, and I'm happy here, which made it priceless. It was a peaceful and loving atmosphere with the kitties. I heard he told people I spent a fortune on the furniture for my apartment. He had to continue his smear campaign, trying to discredit and make me look bad!

Harlow came home for the holidays and was here for about a month and a half. Two weeks before she came home, he sold her car and told her he had to because of me and had to give the money to his attorney, so she had no means of transportation for herself. She had to rely on him, me, and Uber (except Uber went against her budget). He contradicted himself that he only had to sell her car if he was giving his attorney the retainer, which, at this point, he still thought we were in counseling to reconcile. He really sold her car to hurt her, which he knew would also hurt me, while he continued trying to put a wedge in our relationship. I also know he tried getting her to admit she said to him I was the most toxic part of her life by gaslighting her that she said it. I was glad she was home, though, and I loved having her with me and missed her so much. The bad part is that we needed to split time between Dennis and me, but I completely understood because we wanted him to continue paying for college. Even though Dennis still thought we would reconcile, he removed all pictures of me from sight at the house, which was odd considering (I'll let you know later on – just another one of his strategies). I continued to see Ross and was also thankful that Dennis had to continue paying for my health insurance, and I could pay for my counseling sessions with our HSA card.

Sam, the bodybuilder guy Dennis was friends with, worked out with, and partied downtown with, was secretly living at the house. Harlow accidentally found out and was told that on the days she was staying with him, he was staying with his wife, and on the days she was with me, he was staying there. Dennis told her he and Ashley were having issues, but unlike me, they were in counseling and communication. She had found this out right before I picked her up to go to an orthopedic appointment for her knee, and we discussed it on the way. At that moment, I wished I had Ashley's phone number. We were in shock when Harlow was called in to see the doctor. The nurse who came out to get us was Sam's wife, Ashley! What are the odds????? It still gives me the chills to think about the crazy coincidence. Thank goodness we had met a few times before, so I knew exactly who she was. I told Ashley I was glad to run into her because we had something in common, and she asked what it was. I said that our husbands were living together and we needed to compare notes. We exchanged numbers and have been close friends ever since. She told me that Sam had been having an affair, and she threw him out. She also said he was an alcoholic and had been in rehab earlier in 2018 after recovering from pancreatitis. That was interesting news since Sam, Dennis, and another friend had been partying and getting drunk since he left rehab. One day, when Harlow was still in town, she heard Sam and a girl's voice downstairs. She went down to say hi to Sam and met Valerie. She was introduced as one of Sam's friends helping him out. I texted Ashley and asked if she knew Valerie. She said that was the girl he was having an affair with. Well, well, oh, the lies continue.

Harlow went back to school on the last Saturday in January 2019. Before she left, Dennis verbally attacked her, which broke my heart, and made her pay him back hundreds of dollars she was over budget because he confused her about the difference between the exchange rate and what she was allowed to spend. That Monday, I emailed my attorney to proceed with the divorce because Harlow's college tuition and housing were paid for the second semester. That week, he contacted Harlow and commented that he guessed I wouldn't go to couple's counseling to reconcile anymore. He guessed right! Then he told her he didn't need to see Ross anymore because I was the one with a problem and not him. Not long after that, I was told that Kip was coming over to the house and was introduced as a friend from childhood. Yeah, she was, but she was also my friend. At that point, I wondered how long their relationship had been going on. I knew at least he was seeing someone emotionally (and we all know he was doing something with Teresa and possibly with Jenny as well), which is why he accused me of someone calling him to say I was in a relationship. I knew he was projecting; that's exactly what someone abusive or with a personality disorder does. At this point, I had read so many articles about narcissistic abuse that I knew Dennis was narcissistic (to be exact, as I stated earlier about diagnosing him as a covert malignant narcissist with sociopathic and psychopathic tendencies). I knew Dennis was Kip's hero after her husband died 14 years prior, and she didn't date much until then. I wonder if she has had feelings for him and if he solicited her sympathy. I know he was playing the victim like he always accused me of, and I could envision what he was saying to her, along with any other woman he was being inappropriate with. I am so sure he's been telling all of his female 'friends' that he needed a shoulder to cry on because even though he was a Christian husband and tried his best for all these years, his wife rejected his love and was a cruel, abusive, alcoholic and ruined his relationship with his daughter, his poor, poor daughter. "Let's console each other since you are going through something, too!" Sneaky conversations are just as much cheating as anything emotional or physical. So, even though I believe he's had actual emotional and physical relationships with other women, I'm sure he's had sneaky conversations with many. Not long after that, Dennis told Harlow he and Kip were in a relationship, and she told me right away (to be more specific, he told her right before she called me for the European Mother's Day because he had to ruin it). I felt so disgusted and felt incredibly betrayed by her friendship. I had respected her as a Christian woman, widow, and mother, and even when I was picking out the Christmas decorations to take that meant the most to me, I actually took an ornament that she gave me of the nativity scene. Her contact information was still on my phone, as well as her birthday. I was more hurt by her than by him. If a narcissist is broken up with, they need to replace you immediately to make themselves look good. Throughout your relationship with them, they have others lined up to be their new supply if it fits their agenda. That way, people think they are good because they already have someone new, so it must have been the other person with the issues. Also, they don't want someone better than you; they just want someone who cannot see through their lies and give them the attention, admiration, adoration, and affection they constantly crave. After the initial shock, I decided they could have each other because their relationship was based on lies, sin, and betrayal. She may have a reputation as a good and decent Christian widow, but a good and decent Christian woman would not do this. I would have accepted if they had gotten together organically after a while, but this wasn't it. God knows the truth and knew what was going on behind closed doors.

"Narcissistic Abuser: Calm, Cool, and Collected.

After breakup, they immediately find a new relationship partner seemingly overnight. This is a lifelong PATTERN.

The Victim: Disturbed, Panicked, and Confused. Heals alone and moves on to embrace their POWER."

@narcissisticabuse101

I believe way back when Dennis helped Kip when she was widowed, he comforted her and was her hero. I know he was very secretive about seeing her, and I wonder how many 'dates' he took her on without me knowing. I am sure he did the same thing with Jenny, the same with Teresa, and most likely many others. And every time, he would tell these women that I was probably cheating on him or was cheating on him to make them feel sorry for him and try to console him. That opened up their ill feelings towards me and that he was wounded and needed their comfort, along with validating his cheating. I again can hear him saying, "My wife is so cruel to me and is cheating on me. All I ever wanted was to love her and shower her with affection; all she did was reject me. It's my Christian duty to try to help her; she rejected that too. She ruined my relationship with my daughter and taught her to hate men." I'm sure he had the saddest look on his face saying all of that. I know he played the victim to prey on them. All of the times he accused me of cheating, he was cheating on me. He had them all lined up, so he had his choice almost immediately if I left him. I want to know who he cheated with while we were together. I hope these women come forward at some point and talk to me about it. They are his victims also. They were manipulated and played as fools. I want to know their stories of what he told them to gain their trust. This information is also very valuable to help others cheated with and cheated on realize what is happening and the truth.

Harlow only came home over the summer of 2019 for a few weeks. I didn't blame her. She happened to be in town for Father's Day, and Dennis actually left her for 5 ½ hours while he spent that time with Kip and her boys. He also verbally attacked her while she was there and made her cry. Again, I couldn't believe he was doing this to his one and only child, and even though she was an adult, I wish I could have been there to protect her from him. He had every opportunity to make things right with her and chose to attack her. That validates the only times I misrepresented him was when I defended him. He has been and still is truly the boogeyman. I believe after this attack, he put all of his energy and focus on me throughout the rest of the divorce. She and I had a wonderful time. One of the things we did while she was in town was spend the night at the beach, and we went to our favorite restaurant. It was so much fun. She told me later that it was one of her favorite times of the year. I felt so blessed. I wanted to meet her in Europe sometime over the summer but couldn't afford it. I love her so much and was so incredibly sorry she had been and was still going through so much from him. Regardless, my relationship with her and the fact that she was far away from him regularly brought back more of my spirit.

I found out a while ago that Dennis has a secret Instagram account. I wonder how long he's had it. With all the times he stalked Harlow and my Instagram accounts, now I know why. It takes a sneak to think others are sneaky. I also know whom he was following and who was following him, most of whom are single women, a couple whom I knew from our past (and I considered friends), and a couple I hadn't heard of. I am speculating that he had this account to message them secretly. I don't know this for sure, but like I said, he's a sneak. God always knows what is going on behind closed doors. People can represent whatever they want to people and lie their whole lives. But God knows every lie and knows the complete truth. It gives me a lot of comfort and peace knowing this.

I started becoming blessed with friendships. People were coming into my life and back into my life. I was happy that I reconciled my friendship with Jenie. She was still in shock that someone would say she said that. She now realized that was just a tiny taste of what I went through with him. I also met Bonnie Jean. She used to live in my apartment before me.

One day, she knocked on my door and introduced herself, so I invited her in for wine, and we became friends. I became good friends with another girl living in my apartment complex, Kerri, and other neighbors. I had Skye, who is one of my best friends and is always there for me. I had my friendship with Whitney, but she moved to be closer to her children and grandchildren. It was nice to have friends and know that no one would try to take them away from me. With each reconciliation and new friendship, more of my spirit came back. I did remember that since my cell phone was still under Dennis's plan, he knew exactly who I was texting and calling, making me paranoid. Sometimes, someone didn't call or text me right away, and I thought Dennis had gotten to them to ruin it. Of course, he did try. I made arrangements with my friend Maryann to meet for happy hour. She and her husband were the couple we went out with the night before I left Dennis. Her husband, Blake, was the friend whose previous wife was Janice. Maryann and I met at the restaurant Harlow worked at when she was in high school. When Maryann walked in, she said it was quite a production for her to meet me. I asked her why. She said that Dennis was telling Blake he shouldn't allow her to meet me because we were going to pick up guys, that because I'm single now, I'll be picking up guys at the bar, and his wife was going to be with me while I'm doing this. Maryann said other neighbors with whom we were all friends were also part of these conversations. She said she would not be manipulated by Dennis and controlled by her husband. She knows what kind of person she is and what kind of person I am, and she recognized what Dennis was doing. It actually disgusted me that Dennis was using Blake's insecurities to manipulate him into believing this is what we'd be doing. I felt really bad for Maryann and Blake and apologized to her and told her to please apologize to Blake. The last thing I wanted was for anyone to be hurt by hanging out with me, not to mention the other last thing I wanted was to try and pick up anyone at any bar. She is a dear friend, and I'm grateful to have her in my life.

Around April 2019, I realized I could be on Facebook, and no one could tell me I couldn't. I signed up and began to connect and reconnect with many more friends. One day at work near that time, the receptionist walked back to my office and told me someone was there to see me. I assumed it was business-related, but to my shock and surprise, it was Sarah!

She was one of the main people Dennis would continually tell me she didn't like me, so we weren't going out with her and Mike anymore. I looked at her in disbelief. I had her come back to my office, and we chatted for a little while. She said she had heard a couple of months prior that I was no longer with Dennis and wanted to let me know she was there for me. She brought me a gift and gave me a card. The gift was a little wooden plaque that said, 'Blessed are the nice people.' I told her, "Sarah, Dennis has been telling me for years that you didn't like me." She said to me it was Dennis whom she didn't like. I told her he had been reminding me she didn't like me for years, which was why we weren't going out with them anymore. She said that wasn't true; she really didn't like him. I couldn't believe it. He lied to me all these years, leading me to believe Sarah didn't like me. My heart was broken again; how could someone you believed loved you do that on purpose? Oh yeah, because he's a narcissistic abuser and doesn't care about anyone else's feelings but his own. He knew she didn't like him and made up the story about her not liking me. What hurt the most was all of the times he reminded me, over and over and over, year after year after year, to purposefully hurt me and make me feel like I was a terrible person and no one wanted to be around me and wanted to throw me away. Since then, we have gotten together often and have become so close. I consider her my very best friend and love her dearly. I am so grateful and blessed that she reached out to me.

Card and Blessed Plaque

Through Facebook, I have also reconnected with girls I went to high school with, old neighbors like Sharon and Len, and others, which has also been a blessing. Speaking of neighbors, one day, I received a Facebook friend request from Sue Ellen and a direct message. My jaw dropped, and I had tears in my eyes! She was the first of the friendships I lost during the early part of our marriage (not including my entire friend group before we even got married). I couldn't believe it and was shocked and surprised once again. I asked her to talk, and we spoke on the phone for a couple of hours. I told her I knew it was years ago, but if she wouldn't mind, I would like to discuss what happened back then. I told her I felt there was a disconnect that day. I preceded to tell her what Dennis told me, that at the holiday party, he was defending my honor because she called me shitty, that Dan said to him you know how your wife is, that Deidra and Bill were also in agreement, and that he's reminded me of it over and over and over, year after year after year. I also told her I have it on audio tape and in text. And I had a feeling that he was lying about what happened, and that's why we had a disconnect the day I went to talk to her. She told me that she and Dennis were arguing about something at the party (which didn't surprise me because he loved to argue points when someone had a differing opinion). At one point, she said to him, "Let's just agree to disagree" (which I also know he would NEVER agree to disagree with anyone, ever!), and he ripped into her, and she called him an asshole. So, when I went to her house to talk, she thought it was because she called my husband an asshole, and I thought it was because she called me shitty. I should have known, and it made complete sense. And, of course, my heart was broken yet again. That had happened in 2005, and it was now 2019. Our daughter was five, and Sue Ellen was about to have her son. I can't believe that he did this on purpose. He not only made it up so he looked like he was my hero, but it was also because he couldn't face her calling him an asshole. He also ruined my friendship with her and Harlow's relationship with her and Dan. She loved them, and they loved her. Plus, I was looking forward to helping Sue Ellen after she had her baby. He not only reminded me how it was my fault that Dan wasn't friends with Dennis because of me, but also that he was able to reconnect with Bill and rebuild their friendship, despite me, and of course, Bill's wife Deidra didn't want me. Obviously, because Dennis still knew who I was in contact with, he knew I spoke with Sue Ellen, and not long afterward, he was talking about her to someone who then told me.

By taking away my friendships, Dennis stole years' worth of memories and happiness from me, Harlow, and my friends. It's very fitting to quote the saying about the devil: "The enemy is out to kill, steal, and destroy." He killed my spirit and our family and stole so many of my friendships, and at this point, I had no idea he was on a mission to destroy me for leaving him. I was still nervous about all the people coming back into my life and the new people who were coming into my life. In the back of my head, I kept thinking that Dennis could take them away from me at any moment. I was so used to it happening that it was still a fear. Knowing he could still track my phone calls and texts, he knew exactly who I was in contact with. Some friendships did not come back. I believe that for the ones that don't come back, that's the way it's supposed to be, and they aren't supposed to be in my life, and I'm just grateful for the friends I have. I'm not perfect by any means, and I can accept that not everyone will like me. That's completely the opposite of Dennis, who wants to be perfect and have everyone like him.

I was nervous about my first birthday without Harlow and not being with Dennis because I didn't know what to expect. I'm so happy to say it wound up being one of the best birthdays of my entire life! I went out with my sister Madison to a nice dinner to celebrate our birthdays, and we also celebrated with our mom and stepdad. My sister, Taylor, and our friend Cecily came down from New York that Friday. We were under a hurricane warning on my actual birthday, Wednesday, September 4th, but Sarah took me out to dinner that night. We had the best weekend, and it was filled with friends! We went out to dinner and a couple of other places Friday night with a bunch of friends; my dear friend Jenie took us to dinner with her boyfriend Saturday night and then to a few other places, and on Sunday, we went to brunch with more friends, then my favorite wine bar that night, and one last lunch on Monday. I was blown away, and it was amazing! I felt really loved, and it was priceless for my spirit. Since then, I am so thankful that Sue Ellen, Sharon, and I have celebrated our birthdays together, which was wonderful.

I continued to be blessed with people in my life. One day, Bonnie Jean called me out of the blue because she thought I was looking for a new church and that her friend, Melissa, who also lived at the apartment complex, went to a church I may want to attend. Well, this is not a coincidence to me. I had just discovered that the church campus I was going to was canceling that service time. I thought I would have to find a new church, but Bonnie Jean didn't know that. It turned out that Melissa and I went to the same church, campus, and service they were canceling. Before the change, we started going to church together. The first time we went, they announced that night there was a meet-the-church gathering. We decided to go together, even though she had been a church member for 15 years. She knew the new lead pastor and introduced him to me. I told him what I was going through and that my husband and his girlfriend (who used to be my friend) were going to the other campus. He encouraged me to stay and was there to support me. The same night, two girls approached us, Rae and Jade, and asked us to be part of a 30s and above church group. I again told them what I was going through, and they encouraged me to stay and were there to support me. That Sunday, Melissa, Kerri, and many others from church were there for me when I walked into the other campus. I first noticed Dennis, Kip, and Sam when I walked in. I was nervous but walked up with the others to the front, where the group usually sat. During this service, the pastor asked if anyone needed prayer to raise their hands. I raised mine because I could use all the prayers I could get. On the way out, I noticed out of the corner of my eye that Dennis, Kip, and Sam were waiting in the hallway, sort of like they wanted to make sure I saw them to intimidate me. I walked right past them, all smiles with my friends and walked right up to the pastor and his wife to let them know what was happening. He said he was so happy I was there and had noticed me. As I told him my husband and his girlfriend were there, Dennis and Sam walked right by me. Where was Kip? After I spoke to the pastor, one of my friends told me that Kip waited for the guys out by the street. That means she snuck out another door (in shame?). I was so nervous afterward that Dennis would do something to take it away from me, and I even emailed the Pastor's wife out of fear. Then I realized something. There was no way he would ever return to that church because he couldn't have Kip see me surrounded by friends and happy (and normal because I also heard he was telling people I was ill, which is why I was in counseling). Church was another big part of my returning spirit. I felt like a prisoner when I went to church with Dennis, frozen during services with silent tears, afraid of his judgment or of getting in trouble if I did something wrong. So many times, I wanted to fall to my knees to pray from the pain I was experiencing. Now, I could express my spirituality however I needed or wanted. Besides being able to sing, I started raising my hands during worship songs as a cry for God to help me with my broken heart and for healing, slowly turning into gratitude for all his blessings.

I cried myself to sleep many nights and still slept most nights with a tissue in my hand. It's hard to believe this actually happened. It's also hard to believe the pattern of a narcissist and domestic abuser. It's strategic, calculating, and classic, like they check off each thing from a list. How could anyone treat someone else with such hate and evil and choose to be a monster? I will never understand. I continued healing through regular appointments with Ross, which was priceless. When I first started going, he told me that when I was describing the things that were going on with Dennis, my expressions didn't match what I was saying. Normally, when someone describes something, their expressions match what they discuss. He told me it was because I'd had to pretend for so many years and suppressed my true emotions (with a fake smile). I also experienced complex PTSD. I would wake up in the middle of the night, and everything would rush into my head, and I couldn't go back to sleep. It also happened when I spoke to someone about my experiences or if someone else would share their experiences with me. Ross told me he could do therapy to alleviate my PTSD symptoms (EMDR – Eye Movement Desensitization and Reprocessing), and the result would be that I would remember the abuse, but the feelings I felt would go away. I decided not to go through the therapy because I felt that using my feelings would continue fueling my passion for helping others. Additionally, he gave me homework to watch Brene Brown's Ted Talk regarding vulnerability. It was an incredible rediscovery of the importance of feeling emotions. That began my deep appreciation and respect for everything Brene does and stands for.

Slowly, over time, I went through the healing and grieving process. I was also going through the divorce as well, which was just as stressful as what I had gone through in the marriage. It is hard for someone who isn't familiar with nonviolent abuse, as well as narcissism, to recognize what it is and even believe someone would be capable of these actions. As I previously stated, I was grateful that Dennis went to a couple of counseling sessions and Harlow went once. Ross had a complete picture of our family dynamics, which was very important for him being able to help me. For all of the times I questioned myself, each time Ross supported my decisions. He told me that Dennis "had me at pregnancy" with his control over me and treated Harlow and me like we were "defective." He knew that Dennis continually told me I had daddy issues and that I passed them along to Harlow. Ross told me that you couldn't pass along daddy issues. You get them from your DADDY. So, I asked him about my daddy issues and what he saw. He said my daddy issues were that my male relationships had been dysfunctional because I lacked emotional support growing up. I wanted someone to love me, was naïve, and easily taken advantage of, so I picked the wrong guys. Yes, I have daddy issues. He said in the future that I still may not be able to identify when a guy is genuine and decent, and I should bring that person around my friends and family to get their opinions. So ironically, Dennis was one of my daddy issues! Ross told me my heart was in the right place regarding parenting Harlow, and I did what I believed I had to do. He even told me that what I did for her was admirable. As often as I questioned staying with Dennis through Harlow going to college, Ross agreed that was best for her. As many times that I questioned and was sorry how I had to parent her, Ross validated that not only did I not have a choice in what Dennis was doing to us, but with the trauma I was going through, it was hard for me at times to function normally or make decisions. Every one of my doubts was supported and validated. Ross had been so supportive and validating of everything. It had been such a comfort knowing that a professional agreed with my decisions since I've questioned myself many times for many years. Whether I've been validated or not, I will always be sorry because no child deserves to grow up in that type of atmosphere. I realized that when you are with someone that abusive, there aren't any good decisions. They all have consequences, and you just have to make the best decisions with the circumstances you are dealing with. In one of my sessions, he told me he had good news. He said my expressions now matched what I was saying, which was a huge step in my healing. In another session, I told him that since he was a professional and I had been seeing him for almost a year and a half, he could pick up on things that a regular person wouldn't necessarily do. I told him I wanted to be the best person I possibly could, and if there was anything he'd picked up on that I needed to work on or that was wrong with me, please let me know. He told me there was nothing. I can't even express how valuable that response was to me, and it brought tears to my eyes, happy ones for a change. I now stood tall and upright. More and more, I was happy and at peace. My goal for the entire first year after I left Dennis was for healing and to connect and reconnect with friendships, and I met that goal. It felt really good, and my genuine smile had returned.

"A narcissist doesn't break your heart, they break your spirit...

That's why it takes so long to heal."

Unknown

After two years since I left Dennis, I had not been on a date. I learned to be very comfortable with myself and was completely fine being alone. I didn't feel lonely at all anymore. In not dating, I'd gotten to know so much about myself. I consider this a blessing and will always cherish this time in my life and recovery. In my dating history, I've dated men because of how they treated and felt about me instead of how I felt about them. I also regarded their needs and feelings as more important than my own. I craved their love. That enabled me to be easily fooled by Dennis's love bombing. I also learned of my fear of being hurt, abandoned, and rejected. How ironic that I chose Dennis because I was sure he wouldn't hurt me. I thought he was safe, but he was the most dangerous. I thought I loved Dennis, but I only fell in love with his mask and not the monster he turned out to be and mirrored me to fool me. Sometimes, I thought it would be nice to hold someone's hand (which I consider the purist expression of care for someone), go out on a date, or feel affection. I missed intimacy. Even though Dennis's touch repulsed me, there were so many times I just wanted to hold his hand, hug him, or passionately kiss him because I craved those expressions of love. I don't want what Dennis did to me to guide my future and limit my potential for happiness and love in a relationship. I hope that one day, I'll find true love, allow myself to love deeply and vulnerably, and accept that my heart may get broken along the way. I want love in my life and believe I will find it eventually, and it will be amazing. I don't want to feel damaged, but rather the shattered pieces of my heart and spirit reassembled like a piece of Kintsugi, as a metaphor for embracing my imperfections and transforming into a stronger, more beautiful version of myself. I can be broken in places and still shine.

The first person I went out on a date with was a very old friend. That turned out to be the best way for me to be comfortable. It didn't stop the first time he touched me from being triggered. At the time, I didn't realize it and thought it was just nerves, but looking back, I remember my feelings, which were PTSD. Although brief, my time with him was exactly what I needed, and I will always care about him and be grateful. I was also hopeful to be able to have some regular guy friendships. I missed it. I think it's too late to re-establish my friendships with my old friend group since everyone has moved on, and it doesn't seem like it will happen. I will miss Stan, as his friendship was probably the purest friendship I've ever had.

Thank goodness I have so many amazing friends. Since leaving Dennis, I'd been supplementing my income with my credit cards. Still, I started teetering at the maximums of my credit card debt and availability; so many friends were taking me out because I couldn't afford it, especially my dear friend Sarah. I am grateful and blessed with such wonderful friendships, but at the same time, I was embarrassed having them pay my way. Sometimes, I joked with them that I felt like a homeless beggar. Also, during the COVID-19 pandemic and not getting to go out, isolation benefited me since I had no money for entertainment. My parents also had been supportive in giving me groceries and grocery money for several months, especially while Harlow was home from school and when I helped them move. Even my awful financial situation taught me a valuable lesson. In Dennis always wanting possessions as status symbols, I also bought into it. I liked the big house, the nice cars, the extravagant trips, and the expensive accessories. I had never been that person until I was with Dennis, and I've been reminded of what is truly important. I don't need any of that to be happy. I was in the worst financial position I'd ever been and the happiest I'd ever been. So, I guess I'm thankful to have gone through this experience. If I never have financial security, I have treasures with my friendships that are so much more valuable.

The holidays were wonderful with Harlow in town. In 2019, she was able to be here for six weeks. She wasn't able to come home the following summer due to COVID-19 but was able to not only be here for the holidays in 2020 but decided it was safer to stay for a while and stay through Mother's Day 2021. The first four New Year's Eve since leaving Dennis, Harlow, and I spent it cooking together and enjoying each other's company. All of them were so special for me, being with her and my spirit continuing to be restored. I feel so blessed to have such an incredible daughter. I was glad he hadn't verbally attacked her again, and I'm sure she was as well. Spending a Mother's Day with Harlow in town was wonderful, and I had a little bit of a shock. Since leaving Dennis, so many people have told me I look so much better, that I'm not as thin or gaunt, look healthier and younger, etc., and to me, nothing had changed except my spirit coming back. I was shocked when a Mother's Day memory appeared on my Instagram from 5 years prior. I compared that picture with the one from Mother's Day 2021, and the difference was amazing. When I looked at both pictures, it was jaw-dropping how much better I looked now. My coloring is so much better, and I have fewer wrinkles. I couldn't believe the dramatic difference in my eyes. In the picture from 5 years earlier, I can see the sadness and emptiness; this year, my eyes sparkled, and I looked so happy! Wow, I couldn't believe it, which shows what daily trauma does to someone.

Harlow and I communicated frequently when she was away at college. Our favorite thing to do was watch TopChef together through Facetime. Every time she texted me to say she loved me, it was a precious gift. It was amazing to be free to express our feelings and could be ourselves. There were so many times when she was growing up we hung out together, shopped, cooked, watched TV, and enjoyed each other, but when we heard the garage door open, she would go to her room and close the door. We would have to pretend we weren't close because we knew that Dennis would continue trying to ruin it. Tragically, we felt the need to do that. We didn't have to pretend or fear anymore. I still believe I failed her as a mother. When I decided to have children, as I've said many times, what I wanted the most was for my child to have a happy life and family. It breaks my heart that she didn't get to have that. It also breaks my heart that she didn't have siblings, especially because she used to ask when she was a child, but I knew there was no way I could ever have another with Dennis. I was terrified of having another child with him, and until he had his vasectomy, I made sure to use two birth control methods. Another child could have taken on his personality and become a narcissist or abuser. I would have needed to stay with Dennis until that child was an adult as well.

I realize that some of what I've written about could be construed as 'TMI' – too much information. In normal situations, that would be correct. Still, any little detail could ring a bell with someone in a similar situation and be the beginning of the realization that they are in an abusive relationship. Once, when I was at the hair salon, I talked to the stylist next to mine, and we discussed what we were doing during the pandemic. I mentioned writing this book and was asked about it. When I started discussing some details, she recognized that what her husband did to her was abusive. One thing that struck me was that she said he always called her a victim, just like Dennis. That was the first person I had ever spoken to who made that specific connection, but since then, I have heard it quite a bit. Another friend was listening to some of my stories, and when I told her it's very common for an abuser to ruin special occasions and holidays, she recognized her ex-boyfriend did that exact thing on her birthday, and now she knew why. Many abusers read from the same book, so to speak. Sometimes, things I read about make me wonder if there's a manual out there, and they put a checkmark next to each thing they do to you. Remember, for most of my marriage, I didn't realize what he was doing was abuse. Their goals are to condition and brainwash you into believing them and not yourself for power, control, and dominance. They will also do and say all these things to abuse you, blame you, confuse you, and tell you they love you and want to help you and anything else to keep you from leaving. They feel pleasure from inflicting pain upon you. I didn't have the education to diagnose what he was doing and put actual words to his actions, but now I do.

So, with that, I feel it's important to talk about our sex life since sexual abuse can be nonviolent. It did start out amazing because he was love-bombing me. Slowly, through the years, it disgusted me. It turned from loving to just having sex, and not even good sex. It was very mechanical and without affection or passion. Throughout most of the marriage, he continued pressuring me into adding another woman to our bedroom. I thought it was just a fantasy and was happy to play that game. Still, he continued to try and coerce me for it to happen aggressively; almost every time we were together, it made me feel extremely uncomfortable. He constantly said he knew I wanted it and could only be once. I wonder if he had someone in mind. I can't imagine what would have happened had he broken down my boundaries, and I said yes. Would he have videotaped it, manipulated or threatened me into it becoming a regular occurrence, or used it to control me even further? I read other stories that it's very common, even one about a female celebrity who had that happen to her. Thinking about it now horrifies me, and I am so thankful that I always said no. After a while, he introduced porn (a large percentage of narcissist abusers are said to be addicted to porn). Most of the time, I needed the extra stimulation anyway. I faked it more and more through the years until it was difficult to orgasm at all, with the fake smile on my face, but then other times, I wanted to feel something so badly, and it would take forever because he repulsed me. He would get angry if I was tired or not in the mood and would pout and give me the silent treatment. He made sure each time we had sex that I needed to orgasm twice; once wasn't good enough. Well, as nice as that sounds, he was trying to control my body and choice, and it was obsessive, coercive, and unnecessary every single time. Again, if I only wanted to once, he got angry and would accuse me of not being grateful I had a husband who wanted to pleasure me to that degree and would sometimes stop right in the middle. If we didn't have sex enough times during the week, he would say he was ripped off or some other nasty comment, so I made sure to initiate it at least once or twice a week so I wasn't in trouble. When I did, he acted like he was doing me a favor. It made each and every time with him stressful and tense. I'm sure he was also getting it from someone else, which repulsed me even more. At one point, I even went to my doctor to be tested for STDs. He tried many times to convince me to take naked pictures of myself or him take them, and he wanted to video us having sex. I felt very pressured and, thank goodness, never gave in. Even though I always viewed sexual abuse as rape, it's much more than that. He wanted power and control and tried using coercion and manipulation to have me do things I wasn't comfortable with to later use for his agenda, whether he wanted to threaten, shame, blame, or anything else. If he wasn't abusive and I trusted him, maybe I would have experimented more with our sex life. Even though he was not sexually violent, all of these things are considered sexual abuse.

"Post separation abuse is the relentless attempt by an abuser to maintain control by an abuser to maintain control and power over their victims, after separation.

It is often described by many survivors to be worse than the abuses they suffered while in the relationship."

McKown

THE DIVORCE

During most of the divorce, I had no idea Post Separation Abuse existed – Punishment and Revenge

THE DIVORCE PROCESS WAS NOTHING SHORT OF MORE ABUSE. AS BADLY AS I was treated in the marriage, I always knew that he would be much worse in the divorce. I was correct in that assumption. I was thankful at that time my attorney was a family friend and trusted he had my best interest. I viewed him as a fair and honest attorney, and as much as people advised me to hire a shark, I didn't think I needed one, nor could I afford it. All I prayed for the entire time was truth, fairness, and justice, and I thought the law was on my side. I only wanted what was fair and nothing more, but that didn't stop me from being afraid. When you leave a narcissist abuser, what happens to them is called narcissistic injury, and then they inflict narcissistic rage. I knew how evil Dennis was during the marriage; now, he would be worse. For all of the times during the marriage, he reminded me that nothing was mine and everything was his and that I wouldn't get much if I divorced him; he continued that belief and ensured everyone knew it. He was definitely still a monster, and now, besides being the Boogeyman, he had also become the Terminator.

Dennis hired a female attorney at an all-female firm. I believe he thought he could manipulate her and be in charge. I'm sure he talked smoothly at the beginning like he was such a good guy who a terrible woman had wronged. What he probably didn't count on is that he's a male chauvinist who couldn't be around strong women for long. I heard through the grapevine that they weren't very fond of him (I know more but can't say). At the beginning of the divorce, I thought I'd like to buy his attorney a glass of wine as a thank-you for not firing him as a client. Dennis told Harlow that he had the best attorney in town and that it would cost him $100,000 for the divorce, and he wasn't going to be able to pay for college and had to sell her car, which we know he sold almost immediately. I knew this divorce would be ugly and terrifying, and it certainly was. One thing I believed I had on my side was that I knew his strategy when he was fighting someone for money or in court. He makes sure the process takes as long as possible, goes silent, and uses other strategies to make the other person incur more billable attorney fees, and makes them desperate, so they settle for less than they would otherwise. I had also believed that the law would ultimately be on my side, but unfortunately, I found out it doesn't work that way. By the grace of God and his blessings, I had my credit cards, which kept supplementing my salary throughout the divorce, although it kept putting me in a really bad place financially. I kept incurring so much unsecured debt and had no idea what the future held, but I still had faith and hope, along with my attorney assuring me it would be reimbursed.

I knew that because we were married for 19 years, I qualified for permanent alimony in our state. My age and limited education and experience made this extremely important to me. Remember, he made sure during the entire marriage that nothing was ever in my name, not a car, not a house, not the business, not the commercial buildings, not the retirement accounts, not the savings account. This is considered financial abuse for control, so I was financially helpless and penniless. I never earned a single penny in my name until I finally had the job at the beginning of 2018. He made sure, as soon as I was employed, that money wasn't mine either. Also, because I had to escape from our home, I couldn't take what I needed or what was fair. Besides qualifying for permanent alimony, once I started receiving it, my attorney said it should be retroactive. According to the law, it was supposed to be fair and equitable, and I was supposed to be able to continue living somewhat in the same manner as when we were married. That's what I believed. Even when I was planning my escape, my attorney advised me to live as close to a lifestyle as when I was with Dennis, within reason, and not live like a pauper because I'd be reimbursed with my alimony, which would be based on my cost-of-living needs and prior lifestyle.

Initially, there was just a lot of financial paperwork to gather for both parties. I kept asking my attorney to schedule a temporary alimony hearing, but then Dennis and his attorney strategically stalled. We would receive ridiculous settlement offers that were meant to scare me. In one of the offers, I was actually losing money and needed to pay him, along with giving him our "male cat." Even though I knew his strategy, I couldn't help my fear and anxiety. Whenever I checked to see if I had received an email from my attorney or his secretary, my heart would always drop because I never knew what to expect, just that it wouldn't be good. He continued to represent during the divorce that he had me dripping in jewels and furs during our marriage, and he kept overvaluing what they were worth throughout the divorce and financial paperwork. I got appraisals on sellable value for my jewelry, furs, and car to ensure my asset numbers were correct. Dennis had only given me just enough for outward appearances and nothing more than that. It was just enough to talk to others about making himself out to be an amazing husband who showered his wife with gifts, and it was also love-bombing.

Finally, seven months after I left him, we went to temporary mediation. Going to temporary mediation is voluntary; both parties must agree to make it official, and it's confidential to the judge whether it works or doesn't work out. Let's just say it was an absolute disaster! I went in knowing there was no way he would agree to give me temporary support and told both my attorney and the temporary mediator, which neither believed. Dennis was filled with drama and deceit the entire time. At first, he didn't want to be in the same room with me to go over the rules of temporary mediation, and the mediator had to talk him into it. He blurted out in front of everyone that he wanted the divorce done that day and would even jump off the roof to get it done (ridiculous)! After we split up for the mediator to go back and forth to negotiate, she first met with my attorney and me. I told her he was a narcissist, and she thought I was overreacting. She believed what we were asking for was completely fair, considering what he earned, the house, the business, and the assets. Then, she met with Dennis and his attorney for about an hour. When she got back, she had a look of shock on her face, to which I asked if he was being dramatic. When she closed the door, she agreed he was a narcissist. Dennis started crying and said the business was failing, and since he was a high school dropout, he would have to wait tables, and because of me, he had to call Harlow home, and she would want to commit suicide! THAT WAS DISGUSTING! He told the mediator that he read the settlement offers to Harlow and that she was playing us against each other and was responsible for us getting a divorce because she talked me into it. I could not believe he actually said all of that to the mediator. He also said he couldn't afford alimony and was already giving me everything (gaslighting). The mediator told him she saw his settlement offers and that he was really giving me nothing. The mediator also told me she would fire him if he were her client. So, I left that day with no temporary support, just as I suspected. That was Dennis's scheme the entire time. I wonder how many times he rehearsed his lines. It was disheartening and terrifying, but I could do nothing about it. I felt my fate and financial well-being were out of my control, but I still had faith in the law and my attorney.

Whenever my attorney told Dennis's attorney that we would schedule either the full mediation required by our county or a temporary support hearing with a judge, they stalled and said they were working on other settlement offers. When they finally came over, they were complete garbage and a waste of time and billable hours, which I should have known. My attorney didn't help either by believing their crap and not scheduling it like I kept asking. He knew my financial situation was worsening and kept telling me to use my credit cards and that it would be fine. Dennis claimed the business continued to fail, and the house was devaluing even though we had it appraised. So, I continued using my credit cards to pay the expenses that were above my earnings. It didn't stop my fearing the outcome, though, knowing he was such a liar and manipulator and was out to destroy me, just like in the Terminator. At some point after that, I was deposed by Dennis and his attorney, which was more stalling and billable hours. It was pointless because I'd been truthful the entire time, and he thought he would catch me in something. I already knew that he was going on a nice vacation with Kip, which I found out Teresa was also going (triangulation?). I knew he gave away some of his airline points to Teresa for diving lessons. He also asked Harlow if he could visit her over Thanksgiving again and later for her birthday. I found out he went to a charity golf tournament and donated promotional merchandise. I knew he hid gold bars in our safe for one of his buddies when he got divorced so that he could do the same for himself and much more. I also discovered he was delaying billing his clients for months, so the business looked like a loss. I learned from Maryann that Dennis tried to manipulate her husband, Blake, AGAIN by telling him Dennis was deposing her since we talked (of course, he knew that since he still had access to track my calls and texts). Maryann told me that Blake started cursing at Dennis in a restaurant, and their argument was so loud that they left in fear of the police being called. I can't believe Blake was still friends with him. The one very suspicious question I was asked in the deposition was if I ever had Dennis followed. I said no. I didn't ever have him followed, but I thought about it and wished I had the resources. I believe I was asked that question because he was afraid I had discovered something he was hiding from me and was caught. They also asked if I was on medication and believed they would try and say I had a mental problem if I were. The sad truth is that many abuse victims need to be on anti-anxiety medication to deal with the trauma left over from the abuse during the relationship and the additional trauma of the abuse during the divorce and custody process.

Finally, we went to mediation in mid-October 2019. At this point, we had been separated for almost a year. During the mediation process, I learned some disturbing information about how divorces are handled in our state. The law may lead you to believe it's a 50/50 state, but it isn't. First, you don't get to live with the same standard of living, and every one of your budgeted items needs to be necessary. You cannot invest in a savings account, emergency fund, retirement savings, or savings to buy a house. You also aren't allowed to factor in tithing to your church or giving to charity. I feel that being unable to factor in these things violates my rights as a U.S. citizen and human being (life, liberty, and the pursuit of happiness – I guess not!). Also, if you go to trial, judges have their own formula to decide who gets what (in their own opinion), and it's never 50/50; it's all about showing the need and mostly favors the person paying instead of the person who needs it. I was so afraid that I wouldn't be able to support myself, would have to take a second job, and would never be able to retire. Without a savings account or emergency fund, if I had an emergency, whether it be medical, an accident, an extensive car repair, or whatever, I had no way of covering it. I would be screwed with no way out, and how was that fair and just? What if Harlow had an emergency, and I needed to go to her? I didn't have enough money or credit to pay for one flight. Dennis has millions of travel miles and wouldn't budge to give me any of them while giving some to Teresa.

During mediation, Dennis expressed that he believed I should get nothing, and he was extremely difficult to deal with that day. According to the mediator, who was a family law judge for 20 years, Dennis represented that he was the most intelligent person in the room (in other words – narcissistic). Several times during that day, the mediator and the two attorneys had to meet together and strategize because of Dennis and his narcissism. He claimed he couldn't afford to pay me alimony and said his expenses were just as much as they were when I was still with him, he wasn't making any money, and the business was still failing, which were all lies. Much of his strategy against me was using Harlow's college tuition and living expenses as leverage. I wanted to ensure that it wasn't taken away and written into the settlement agreement so it would be binding since he kept threatening it. In our state's divorce cases, once a child is an adult, you cannot factor any expenses for them if you go before a judge in a trial. Dennis knew my top priority was her college, so he used it against me as a weapon. Besides fearing Harlow's college and my financial well-being, I felt the mediator and my attorney pressured and scared me into taking a deal. The whole agenda of a mediator is just to get it done, and it has nothing to do with truth, fairness, or justice. So, at the very end of the day, we did agree on a settlement, which was much less than I should have gotten, but since he thought I should get nothing, I was ready to just get it over with and cut my losses. Because it was late in the day, Dennis's attorney later typed up the agreement and sent it to my attorney. That took 2 ½ weeks. When we received the paperwork, most of it was changed from what we agreed upon that day. I could not believe the law allowed that to happen, and there was nothing I could do about it! It was also shocking that any attorney was capable of this unethical practice. I trusted we agreed in good faith, but apparently, good faith has nothing to do with the law or her morals. It took another FIVE months of negotiating back and forth to get back to what we agreed to in mediation, which equaled more stalling, threatening settlement offers, attorney fees, and debt. Every time they sent offers, they continued to devalue the house and lower my alimony to scare and threaten me. They kept using the strategy that it was a one-time offer as control and also to scare me into action. I knew what he was doing and didn't want to give up. He continued stalling to hurt me and postpone giving me anything as long as possible. I kept asking my attorney to schedule a temporary alimony hearing, and he kept dismissing me and said just to use my credit cards, which would be reimbursed later. I was ready to go to trial if needed, even though I was very close to running out of credit. My attorney could have deposed his bookkeeper and girlfriend if we went to trial. That would have shown how he was still living well, traveling, and so forth. We would have been able to ask Kip when she started seeing Dennis, what travel and going out they had done, if they ever saw each other socially when I was still with him if he was paying any of her bills, or if she was hiding anything for him. We would have been able to ask Amy if she delayed billing clients and other business questions to prove Dennis was lying and strategizing with the business. If either of them lied, they would be in contempt of court. Unfortunately, Amy resigned before we could depose her (wonder why?), and he probably would have manipulated Kip to lie for him, as he previously tried with me. It's tragic that because he owns his own business, to try and prove he was lying and manipulating his numbers, I would have had to hire a business valuator or forensic accountant, which I didn't have the financial resources to do and was in fear that if we tried to require Dennis to pay and failed, I would be on the hook.

Towards the end of February 2020, almost a year and a half after I left Dennis, we finally came to terms but hadn't signed yet. To save Harlow's college tuition and expenses, I took a monthly alimony number that was much less than my needs, and I expressed to my attorney and the mediator that I'd have to get a higher-paying job to make up for it. I also gave up permanent alimony and accepted 13 ½ years, gave up retroactive alimony, and gave up reimbursement for all of my attorney fees. I also took less than what was fair for the value of the business (because he was lying and saying it was worthless), the commercial buildings, 99% of the possessions in the house, and gave up getting any of the items I saved from Harlow's childhood, which was heartbreaking. My most important issue was Harlow's college, which would now be binding, and Dennis could not make her come home. That was worth everything I gave up.

I had reached the point that I had exhausted my credit limit and had also reached the point that I couldn't pay my rent, utilities, and the minimums due on my credit cards by March 1, 2020. I knew it was coming and had prayed about it and asked everyone I knew for prayers. On February 28th, I lost my job. It was the blessing I was asking for because I received enough severance to pay my bills on March 1st. It was a miracle! I knew I wouldn't be able to pay my bills on April 1st without a job, but I knew I would be fine. My prayers were answered for March; I knew they would be for April. I was right. We both signed and notarized the mediation paperwork in time for me to receive my first alimony checks for February, March, and April right before the end of March so that I could pay my bills. I found a new position that started in mid-April, which meant I'd be okay moving forward with alimony but had a great deal of unsecured debt to pay off. I hoped the house sold quickly and I could get the other portion of my settlement. My new salary and alimony would be enough to support myself, which made me extremely relieved and grateful that my struggles seemed to be ending.

Right before I started my new job, I changed my place of employment on Facebook and LinkedIn. I didn't realize it would post, I just wanted to update my information. I found out that one of my LinkedIn contacts (a minion) told Dennis about my new job. Even though it was between us signing the mediation settlement and a judge finalizing it and notifying my attorney immediately, I believed there wouldn't be an issue. Boy, was I wrong. On my first day at work, my attorney contacted me because Dennis contacted his attorney. They wanted to know what day I was offered the job and my new salary. I didn't realize that case law allowed them to readdress the mediation before the judge finalized the settlement agreement. I knew my old salary plus the negotiated alimony would not cover my monthly expenses, which my attorney was aware of, and I needed either a new job or a second job anyway. My budget clearly showed it, but that didn't matter to them. It was yet more abuse, stalling, lying, and attorney fees. Yet again my attorney also failed me by not informing me of all of this ahead of time.

I'm sure to Dennis' friends he'd been making me out to be a gold-digger who wanted to destroy him, which was projection and a smear campaign because he was out to punish, gain revenge, and destroy me. I found out that a couple of his buddies were talking about me that I was flaunting my new job and trying to still collect money from Dennis. This wasn't Jeanelle trying to 'collect' anything! I'm entitled to alimony and a settlement for everything we worked for the almost 20 years we were together that he took from me, and I had to give up. I can't believe Dennis so manipulated these grown men, and they believed his lies. How much did they think I was earning? Both of these men are multi-millionaires and CEOs of major worldwide companies (you know – captains of industry)! I love how they were talking about me but either didn't want to know the truth or didn't care while saying all the while that they were remaining neutral. You would think people wanted to know the truth, but instead, the flying monkeys stick together (now I realize what that expression means). I'd instead call them minions from Dennis's favorite movie. I guess he likes that movie because he sees himself as the villain who has minions he controls and manipulates. Neutrality, and when they stick their heads in the sand, it's enabling and validating the bad behavior and abuse.

"We must take sides.

Neutrality helps the oppressor, never the victim.

Silence encourages the tormentor, never the tormented."

Elie Wiesel

I also had the opportunity to talk with another mutual friend, who said to me that Dennis loved me so much and was hurt badly by my leaving and he could see the hurt on his face. They even spoke about it in private at an event Dennis and Kip were there together. I guess he, believing Dennis was such a good guy (mask), had no idea what Dennis was truly capable of and didn't realize it was odd for Dennis to start a relationship with Kip within just a few months after I left (and now were playing family), while he's telling him how much he loved me and how much I hurt him? Maybe he wasn't aware that Kip was my friend also, and we had hung out together a lot when our kids were small and as couples before her husband died. At this point, I think there are so many stories out there about me that were being told depending on Dennis's agenda with that person, along with a mask of sadness. I wish I could get all his friends together in one room and ask them to talk about what Dennis said about me while we were together and since I left and see how many different stories are out there. It would be entertaining, to say the least. The manipulation continued, and Dennis happily told people what he needed to for others to feel sorry for him as the victim and make me look like the villain. I heard from another friend that Dennis was attacking the character of Kip's only true boyfriend since her husband died. I wonder if Kip knows that, and I wonder if her old boyfriend knows as well (who also went to school with us)? Dennis had to attack his character to make himself look better, another disturbing thing a narcissist will do for their agenda.

The entire time, I've put up with Dennis believing he didn't need to give me anything, so when we came to what we agreed upon, I just wanted it done and gave up so much of what was fair and just. Because I started a new job with a higher income (but still below my needs), he wanted to terminate or cut my alimony permanently, and I couldn't do that. With the current salary at my new job plus alimony, I was still not earning a third of what he was earning. The entire time we were going through the divorce, he represented that his business was failing and making no money. It was a blatant lie, and since I was a bookkeeper, I could see in his financials that he was making money and trying to hide it throughout his Profit and Loss report, along with his other financial paperwork, credit card statements, and bank account statements. He was like the boy who cried wolf! And he started crying even louder that his business was failing during the COVID-19 pandemic. Now, I had to worry about the pandemic and how it would affect my divorce settlement. He claimed his business would take years to recover, which was just another lie and strategy. I'd seen on the news and know of others in his business doing incredibly well selling hand sanitizers, face masks, and other personal protection items. I offered to fairly postpone my alimony while his business got back to 'normal,' along with my attorney pressuring me to. Still, Dennis was just using the virus to manipulate the situation and outcome of the settlement, along with the business's manipulated financials. So, I was not getting anything yet again, with more stalling, lies, manipulation, attorney fees, and debt. He lied about everything the last year, so how would we know he wasn't lying now? Not only was he actually lying, but I have the paperwork to prove it. I was already in dire financial straits, and it would take me a long time to fix all of that, years! I had recognized, though, that because I had a large monthly amount going towards the minimums on my credit cards, I was again close to being unable to meet my needs with my current salary. I was barely getting by, and at some point, again, I wouldn't be able to pay all my bills. I even had to stop paying my attorney at the end of 2019 and was extremely thankful he understood what I was dealing with, as so many victims and survivors like me are left representing themselves because of their financial situation (pro se).

I was grateful we filed our 2019 tax return jointly because it proved he was lying. I made less than a quarter of what he made in 2019, and he still got to keep the business, the commercial buildings, have two vehicles, travel, golf and go out, live in our house, and keep almost all of our joint assets. The business also did make money, which contradicts his statements and paperwork. He received an IRS refund of approximately four months of my take-home pay. None of this was just or fair. And now he wanted to take more away from me. It was just disgusting, and I couldn't imagine a judge wouldn't see this. I had no idea the trauma I was still going through; my stress level was at an all-time high, and I felt I could have a panic attack at any moment. I had to continue praying about this instead of being able to start my new life like I should have been. He wanted to eliminate or severely reduce alimony and now wanted me to pay his attorney fees to scare me. I couldn't even pay my own attorney and wouldn't be able to for a very long time. I started praying for our attorneys and our judge that they not only saw the truth but would seek real justice and fairness. He told everyone I fraudulently obtained my new job before we signed our agreement. No, that's not true, and we have proven it, and he was continuing his smear campaign to everyone possible.

Again, I ran into another one of his very good friends. He kept asking how I was doing and then asked what was happening with the divorce. He heard about my new job (I'm sure all of his friends did) and I was able to tell him the truth. At one point, he told me that Dennis has issues with women. I agreed with him. I still can't wrap my head around these men who know what kind of guy Dennis really is and continue their friendship with him. This friend was there when Dennis verbally attacked another friend on a guys' trip and didn't agree with what happened, along with his neighbor whom Dennis verbally attacked and smeared after he did computer work for him. He was also with Blake when Dennis was manipulating him in the restaurant and part of the huge discussion about Maryann and I going out together. Now he's telling me he knows Dennis has issues with women. I don't get it. It's validating the behavior, and that's not okay. What are the Bible verses?

Proverbs 13:20 CEV "Wise friends make you wise, but you hurt yourself by going around with fools."

Also 1 Corinthians 15:33 CEV "Don't fool yourselves. Bad friends will destroy you."

I guess I really should understand people looking the other way and not getting it. It's so incredibly hard to know what someone else is going through when you haven't walked in their shoes. At the same time, yet again, neutrality only supports the abuser, minimizes the victim and the truth, and is revictimizing and retraumatizing. That's another reason I wanted to write this book – to raise awareness and understanding of what all types of abuse look and feel like with the hidden evils behind millions of closed doors. Dennis was still representing he needed as much for his lifestyle as we did when the three of us were together while saying he was barely earning any income and claimed he was earning less than me to instill fear again. He lied and grossly underreported what he paid himself on his financial affidavit (perjury), which I saw on his actual reports and bank statements. If he had money issues, he would have needed to give up many things to save money. He was still paying to have the house cleaned, lawn maintenance, and pool cleaned, still had two vehicles with car payments, and was still going out with his girlfriend, traveling and playing golf (I know all of this because I have copies of all his credit card and bank statements). He still had his car washing and massage memberships and had added second memberships to both (for Kip?). Since he had mortgage forbearance, he didn't even need to pay to live in the house while I struggled to pay my rent.

Through the divorce dragging on, I kept learning new things. We had to provide new financials because we would be having a hearing with a judge. Going through the 733 pages of his paperwork, I could see from his 2019 business tax return that the business grossed almost $2 Million, the biggest year the business had up to that date, during Covid. He went on trips in 2019 and early in 2020 with Kip and also with her boys and there is a lot of money being spent on them and going in and out of the business. It was valuable information not just for my case but to educate others. This is considered legal abuse, post-separation abuse, and vexatious, and all are very common when you leave an abuser. He was lying, manipulating, and stalling to instill fear and exhaust my resources so I would give up to punish me and gain revenge. The laws in this country allow it to happen. I have read so many stories that are just as bad and even worse, especially when minor children and custody are involved. A friend of mine who went through something similar said "The courtroom is their playground."

His dragging this on was preventing me from starting a new life, which was also part of his abuse – future abuse. I was stuck in my apartment and couldn't buy a home of my own. I had found a perfect condo, but because we are still married, he would have to approve my request. Regardless, I wouldn't have been able to qualify because I didn't earn enough income without alimony, had no funds for a down payment, and had all of my unsecured debt and my credit score dramatically decreasing. My future was still in his hands, and he didn't want me to have one. He wanted to destroy me, and his attorney was his accomplice. She was an abuser as well. At first, I respected his attorney for doing her job, but the longer this continued, the more disgusted I was with her. She knew he was paying her tens of thousands of dollars to hurt me. She saw it and knew it, and it's a vile way of earning a living, blood money. You would think Dennis would have wanted the divorce to be over to make an honest woman out of his girlfriend, considering we were still married over two years into their dating relationship at this point, especially since she considers herself "God's girl." But I've realized and have read that winning is much more important to him than any person, even his romantic relationship. I actually wished she was important enough to him to be willing to end our marriage. I was okay with them being together – better her than me. I was still his target of abuse, and that was his motivation. The longer the divorce went on, the longer he could continue blaming me and using it as an excuse for his behavior, along with seeking revenge for my leaving. Narcissists will happily drag you into court, are greedy about everything, try to win at all costs, and then blame the victim. He still believed that everything was his, nothing was mine, and I didn't deserve a penny. This fight of his was so counterproductive. Plus, he was willing to spend a fortune in legal fees for this ridiculous fight. He was hurting himself too but obviously didn't care because he viewed it as a game.

At this point, I knew the divorce fight was far from over and maybe starting from scratch. I had no idea what I was going to do. I couldn't support myself, and my budget was devastating. I couldn't even begin paying my attorney or any other debts. Since I was on my new job's insurance, I no longer had access to the HSA account and couldn't afford to see Ross anymore. The only thing I ensured was that I was tithing to my church because I was faithful God was providing me blessings every step of the way through the divorce. I couldn't afford to continue with this fight, but this wasn't just about me and Dennis; it was also about justice, the law, and bringing awareness and change for the future of others. I was fighting for that besides myself. I knew the law was unjust and unfair, and the fact I was in a nonviolent abusive marriage had no validity in this divorce and when we got in front of a judge. Dennis was willing to manipulate everything to his advantage. He's a master liar and would do whatever it took to make everyone believe his business was failing and making no money. I expected that, at this point, I would lose this battle. I also believed that it was for a reason. I believe everything I went through since we've been together was to help others. My loss will fuel my passion for bringing awareness and change to help those after me. I was hoping to see this to the very end.

During the divorce process, he must have been going through the house because he emailed me that he was dropping off some of the things I had requested at my stepdad's shop. Some of the items were listed in our mediation agreement and some additional Christmas decorations. When I went through it all, I noticed he included the cards we gave each other on our wedding day. I also received the portrait of me he had painted and gave me the last Christmas we were together. When I originally received it, I thought it was really beautiful. It was bittersweet, and I cried that day, knowing it was just another shiny object to make himself look like he was a loving husband. I didn't take it when I left because I feared it would get damaged and regretted it. I saved a special place for it above my sofa, where it now hangs. During our emails back and forth, he mentioned the cats and that he missed them. He only paid a little attention to the female, but the male cat would hang out with him when he watched sports. Out of compassion, I actually told him that I knew he particularly missed the boy, and if he wanted, he could have a sleepover. Dennis didn't respond to that, but he adopted a couple of kittens only a week or so later. I got my answer and knew he couldn't have agreed because it gave me control. Regarding the cards he included that we gave each other on our wedding day, I actually found it interesting he found them and was motivated enough to want me to see and read them. I was entertained by that and guessed he was sending me a message. I wonder what it was? I wished the things we wrote in those cards were true. Even on our wedding day, I was filled with fear but with the hope it would get better. I guess he didn't realize that I left him because of how he treated me and all the things he did strategically to hurt and control me. He still thought it was all me. It's twisted. I sometimes wish I knew what was happening in his head, both when I was with him and now that I'm not. I wonder what caused him to become this way. You aren't born a narcissist or abuser; something happens during your upbringing to cause your personality and behavior to change. I don't think I'll ever know, but if he had died during our marriage, I would have donated his brain to scientists to see if there was a connection.

Both Dennis and I were deposed leading up to our February 16, 2021 court date, finally getting in front of a judge, but due to his wanting to terminate or permanently reduce alimony, plus set aside the entire Mediation Settlement Agreement. His attorney tried to paint a picture that I fraudulently lost my job and obtained a new one and that I should have filled out a new financial affidavit. My attorney disagreed I did anything fraudulent due to my reporting it to him that day. It would have been my attorney's responsibility to have me fill out a new one. I was able to express my financial problems, and at one point his attorney insinuated that I should downsize to a one-bedroom, one-bathroom apartment. Not only would that prevent Harlow from having a place to stay with me, but why was it necessary for me to continue to suffer while Dennis still lived in our 5-bedroom, 5-bathroom million-dollar house? I didn't get it! Dennis's financial paperwork proved that the business was still making a lot of money, and he was still paying himself a lot. Still, his legal team was trying to use manipulation and smoke and mirrors to deflect the truth. Unfortunately, because their strategy was his inability to pay me because of the pandemic, it looked like all of the times he lied last year that his business was failing were no longer admissible because temporary mediation and mediation were confidential to a judge. He wasn't under oath all the other times he claimed his business was about to shut its doors while grossing just shy of $2M in sales. And this year the projection up until our deposition had him surpassing that in 2020. He even claimed during the deposition that he had been trying to sell his Mercedes for five months – really??? More lies and who knew what he could manipulate when we got in front of a judge. Dennis could also pay himself considerably less due to the forbearance of the mortgage. Of course, my tithing to church was a huge issue, and all my friends paid for me to go out. Dennis's attorney had me give all the names of those I remembered. I wondered if he would contact any of them to try and ruin my friendships by claiming I really did have money to go out and was giving it away to church. We all know he wasn't tithing to the church, even though he's a devoted Christian! His attorney also asked again, as with the first deposition, if I had Dennis followed and if I was taking any medication (even though I really needed it). It was funny when my attorney asked Dennis about one of the trips; he responded that he was invited to go with other families. My attorney asked whom he went with and he said "A girl I date and her kids." I wanted to laugh at that statement. It's not a girl he dates; she has been his girlfriend in a relationship for two years! I was a little upset right before the deposition because I was made aware that Dennis was videotaping me and if I wanted him videotaping, it would be about $300, plus my portion of the court reporter. I started crying because I wasn't planning on those costs, but I really didn't have a choice. Because the depositions were virtual, I was at home, and the cats kept jumping on my lap. At one point my boy cat had his tale in my face, and Dennis commented. I held him up so Dennis could see him. Not long after the depositions, my guy best friend, Sonny, received a fake Instagram friend request. It was actually hilarious and predictable.

On February 16, 2021, we had our hearing for the first time in front of the judge. Dennis's legal TEAM had over 30 exhibits with many charts and graphs trying to manipulate the judge into believing he wasn't making any money (smoke and mirrors). The financials clearly showed that the business, yet, again, even with Covid, surpassed all other years with gross sales. He was now representing that one of the other sales reps, Gary, had a 275% increase in sales for 2020, and Dennis's sales were dramatically down. Dennis was also representing his pay reported on his Financial Affidavit was much less than what I saw he was actually paying himself with salary, distributions, car allowance, and other personal expenses the business reimbursed or paid (it all showed on his QuickBooks reports, credit card statements, and personal/business bank statements). I really believed our case to prove he was lying, and my needs were very strong, and I was confident that day.

Not long after the video hearing began, my attorney stopped and asked to call me. In our conversation, he voiced how concerned he was about how judges favored those paying alimony concerning the uncertainty of COVID-19. He said we should put off the hearing, agree to abate alimony, and reschedule the hearing later. I voiced my frustration and didn't want to give up that day, and I also told him I couldn't afford to keep going without any support, as my credit was exhausted and I wasn't earning enough to pay all of my bills. I also reached the point that my credit card balances were incurring over $300 each month in interest, and not long after that, one of my credit card balance transfer deals ended, and I was incurring $600 each month in interest. I was shocked, stunned, and confused that I needed to concede temporarily. It made me sick to my stomach that I had to decide to postpone yet again and continue with no support at all. The injustice of all this piled up higher, along with my debt and anxiety. We rescheduled the hearing for May 27, 2021. I was hopeful that by then, things would be different. I was incredibly disheartened, and in shock that I yet again had to postpone any kind of financial support, that my financial situation was so dire, the legal system was so flawed. My attorney did nothing to help me, and quite a few things hurt. I kept thinking to myself what an injustice it was that I couldn't tell the judge the truth that my husband was a nonviolent domestic abuser and should be held accountable, how I had to escape to leave him and had to give up almost everything, and that Dennis had been lying about his finances and ability to pay support for over two years, leveraged/threatened his daughter's college to scare me into accepting less, and this was all considered post-separation abuse.

On May 21, 2021, two and a half years after it began, it seemed my marriage was about to end. I was ready to fight the battle in court the next week, on the 27th. Still, as I looked at all his financials, the now 47 exhibits his legal team prepared to attack me and provide as many smoke and mirrors as possible to gaslight everyone, the requests to the judge, and the uncertainty of my financial situation, along with what the judge had the power to decide, my attorney pressured me not to go forward with the hearing, so I conceded and took a terrible settlement deal. I didn't want to, and I felt incredibly defeated. He also scared me that I would have incurred an additional $10,000 in legal fees on top of the $20,000 I already owed him. I was afraid and didn't know what else to do, but at least Harlow's college could not be taken away.

No truth, no justice, no fairness, and no accountability!

There was such an atmosphere of uncertainty and fear with the vicious attack against me. I could feel my emotional well-being taking a huge hit and myself breaking down mentally and emotionally. I knew I had reached my point financially that I couldn't take it anymore, and preparing for this battle would consume me to the point I wouldn't be able to hold it together during the hearing, remotely as it may be, in front of the judge, the attorneys, Dennis, and the court reporter. I also believed that even though his lies and manipulation were so blatant and visible, he and his legal TEAM would have created enough uncertainty through the exhibits and attack that the judge may not have given me anything more than what I agreed to in the offer that came over that day. I lost all faith in my attorney, and he proved his representation was worthless. I was also terrified because Dennis wanted me to reimburse him for everything he still paid for when I first left him, like my insurance, cell phone, and all my therapy sessions with Ross when I used the HSA card. They painted me into a corner, including my attorney, and I saw no way out than to take the deal. I agreed to a fraction of what we had agreed to pre-Covid. Oh, Covid, as much as the past year and a half has been fantastic for my spirit, wisdom, and friendships, Covid assisted my husband in his quest for revenge and his attack to destroy me financially.

Everyone relating to this battle, Dennis, his legal team, the judge, and my attorney, could walk away unscathed, except for me. The most important question I am forced to ask is why? Why did my husband need to continue to abuse me legally and financially? He worked tirelessly in the presence of his evilness. His goals were to punish and destroy me through this calculating revenge. He, indeed, was the Terminator. His attorney wasn't much better. She took every penny he was willing to pay her. He spent approximately $100,000 in 2 ½ years just on his legal fees. It was like a premonition when he initially told Harlow it would cost him $100,000 for the divorce! Why did he need to spend that much just to hurt me? That doesn't even include all the manhours he spent himself that could have been used to generate sales and run his business (or be with Kip). His attorney should be ashamed to be an accomplice to post-separation, financial, and legal abuse. She knew exactly what he was doing and was still happily racking up billable hours in her war strategy against me, which was vile and repulsive. Yes, she is an attorney, and it is her job to represent her client, but she also participated in the abuse, which should not be included in her oath as a family law attorney. I knew she was fully aware of who he was and what he's done. Isn't there a famous quote, "Justice has nothing to do with the law?" That statement disgusts me because I know firsthand how true that really is. This battle, and every step I took through these 2 ½ years, showed me how flawed and ugly the law is, especially toward domestic abuse victims and survivors.

My attorney also knew what I was facing in the hearing, and as I voiced my frustration and anguish, he reminded me that he didn't know what the judge would decide, but it seemed as though things were stacked against me because of COVID-19. I felt he pressured and coerced me to take the deal offered, and in that conversation, he even told me certain judges don't like awarding alimony because they have been divorced and are paying it themselves. He also told me his reputation with the judge was on the line if I didn't take the deal. I was shocked, appalled, and disgusted that it would even be true and communicated to me with such a matter of fact by my own attorney. It also made me realize he didn't have my best interest and only his. He really didn't care and had given up way before this day. He was fully aware of my devastating financial situation. He did nothing to help me, even though I begged him many times that I needed temporary support and was accumulating a considerable amount of debt at his encouragement. It was just more appalling truths of the law. I felt so defeated and realized there was no way from the beginning that Dennis would be fair or stop fighting me until I gave up. He left a path of destruction and killed his target. Even if I had hired an aggressive attorney, he would have fought harder, and I would have incurred much more debt.

Knowing his strategy going into this divorce, I should have realized he would never have allowed me to win or be fair with me and would continue fighting until I gave up. I feel like it was a train wreck that I saw coming, and not only was I unable to stop it, but it also ran me over. I suffered during the entire marriage, I suffered just as much through this divorce, and I will continue to suffer with my devastating financial position. Yes, he won this battle without a shadow of a doubt, but this was indeed just a battle, but it's not the ending. I get to decide what my ending will be. Maybe this is how it was supposed to be. Maybe this will fuel me to continue my fight and advocacy against all types of abuse and injustices in the court system. This is more wisdom and experience to help others. I have become another casualty of what happens when you divorce someone like my husband, a narcissistic abuser, the Boogeyman, and the Terminator. I continued reading articles and connecting with survivors who gave in and suffered the consequences of the wrath that plagued them. I also needed to be grateful that I was spared the added despair of a custody battle. Even though I had the information needed to show the truth, I learned that the truth doesn't matter in the eyes of the law. Dennis was willing to deceive, lie, cheat, manipulate, and fraudulently report anything for his agenda. He has and still does not believe that rules and laws apply to him, and he feels he can get away with whatever he wants.

Family law is a game. There are many players, with winners and losers. The winners are those who use power, control, aggression, strategy, money, deceit, manipulation, and weaponize fear and uncertainty through threats to win at all costs. The losers in this game most likely are the ones who need the laws to protect them in the first place. The law is only fair when both parties are willing to be and is based on people telling the truth. It's just not set up for liars, cheaters, and manipulators who are willing to go against the law, and their taking an oath to tell the truth is completely worthless. I really wished I hadn't given up and gone along with the hearing. I regretted it, but at the time, I felt that throwing in the towel was the right thing to do, especially with what my attorney said to me (technically, I believe his license to practice law should be taken away). I'm unsure because I saw the numbers in Dennis's paperwork that clearly showed the truth. I'll have to wonder if the judge would have believed the lies, smoke, and mirrors or if he would have seen right through them and awarded me what was really fair. We'll never know about me, but every bit of this will be used to at least try and help others moving forward. I'm yet another statistic of the severely flawed legal system. After I settled, I asked if the judge could sign the paperwork on June 1st, which is Narcissistic Abuse Awareness Day. If we settled on the 21st of May, I thought the paperwork would have been finalized around then, but it wasn't. I checked my email multiple times daily to see if the divorce was finalized. On the morning of July 8, 2021, while I was at work, almost a month and a half after I settled, I received an email from my attorney's assistant that the judge finalized the divorce on the 7th. I immediately broke down and couldn't stop crying for the rest of the day and night.

My emotions got the best of me, and I wished I could have gone home, but I had too much work to do. I wasn't crying because it was finally over or I was finally free. I was crying because I still couldn't believe how much Dennis wanted to destroy me and succeeded. Every bit of abuse weighed down on me from the marriage and divorce, and I felt incredible pain, trauma, and heartbreak. Even going into this divorce, knowing he would fight with every ounce of who he was, I hoped he would realize at some point to be fair, if not for me, for the future dynamics of our ties with Harlow. If not for that, I mistakenly had hope and faith in the law and my attorney.

Well, he 'out-dicked me,' and I let him, but I never wanted to be a dick myself. I lasted as long as possible but was no match for his evil. I was naïve to have thought things would have ended well for me, and even though I was proud of my perseverance and determination, I was having a hard time forgiving myself for not knowing better, for having to give up, and not having much of a choice. He was the Terminator and wouldn't have stopped until he got me exactly where he wanted me, which was emotionally and financially devastating. All the times he threatened me during the marriage that everything was his, nothing was mine, and if I left, I would need to leave with nothing and wouldn't get much in the divorce, he made sure that came true. I failed, my attorney failed, and the court system failed. I also realized that, as I experienced a constant state of survival throughout the relationship, I was in the same condition throughout the divorce. That night, I reread the 22-page letter I wrote to Dennis months earlier, finally using my voice to tell him only some reasons I left him. I felt it was appropriate, and I cried through all of it. Besides work, for the most part, I kept to myself for almost two weeks. I felt as though I was in shock and wasn't in a position or had the desire to celebrate, nor the money. I needed to wallow in self-pity for a while before I picked myself up, brushed myself off, and figured out what was next. I asked myself how to fix my financial situation and put those pieces of my life together.

Thank the Lord I hadn't left him while Harlow was a minor. I realized how much harder he would have attacked to hurt and take her away from me. I got a taste of what other survivors go through, although it could have been much worse. In this aftermath, I thought about all of the others who were forced into homelessness or bankruptcy. Then, I realized I was over the limit on my credit cards, my bills were being rejected, and I had never been in a worse financial position in my entire life. WAS I NEEDING TO GO BANKRUPT NOW? I felt like I went through such an incredible amount of trauma and was about to start more. I started over when I left him, and I was again starting over after the divorce. Besides my financial situation, I was hurting over him, ensuring I didn't get any of the things I saved throhout Harlow's childhood. As a mother, it was so special as she grew up to save specific items with sentimental value and to one day reminisce with her. From the day she was born, I saved so many bins of meaningful items, from her first outfit, her Christening dress, other special outfits and uniforms, toys and dolls, and so many other things. It actually broke my heart when I asked for them in the divorce; he wanted to dismantle the carefully saved items in his strategy against me. I knew he didn't care about any of those things and had no idea what I saved and just used it against me to hurt and manipulate me. I finally agreed to keep them intact for Harlow's sake; they are all in his possession. He took all of it away from me and stole my future memories with her and possibly her children. I wonder if I'll ever see any of it again.

I received several opinions during the divorce, and when it was finalized, what I did wrong and should have done. People kept telling me to call his bluff, not worry about Harlow's college, and that she could pay for it herself, but she was worth the sacrifice of my overall financial well-being. One person even called me an idiot and stupid. Not one of these people has had the experience of being with a narcissistic abuser like Dennis. Not one of them had also dealt with this level of post-separation abuse. Even though some had bad marriages or divorces, they did not understand whom I was dealing with and what he could do. None were in the financial position that I was in. They also didn't realize that when you are dealing with someone like him, who owns his own business, Dennis had the capacity to manipulate and lie about his income, the business's books, and the stability of the business, also using Covid and his own child. He didn't even care about his accountant or how this could affect him. His accountant has said numerous times in similar words that Dennis does what he wants, and there's nothing he can do to change his mind. Dennis was never going to give up and was willing to do anything in his power to win to hurt me on purpose, and he had the resources and evil heart to succeed. Everything regarding this divorce was a worst-case scenario for me, and the only good thing about it was it wasn't for custody either. I had requested to change my last name. It made me sick having his last name, and I wanted to change it back to the one I was born with. My upbringing may have been dysfunctional, but nothing compares to my marriage to Dennis. I never wanted to be called by that last name again, but it wasn't valid in the divorce paperwork. Since I was adopted by my sister Madison's father when I was eight and my birth certificate was changed, I now need to file separate documents for a formal name change with the courts. Since that would cost an additional $500, I could not do it immediately. Maybe there's a reason I was supposed to have his last name still.

I continued not sleeping well. My average was 4-5 hours a night; I was extremely restless and would toss and turn all night. I would wake up in the middle of the night, and everything would rush into my head. I tried taking many different supplements, but they always stopped working. In the weeks following the divorce being finalized, I got less sleep than I normally did, averaged 3 hours of sleep a night, and would have to talk myself out of panic attacks. I noticed I was talking to a friend about how Dennis destroyed me financially and that I most likely needed to go bankrupt. I had a smile on my face while telling her. It was almost like I felt I didn't deserve to be upset or show my emotions or pain, like when I was still with Dennis. That night, I had a nightmare: I was forced to be with him again, and he was in bed with me at my apartment. He kept me awake like he always would by watching TV, moving around, and doing anything else to disturb my sleep. Then he started talking to me and told me he wanted to buy me a gift to love bomb and gaslight me. I felt so helpless and woke up in a cold sweat and anxious.

In the aftermath of the divorce, I felt the reality of what Dennis purposefully and calculatingly did to my finances was retraumatized and emotionally imploded. I was seeing someone for only the second time since leaving, and because I was completely falling apart, that fell apart as well, although we remained friends. I had to decide if I was going bankrupt, and I was also considering downsizing my car and apartment. I was hurting again that if I gave up my 2-bedroom, 2-bathroom apartment for a 1-bedroom, one bathroom, that meant Harlow would no longer have her own room or bathroom with me. My heart was broken yet again. It was already painful that I had to limit going out with friends, among other things, including giving up tithing. I realized I never earned enough income to tithe in the first place, and because it was charged to my credit card, it added to my debt and helped me reach financial exhaustion much quicker. I didn't have the answers and didn't know what to do. I was so afraid for my future; this was the worst financial position I had ever had. I had to grieve and heal all over again, and I also needed more counseling and medication for my anxiety and to sleep at night. By the grace of God, I was able to keep my apartment and was extremely grateful; however, I would not have been able to qualify for any other apartment or rental anywhere else, even downsizing in my current location. Not long after, I visited my friend, Jana, who had recently moved back to town. Her new house was so beautiful; it could be my dream house. Right after walking in, I had tears in my eyes, and as my voice was cracking, I commented to her that I wondered if I would ever have a nice house again. Then I thought I'd been so incredibly blessed being in my apartment. I've met so many wonderful people that I consider forever friends. So, it's almost like I am in a big house, with many rooms and many family members. I recognized it was my favorite place that I have ever lived.

After the divorce was finalized, I was re-baptized at my church by the pastors whom I love dearly. Even though many of my challenges remained, it was important for me to mark this time in my life as a positive beginning. It was a pivotal part in the returning of my spirit. The picture that was taken by the church photographer shows the pure joy on my face, as well as my pastors.

"I will destroy you, you will be homeless and penniless and I will take the kids away from you."

"At the end of the relationship is When the Mask can come Completely Off and you see the Real Person, hidden in plain sight all along."

Maria Consiglio

7

SALE OF THE MARITAL HOME

In the height of the Covid seller's market, of course, more manipulation

AS STATED WITH THE DIVORCE, THIS WAS A GAME TO DENNIS, AND HE didn't care how long it took and how much money it cost; he was out for revenge and was willing to spend as much energy, time, and resources as possible to hurt me. He was willing to do the same with the sale of the house. His motivation for revenge, to punish me, and to stall and prevent me from receiving alimony and any of my settlement, was enough for him to lie and manipulate the sale of the marital home. With Dennis claiming his business was failing during the pandemic, at least Dennis's attorney finally convinced him to list the house for sale in June 2020. Neither of us would receive any of the profits from the sale until the divorce was finalized (yet another way to manipulate and strategize). I had hoped it would motivate him to end the marriage faster, but it did not. It took a couple of weeks for him to send a list of 3 realtors for me to pick from. Then he stalled as long as possible by having his minion attorney friend nitpick the entire realtor contract and request many changes. This took around two months. Then he stalled the pictures of the house for another couple of weeks by using an electrician, making the house a mess with his electrical work. He also didn't allow a sign in the yard until his attorney told him he had to because he claimed it would set him up for the house to be robbed. He didn't allow a video open house because he said it would allow someone to case it (he used those words) to also rob him. It took until February 2021 for a broker open house and a 3-D of the home online because he used Covid as an excuse, even though safety protocol was being followed and the market was extremely hot. It was discouraging that houses were selling left and right for way over asking, but barely anyone was even requesting to see our house. I knew it wasn't the easiest sell because it's a historic home built in 1919. Even though it was a 5-bedroom, 5-bathroom, 4300 sq ft+ home with a pool, 2 kitchens, a 4-car garage, 2 porches, and a deck, and appraised for $1 million, it still needed some renovations and would take a unique buyer to see the charm and incredible potential.

The only genuine offer we received by mid-June 2021 was very stressful. When the offer was being made, and our realtor had us in a 3-way text and email, all of a sudden, Dennis started texting and emailing me directly. Besides a few emails regarding the specifics of the divorce, this was the first real communication with him since he was trying to reconcile. I felt myself shaking, kept feeling myself hold my breath, and then breathing shallowly. I did it over and over, and it made me lightheaded. I went through tears, my body tensing, especially my neck and shoulders, and my jaw started cracking and felt tight. I realized I was experiencing PTSD, and it was actually interesting how noticeable it was at the time I was triggered and realized in those moments how it would be if I had to deal with him regularly through custody sharing and what others had to deal with and feel on a regular basis. Here are some of the things he said to me in his texts when we were texting with our realtor, and then he sent to me directly – this negotiating began on 6/16/21:

He reminded me that he wanted 90 days to vacate once the house went under contract. I knew that was one of his strategies to kill any deal, so I offered to help him pack the house as long as someone else was there with us (a witness). He declined and said he wouldn't be comfortable (playing the victim?). The next day, he agreed with our realtor to accept 30 days. That, to me, was a miracle. On the morning of the 17th, he started texting me at 7:06 AM with "*Good morning.*" So, he destroyed me through the divorce, and now he was being nice to me? He was lol'ing me, Ty (for thank you), and then when we were also communicating with our realtor, he texted me, "*U rock!*" (UNBELIEVABLE) We went back and forth between the 3 of us and the 2 of us with numbers and reminding our realtor of all of the improvements we made and other general information. He also texted, "*u r doing great!!*" (WHAT????) At one point, I told him that if he really wanted to keep the house, I'd be okay with it, and he said it was too much for just him. He reminds me how the realtor was such a prick when we bought the house, and this buyer's realtor was the same. Many texts were back and forth about the price and trying to get as close as possible to the middle of what we wanted to sell and what the buyers wanted to offer. It went on for a couple of days. At one point, he mentioned that his dad was watching us from heaven and that since we hadn't come to an agreement, we should raise our price from the day before. I told him I just wanted fair negotiations, and he agreed. He then said he hoped to make me smile to start my day (What the F??? And, his dad was definitely watching from heaven and now knows who his son really is and all of his horrible abusive behaviors). I was trying to be nice and professional, and at the same time, I just wanted to get whatever we could out of the house sale.

Then he texted *"I truly am very very proud of your strength in this...no matter what ur the mother of our child and I want her to c this...as u know I tend to go on and on and this is one thing I can't wait to brag about u to her...u have been incredible and I am truly proud of u...I think u already know this but I feel I need to say it just in case... lets have A GREAT DAY TODAY and get this done fairly for all!"*

Again – WHAT THE F – laughable and crazy!

I told him, *"I appreciate your kind words – all I'm seeking is fairness in all of this,"* and he said, *"I fully agree,"* which confused the hell out of me that all of a sudden he wants fairness??? He wants to stay "quiet" quite a few times as a strategy (which I know from experience) and again calls the other realtor a prick. We had lots of texts on the 18th and 19th, and late Saturday the 19th, I thought we were still going back and forth on the other items in the house the buyers wanted, so I didn't sign the contract until Sunday morning the 20th (Father's Day). He texted at one point that day, *"And, thank you with all my heart for having Harlow, without her today would just be day...she is the best thing ever and thank you."* (Again – WTF!!!) I did say *"You're welcome, I feel the same – she is the best thing ever – so beautiful, smart and talented."* He says, *"The harp, I melt when she plays, I can't wait to hear her sing with it too...she has truly blossomed into the wonderful adult we hoped...I told her the one word I use to describe her is kind...can't think of a better way I would want to."* Well, I guess it's better that he's not attacking her character anymore! I told him I still have the school's harp they lent me while Harlow was in town, and he offered for me to borrow his truck, joked about how I loved driving it, and said Lol (Crazy!)! I responded it was hilarious and that I appreciated the offer and would let him know. Unfortunately, the offer on the house fell through because they said it needed to be done by Saturday night, and it wasn't until Sunday morning I signed it and never got a good answer as to why that was an issue. Still, I did apologize to both him and our realtor. Later, I wondered if all the flattery by Dennis was to manipulate me into making sure our number was too high and the deal would fall through. Unfortunately, I will never trust he doesn't have a deceptive personal agenda. That Monday morning, he passed me at the post office. He did it on purpose because he knew when I went each morning to pick up the office mail, from when he saw me when I started my job. He said *"Good morning"* in a very nice voice, so I said it back to him. I then started shaking and didn't stop for a couple of hours (PTSD). Was he delusional, or was it sneaky manipulation?

Our realtor re-scheduled the broker's open house, which was canceled during our negotiations, but hardly anyone showed up. Then Dennis decided he wanted the For Sale signs removed and still refused to have a regular open house when our realtor kept suggesting it as one of the best ways to attract potential buyers. Dennis knew he could again manipulate and stall the sale of the house because it was after our divorce was finalized, and I would need to take him back to court, which he also knew I didn't have the financial resources to do so. This was just another game for him, which continued the trauma and drama to hurt me. Dennis also tried to cancel that broker's open house because he was in the hospital with a kidney stone and needed surgery due to the stone getting stuck. I kept thinking this may be the start of karma and wondered if they needed to slice into his penis (I know that's not nice, but I really hoped so).

Late afternoon on Saturday, July 24th, I went to get my car washed. It was filthy, and I wanted to get a price at the Mercedes dealership the next day to see if I should sell it. I decided to stop at Trader Joe's for my weekly groceries on my way home. When I walked out with groceries towards my car, Dennis passed me in the parking lot and said, "Hi, how are you?" I said, "Fine, and you?" He said "Fantastic" in a very sarcastic way. I know he goes to that car wash (remember he has the car wash memberships), so I wondered if it was a coincidence or if he followed me. I looked around for his car and saw his Expedition in the last spot on the end, backed in. Dennis never backs into parking spots and especially wouldn't in his XL Expedition. I suspected he either followed me or saw my car in the parking lot and parked where he did to watch me come out so he could purposefully pass me. I wonder if his agenda was just to engage or to intimidate.

Our realtor had, over time, become very disheartened dealing with this sale and all of the obstacles she had to overcome. The sign and open house were really getting to both of us, and she sent a carefully worded email on August 3, 2021. That got me angry; he was causing her a lot of stress and frustration, along with the lies, manipulation, and stalling. So, I emailed both of them after rereading the wording of our MSA and the separate confidential agreement dealing with the price of the house. Here is my email with Dennis, copied from that evening:

Chelsea,

Nowhere in our Mediation Settlement Agreement, or Executed Confidential Sale of the Marital Home Agreement does it say there would not be a sign in the yard, nor does it say we wouldn't have an open house. It does say the following:

1. *Former Marital Home. a. The Former Marital Home shall continue to be held in the joint names of the parties as tenants in common after entry of this Final Judgment. The parties shall continue to list the property. The parties shall consider the advice of the listing agent in changing the sales price for the property. The parties shall accept all reasonable offers as defined in the Confidential Agreement Regarding Sale of Former Marital Home. Both parties shall cooperate in good faith and perform all those acts and execute all those documents necessary to effectuate the sale of said home as soon as practical.*
2. *both parties shall consider the reasonable recommendations of the listing realtor.*

The reasonable recommendation of our realtor, Chelsea, has a sign(s) in the yard. The reasonable recommendation of our realtor, Chelsea, recommends open houses, and broker's open houses. Other reasonable recommendations of our realtor have been either ignored or have been denied by Dennis.

The feedback I received from 5 realtors that I know personally is that both a sign in the yard and open house (as well as broker open house), are valuable tools in selling a house, and are standard practices.

If Dennis really wanted the house sold, he would agree to your very reasonable recommendations. Since Dennis is not agreeing to your reasonable recommendations, we should agree that Dennis is stalling the sale of the house for his personal agenda. His personal agenda is that as long as the house does not sell, he does not have to pay me any alimony or any of my settlement. As long as Dennis remains in the house, I have to reimburse him for half of the mortgage while he remains living there. He has more motivation to not sell the house than to sell it. This is why he has stalled numerous times throughout this process, in numerous ways. This is also why he has tried to manipulate both of us on numerous occasions.

If after stating all of this, he still does not agree to your very reasonable recommendations, then everything I just said is the absolute truth.

Please let us both know your reasonable recommendations, as our realtor. Let's see what happens next.

Thank you Chelsea for all you have done throughout this process. Thank you for all of the work you have put into trying to sell the house, your kindness, your professionalism, and your patience. I apologize to you for the unnecessary stress the sale of this house has caused.

Sincerely,
Jeanelle

Not long after that, I had a nightmare. I dreamt that Dennis abandoned the house and bought a big, beautiful, expensive new house. I felt so helpless because his agenda was to hurt me that he was doing fine financially and was happy he successfully destroyed me. I remember in the nightmare screaming and crying while he had an evil smug on his face and was happy with what he had done to me. I believe I had this nightmare because I just finished watching the second season of Dirty John, which was about Betty Broderick and legal abuse. I was thankful that this type of abuse was the show's main plot, and I hope it will bring more awareness and understanding to the public. Maybe one day, my book will become part of the series......Netflix, feel free to call me! I already know I want Margot Robbie to play my part, please!

Chelsea emailed both of us that afternoon. She tried so hard to be bubbly and professional. She suggested smaller For Sale signs and a video open house to appease us both. I wrote back that she was the expert, my only agenda was to sell the house, and approved anything she believed would help the sale and bring potential buyers. After that, he went silent for a while, and Chelsea ordered the smaller signs without his approval as an important way to attract potential buyers. Chelsea had a couple of showings in mid-August and again in mid-September. In mid-October, we received an offer that was too low, and we started negotiations. On October 22nd, I received an email from Dennis with the subject line "house sale and settlement." I'm inserting a lot of it below and initially thought about leaving out all the numbers, but then decided it was necessary, which he goes round and round to gaslight and manipulate me:

> I anticipate the buyer will take our counter offer but will require me to be out in 60 days. You know I can say no to that deal. I am not interested in not selling the house, but I am interested in settling our entire divorce when we do so. I would like to work out with you, before the time will expire on the new contract they submit, a settlement of the alimony portion of our divorce to come out of the closing split. Then we can both be entirely done with this and move forward, except for the things we still need to give each other (pictures, baby teeth. etc.).

When I look at the rough numbers if they give us $950k I have been told to factor 9% as our closing cost, realtors, etc. – so that would leave us $864,500 roughly to pay off the mortgage.

I will pay 2 more mortgage payments, so the payoff will be approximately $574.000, leaving $291,000 to split.

We each would receive $145.5K.

We then have a settlement that I owe you $77,603 for, and you will owe me back approximately $90,000 (repairs after inspection and some loose ends, last 2 mortgage payments, etc. to still factor)

So your net will be about $132K and mine will be $157K.

I know you have debt based on what you submitted in your FA. When you pay that off, you will have whatever is left (if CC's, your parents and attorney are $90K, that will leave you $42K).

This is where I think it is advantageous to both of us to settle the alimony. Rather than 8.4 years for you to get $100K, I am willing to give you $60K from my portion of the settlement to get this done. This is not an offer to get a counter offer, it is a one-time offer. That way we each would net around $100K once done with our debts, which seems very fair to me, and you will have enough for a 20% down payment on the $400K condo that you said you wanted to own, and still have a cushion.

Please review this with whomever helps advise you and let me know as soon as you can, it will effect both of our lives and what we reply to the offer. I would like to do it either way, 60 or 90 days on the offer, that is up to you if you are OK with any deal and having this happen. I am not sure you realize what your net is going to be, that is why I have taken the time to lay it out for you, so that you are not caught off guard.

It is funny that I offered you $950K for the house almost 2 years ago to the day and you said no. Imagine how much better off we both would be right now if you realized I was truly looking out both of us, and ended everything at mediation. I *am trying to help us both again, I hope you can understand that this time.*

Best,
Dennis

I did not respond to this email. He was trying to buy me off by giving me 60% of my total alimony up front and manipulating me by dangling cash to pay off my debt, which he obviously knew I had. He put in there that it was a one-time offer like he did so many times in the divorce to have control and scare me into action. He failed to write how I'm paying him back half of Harlow's college tuition and expenses for two full years and half of the mortgage for two years, which is reflected in the number I owed him. I expected he would pad his numbers; he was always a schemer, liar, and cheater. I was fully aware she was way under budget last year, and he made sure to give her the overage because he not only looked overly generous (hero), but I had to reimburse half of it. Negotiations continued in a three-way conversation with our realtor. Dennis wanted 90 days to close, which would first work with the buyers so they had time to sell their house; however, it was under contract immediately, and they wanted 30 days. Dennis declined and then texted me directly:

Dennis: From the email yesterday get u $60k immediately...if I get inconvenienced to move out in 3 weeks, my effort gets you $25k more...I would tell them $975 to get me out so fast... they are at $925 so u would have $85 ($60+$25) based on my effort...I know u hate for me to get any credit for doing anything nice but there it is...$85k of $100k that will take 8 + years immediately is a huge win for you and gets us closure... ur call of course, I can do the 90, they will wait and pay $925 and that is that, but we have a chance to use their time to our financial gain if we work together...please don't label this manipulation, this is purely a business deal at this point and u control the outcome

Me: No

Dennis: Ok….90 days it is…u insist on sticking to the letter and not working together so I will follow your lead

Me: When you say don't label as a manipulation, it's gaslighting me that it really is manipulation. You just proved it

Dennis: Lol..always the victim…even when u get your way… narcissism has no boundaries

Me: Blame shifting, projecting, and scapegoating

Dennis: Lol…u made ur decision…stop abusing me…we both live with your decision…not mine, yours, and I am ok w it.

There is no blame, u stuck to our agreement

The deal will happen, just at the lower price since we don't have power

STOP ABUSING ME???????? NARCISSISM HAS NO BOUNDARIES????? REALLY??? Quite a bit of projecting in just a few sentences!

Me: We do have power, you just took it for yourself

Dennis: U getting $25k extra for me putting everything into storage and living in an Airbnb was for me?? U live in odd world of perception..if I got u $50 from my effort I guess that have been even more for me

Me: You're trying to get me to take a deal that $40,000 is taken away from me out of alimony. You've already fucked up my financial situation over the last three years, and I can't let you do any more damage. You're trying to use it to your advantage. I knew you were lying the entire time about your *financial situation throughout the entire divorce. This was a game to you, and you were willing to spend any amount of time and any amount of money to hurt me.*

Dennis: My heart truly breaks for you...you left, you filed, you requested so much info...every, everything multiple times for years in a no cash business that you can't hide anything.. you purposefully hid info to try to gain on me and filed a temporary hearing while doing so to also try to gain and put unfair pressure on me and you got caught..you controlled all... the respondent only responds...I asked u to let Jerry handle (his minion attorney friend – there's no telling how badly I would have been screwed if he was both our attorney for Dennis believing I should get nothing as he always threatened), *u chose a different route...please, take responsibility for your actions...you just assumed a huge favor of me to get u $25k more, I asked u a favor in return, where u would ultimately sacrifice $15k that wouldn't even be in your pocket until 2029 but would get u $85k now to help ur situation, I felt that was a great offer that I would take if the roles were reversed...u chose not to do that favor in return if I did mine, which is fine...please don't blame me for your decisions...and that is all they are, decisions that make u happiest, which I am ok with*

I was incredibly stressed by all of this communication and manipulation. I felt myself shaking and holding my breath, and I couldn't imagine how much worse I would have felt if I hadn't been on anti-anxiety meds and in therapy. I couldn't take it anymore, didn't respond, and decided to turn him on silent. The 3-way texts continued during this text trail. The buyers agreed to a higher price to have the house in 30 days. Dennis said 90 days was his only stipulation, and I controlled the price. I said he agreed to 30 days last time and purposefully tried to kill the deal. We went back and forth, and he said he was desperate to please everyone (LOL) and learned it's a bad way to live, and 90 days is the standard (gaslighting again – 90 days is never standard, which is how he fooled me during our mediation settlement). I reminded him that 90 days is only his standard and no one else's, and he has had time to go through his stuff and identify another place to live. Our realtor gets very frustrated and keeps trying to see if we could agree, and Dennis says:

No 90 is 90...holidays coming, Harlow home...not good to upset that situation anyway...God looking out for us

Find a new buyer

(GOD LOOKING OUT FOR US???)

I was texting Chelsea directly, as was Dennis. I let her know he was trying to manipulate me into taking a deal and giving up my rights to alimony, and he told her the house sale was up to what he was offering me. She told him this wasn't the time for a side deal, and it was not acting in good faith selling the home (of course, he needs to continue controlling, manipulating, scheming, lying, etc.). The next day, she tries again. Dennis says he asked a favor in return from me for a favor (gaslighting......as well as delusion), and since I won't return the favor, we were stuck, and it was out of his control. I said I was advised that his using my financial situation as leverage and not agreeing to a fair offer was not a favor but blackmail, and he advised me that if I signed the deal, he would agree to the offer, but if I didn't, he wouldn't. I mistakenly called it blackmail because I'm not up on manipulation tactics. Dennis calls me out – it's too funny not to transcribe:

Dennis: U need to learn what blackmail is....or your advisor does...this is a give and take...u r just taking...that is greed and selfishness...but that is fine, I am used to it...was hoping to see some growth and spirit of cooperation vs. making it all about ur gain exclusively...

I laughed every time I reread all this – he's genuinely delusional and believes himself. Then he sends a screenshot of the definition of blackmail and the definition of give and take. Chelsea then sends a screenshot of forgiveness. I say that giving up my rights to alimony is not give and take, and he uses my financial situation as leverage and coercion. Chelsea continues her frustration, and Dennis says:

> Dennis: I can only give if I get back...I can't be coerced, bullied or forced into giving in to a demand that hurts me without getting something in return...as I have said, I am willing to give to get...Jeanelle has only been willing to get...one way deals are not fair I will not ever again take an unfair deal.

(WTF! Coerced, bullied, or forced????? Complete projecting and blame-shifting)

> Me: When you threaten the deal unless I give in to your demands, that's considered bullying.

> Chelsea: You people are killing me!

> Dennis: Me too...we r right there...teamwork and cooperation would be so great right now

> I didn't threaten the deal, I answered ur request w my request... respondent responds

> Me: Teamwork is not giving up my rights for your demands. Teamwork would be you being reasonable and not preventing the sale of the home.

> Dennis: Ur right, I'm not giving up my rights for your demands....christ almighty stop embarrassing yourself

> I have the right to 90 days

> Done

> U want me to give up that right...and it is HUGE, but u offer nothing n return except name calling

I again reached a heightened stress level and couldn't take it anymore. I was at least happy that I stood up for myself and called him out, even though he was trying to gaslight, project, and blame shift. I texted Chelsea that I would no longer communicate in a 3-way text or email, so she suggested we stop texting for communication because it was non-productive. Dennis agreed and said we were at an impasse and to make sure the buyers knew 90 days was firm. Later, I spoke with Chelsea on the phone. She knew he was not being fair in these negotiations and was trying her best to get him to be reasonable. I had told her a bit about why I left Dennis, but during this conversation, I got very specific and believe she finally understood. The next day, she texted in the 3-way the buyers were willing to negotiate 60 days at the number we were agreeable. I texted Chelsea that I would not communicate with Dennis and have it silenced on my phone. She asked me if I'd give up any of my portions to appease Dennis, and I agreed to $5k (how much more can he take from me?). She gets him to agree, and we finally go under contract, with a closing date of December 21, 2021.

At first, I was nervous Dennis would try and ruin it, but then I realized he wouldn't do that because too many people were involved for him to show his true self. Of course, he found a place to rent fairly quickly, had Kip's help (she was useful to him), and moved in time for the closing. Leading up to the closing, I asked Chelsea a few times to make sure Dennis sent receipts for all of the things I needed to reimburse him, and he completely ignored the request, although she sent me invoices for the handyman who made repairs after the inspection. The weekend before the house closed, he emailed the title company (his friends – useful again) and me the list of what I needed to reimburse him. It was a list of amounts for half of Harlow's tuition, living expenses, travel, and cell phone from the beginning of 2020 to the end of 2021, my share of HIS mortgage, my share of house repairs, the $5000 I agreed to for him to move in 60 days, and HSA reimbursements (FOR MY THERAPY). He not only did not provide any receipts, but nowhere in the MSA was I supposed to reimburse him for the HSA expenses, and I was only supposed to reimburse him for repairs directly relating to the sale and not all the other bullshit he had listed. He also rounded down the amount I was supposed to receive from the number in the MSA. I knew he would do it, and at least he didn't disappoint me. I wound up paying him over $90k from my portion, which disgusted me. We closed as scheduled, although I had the closing agent at my office help with my portion of the paperwork, so I didn't have to communicate or see Dennis.

Finally, that chapter ended, which was a huge step forward with my financial difficulties, although not the end. First, I paid my parents back the money they lent me back when I was leaving (escaping) Dennis. Next on my list were car repairs and arranging to travel for Harlow's graduation. Also, I was waiting until the two credit cards were sent to collections so my bankruptcy attorney could help me negotiate settlement payments. I am not planning on paying my divorce attorney another penny for his almost worthless representation, and he can write it off. My hope for the rest is to have enough for a down payment on a condo when the time is right, and my credit is repaired. In perspective, the grand total I ended up with, both the settlement and all of my alimony, doesn't even add up to one year of Dennis's earnings. In addition, for the first six months of my alimony payments, all of it + went to Harlow for her monthly expenses and then a portion for a few months afterward. Less than ten months after the house sold, Dennis purchased a new home for $875,000.00! It's also bigger than the house we sold, so I guess he really does need all that space for one person. I also heard he was doing a lot of renovations because, obviously, he can afford it. Without a shadow of a doubt, it validates to the world he was lying about his finances, just like I knew he was.

"One day you will tell your story of how you overcame what you went through and it will be someone else's survival guide."

Brene Brown

MY ADVOCACY AND ACTIVISM

Along with many other survivors and organizations bringing awareness, education, and understanding of what all types of domestic abuse look and feel like - A powerful movement is spreading worldwide to protect all domestic abuse victims and children - This is only the beginning

SINCE I LEFT DENNIS, I HAVE STARTED GETTING INVOLVED IN SEVERAL things. I have more than just a desire to heal and move on; I believe it's my purpose to tell my story and educate the public about the hidden evils of all types of abuse. Since society tends only to believe what they can see, I want to show them what it looks and feels like behind closed doors, hidden from the outside world. As much as I support victims and survivors who can't or don't want to tell their stories, since I'm willing to, I will use my voice because if I kept silent, I would support both abuse and abusers. I was so fooled by Dennis's mask of perfection and Christianity and didn't have the words or meanings to know what he was doing, just that the things he did and said were evil. Now, I consider his abuse torture and terrorism, and I consider him an intimate partner/family terrorist. I felt controlled, powerless, dominated, and my boundaries were broken down. That's precisely what he wanted, and he premeditatively chose every bit of the threats and abuse to reduce me to nothing, strip away my autonomy, and keep me that way to feel broken so I wouldn't leave him. I am heartbroken that it happened and felt I could do nothing to protect my child or me or stop it due to my lack of awareness and understanding. My heart also breaks for any other human being or living creature that has been or is being abused in any way. I would never want any intimate partner, safe parent, child, or anyone else to experience even a fraction of what we experienced, and I know so many have it much worse. I want that to change, and I hope my story and advocacy will help. I believe every door that has opened for me since leaving (escaping) leads toward my purpose, and I will continue walking through each one. The only way we can begin to reduce and prevent these evil and sadistic acts is by bringing awareness, education, and understanding to victims and survivors and the general public, law enforcement, and lawmakers. Everyone needs to understand every bit of it, and I won't stop until that happens.

> "The ultimate tragedy is not the oppression and cruelty by the bad people but the silence over that by the good people."
>
> Martin Luther King, Jr.

The first door was a bill that my state's House of Representatives and Senate filed. At the beginning of 2019, I was watching the news and saw a story about the proposed law in the state legislation. I read what changes they wanted to make and felt they were unjust. I wrote several letters to many State Senators and House Representatives involved with the bill, including the Governor and Lt. Governor. I felt it was my duty to tell some of my stories so that possibly one person would read them and could make a difference. The bill did not move through that first year. I continued my involvement in the next three sessions, which had the same result. This led me to get involved with other bills and advocacy groups. I also became friends with my State Representative and walked with her in the 2020 and 2022 St. Patrick's Day Parades.

The second door was becoming involved with my County's Domestic Violence Commission that the County Mayor began. After hearing about the committee, I met him at an event and asked him about becoming involved. He said the committee was formed, but anyone from the general public could attend the meetings. He put me in touch with someone on his staff and attended the meetings. Anyone from the public can speak, so I spoke at both I attended in person before the start of Covid. It was spontaneous for the first time in December 2019 because I hadn't prepared a speech. At the second meeting in February 2020, I prepared and presented a 3-minute speech, a snapshot of what I went through. They asked me to become part of the sub-committee on public awareness, and I was honored. At that time, I still didn't have much of the information I now have learned.

In 2020, I participated in a remote meeting with a domestic abuse judge, one of the leading domestic violence committee members. In this meeting, several survivors of domestic abuse, including me, told her about the challenges in dealing with the legal system during and after leaving our abusers. There is a definite need for awareness and change to provide the support needed to navigate through the courts. It gives me hope that my county is trying to address issues in all aspects of domestic abuse to assist victims and survivors better.

"Dear Family Court Judges,

When you give an abuser an inch, the Post Separation Abuse goes a mile (and the harm, trauma, and suffering escalates). When you hold abusers accountable, you allow the space for healing & peace."

Victims-Survivors of Coercive Control/
Post Separation Abuse –
Custody Peace custody-peace.org

My best guy friend Sonny, who works at a radio station, offered for me to record 15-second PSAs to bring awareness of domestic abuse during October 2020, Domestic Abuse Awareness Month. I was also interviewed on a radio station's talk show hosted by an attorney under my pseudonym. In anticipation of the interview, I signed up for an email, Instagram account, and Facebook under Jeanelle Maraid. Through the Domestic Violence Commission that October, I participated in a video PSA that will air through county events and other venues to spread awareness.

I attended a couple of Zoom meetings during October 2020, one for our area's main shelter for domestic violence victims/survivors, and the other one was with my Representative and a Senator who co-sponsored a bill for domestic violence that was introduced that session. I set up a call with my Representative for November 20th to ask her for them to include nonviolent, coercive control language in their bill. During the call, she was highly interested in introducing a bill but could not get one filed. I posted on social media daily during the month to bring awareness and understanding to the different types of abuse, the cycle of abuse, and the different tactics and strategies nonviolent abusers use. I had learned a lot up until that point, and much of it was incorporated into the beginning of this book. If interested, they can still be found on Jeanelle Maraid's Instagram and Facebook.

Reading articles and listening to podcasts, as well as following others on social media who went through similar situations, has helped so much identify what actual abuse includes and explain it. I have also done a lot of research on websites online. I had nowhere to turn to for a long time and did not understand the severity, and others were going through the same things. This education helped connect the dots and put the puzzle pieces together. Victims, survivors, advocacy groups, and activists are now beginning a movement to raise awareness about nonviolent abuse across the country and in other countries (coercive control) and for the protection of children. You now know domestic abuse is about power, control, dominance, and breaking down boundaries. Power, control, dominance, and breaking down boundaries are the whats and whys, and abuse tactics are the hows. It often starts subtly, escalates over time, and seldom begins with physical or sexual violence. We need to look at the whole picture, as violence is only a tiny aspect of the large umbrella of domestic abuse. It's time for meaningful and valuable changes in the law to prevent domestic abuse instead of reacting to it after it takes place only when it's physically violent. Both law enforcement and the court system need extensive training on not only domestic abuse when a victim is with their abuser but also post-separation abuse after leaving. Bringing awareness will help lawmakers understand what all types of abuse look like. I am hopeful they can open their hearts and minds to bring real change that will not only help victims and children but also put in place procedures for abusers to get help through mandated counseling and programs that address the reasons for their behavior and mental and emotional issues, not just put a band-aid on it.

I connected with a woman on social media whose daughter was killed by her abusive ex-husband, which was heart-wrenching. When he was up for parole, I wrote a letter to keep him in prison. She has a couple of Facebook accounts – Rise From The Ashes and Ashley's Closet, in honor of her daughter to bring awareness. She had a non-profit, and I was on the board, but it didn't make it. Her goals are to not only help victims and children directly but also help change the laws in our country to protect them from all kinds of abuse. Children in the court system are treated as objects, and their safety is less important than the manipulative strategy by abusers using the language 'parental alienation.' When a child has been forced into custody with an abuser, the likelihood of them having emotional and mental trauma is highly likely and, more often than not, undetected or unaddressed. A quote says children exposed to family violence show the same pattern of activity in their brains as soldiers exposed to combat. Domestic abuse tends to be generational, and the children of abusers have a very good chance of becoming the next generation of abusers or victims, as well as other tragic and preventable issues. I hope that bringing proper awareness may help prevent bullying, murder, suicide, addictions, and even mass shootings, as domestic violence is a gateway to these and most other acts of violence. I feel it's a travesty and injustice to our children who are forced into relationships with abusive parents mandated by judges and forced to attend reunification camps to reconcile with abusive parents. When people say that every parent has the right to have a relationship with their child, and every child should have the right to have a relationship with a parent (even an abusive parent), it's teaching our children not only to tolerate abuse but that it's a normal part of life.

Our children deserve better than that and should be taught that all types of abuse are wrong and that they will be protected.

I remember when Dennis told me Harlow would abandon me at 22 or 24, and then finding out, he bragged to his friends during the divorce that he would ruin my relationship with her. I participated in a Zoom meeting regarding the estrangement and separation of adult children who turn against and blame the victim/survivor and support the abusive parent who turns from aggressor to hero and strategizes to ruin the child/parent relationship with the safe one. It also concerns trauma bonding, Stockholm syndrome, or the fact that children still seek love and attention from that parent. The group who led the seminar said it is prevalent, and for this particular meeting, over one thousand parents and grandparents signed up. I met a new neighbor recently who is divorced from her abuser and has two adult children with him. The father is in financial control of both her son and daughter and has threatened to cut them off if they are in contact with the mother. The son has not spoken to her in a decade. I also have a friend from high school who is still the target of her abuser many years after their divorce. She tragically lost custody of her children because he convinced the courts she was unfit and used an auto-immune disease to say she was abusing them through Munchausen by Proxy. Through the years she would make secret trips to see them, so they knew she loved them. Now that her children are adults and in contact with her, he is threatening to take her to court for back child support. These are two very real and common examples of what an abuser is capable of post separation using children to continue control and destroy the relationship with children and the other parent. My heart really hurts for both and all their children.

"Abused children have been taught that love can coexist with abuse.

This shapes our adult perceptions of love. As we would cling to the notion that those who hurt us as children loved us, we rationalize

being hurt by other adults by insisting that
they love us."

Bell Hooks

I wrote an article about adding post-separation abuse as an additional
stage of the Cycle of Abuse. What I went through during the divorce,
along with some of the most horrific stories I've read, has taught me
that abuse not only doesn't end when you leave an abusive relationship,
but it usually gets worse. The abuser seeks to punish and gain revenge,
and for a violent abuser, the victim is up to 75% more likely to be
murdered, along with children. It was posted by some of my advocacy
groups on Facebook.

During Domestic Violence Awareness Month in 2021, I posted on
Instagram and Facebook again daily in October. That year, it was even
more important to me due to the police footage and then the murder
of Gabby Petito. It was incredibly apparent to me that she was a victim
of many types of abuse from her boyfriend, seeing her trauma and
despair. He was calm, cool, and collected to the officers, manipulating
them into believing he was the victim and she was the abuser within
the first few minutes. He also had Gabby believing it as well. This
was not only heartbreaking but also tragic and disheartening that law
enforcement was unaware of the actual signs of abuse. I heard that
Gabby's parents filed a lawsuit against the officers/police department.
I hope they receive justice and it leads to more education in all law
enforcement training. Physical markings are only a small percentage of
what victims of domestic abuse go through. My 2020 posts represented
so much information I had researched and learned, and the 2021 posts
were a lot more personal, with some of my stories woven in. Each day,
I found a quote, some with a picture, that went along with the day's
theme. The last post had three quotes with pictures of angels and prayer.
I was proud of the posts in 2021. My writing had somewhat improved,
and my posts had hundreds of shares, meaning thousands likely saw
them. Also, that October, I sent emails to the five news stations in my
area in hopes they would be interested in doing stories about domestic

abuse and violence, especially due to the circumstances surrounding Gabby Petito. Later in the month, I sent follow-up emails but never heard a word, which was incredibly disappointing.

That November, I started writing to the State House of Representatives and Senate that someone would introduce a bill including coercive control language. The Senator's office I was familiar with contacted me to let me know they did file a bill that not only adds coercive control language to domestic violence but also protects children from being placed into custody with abusers. This bill was named after a little boy after the judge gave custody to his abusive father, who ended up murdering him and committing suicide. I offered to help in any way possible and was put in contact with his mother. The Senator's office also introduced me to others involved, and I joined their organizations. Each member has tragic and horrific stories of losing their children to their abusers by the severely broken court system. This organization was involved in trying to get that bill through the House and Senate to be passed into law, but unfortunately, it didn't move through during the 2022 legislative session. They are also supportive of VAWA – Violence Against Women Act. By reauthorizing this Act, it puts national protections for domestic abuse victims in place, adds coercive control language to domestic violence, and protects children from being put into custody with abusive parents. It includes Kayden's Law, which afterward passed in Pennsylvania, similar to my state's filing of a law named after the little boy. Angelina Jolie gave speeches to U.S. politicians, urging them to vote to support VAWA. President Biden also urged them to move quickly, and he would sign it immediately. It did pass in both the US House and Senate, and with the President's signature on March 16, 2022, it was reauthorized. With the Violence Against Women's Act, many groups are beginning to join forces with national organizations, such as One Mom's Battle, Custody Peace, National Safe Parents Coalition, and others. These, along with other groups and organizations, were formed by advocates and parents who lost their children to their abusers and could not keep them safe. In doing so, their main goals are to protect children moving forward, save them from going through what they and their children experienced, and bring awareness and changes to the tragedies of the family law court system. There has also been a lot of media coverage of celebrities regarding their experience with domestic abuse and child custody issues. Hopefully, this will only add to bringing awareness during and after relationships.

> "As a child I never imagined that all of the real monsters in the world would be humans."
>
> Mobeen Hakeem

We spoke about my advocacy when I walked in the 2022 St. Patrick's Day Parade with my Representative. She told me that at the beginning of that year's legislative session, she went to the Senator's office and asked if she could file a bill that added coercive control since I'd been asking for the last couple of years. It was a massive honor to believe I was even a tiny bit responsible for adding it to that bill. In one of the group's Zoom meetings, someone asked the boy's mother how she was doing, significantly because the bill didn't move in 2022, and she was planning the first anniversary of her son's death. She said she was trying to get used to no longer being a mother. That was heart-crushing to hear and is just another reason why laws need to be changed to recognize all forms of abuse to protect children from being placed into custody through the court system with abusive parents. Judges and other court appointees force children to have relationships with abusers despite overwhelming evidence of abuse. Children, and even older children who fully understand and voice the abuse, are being forced into reunification camps to reunite with their abusers. Also, if a parent has been abusive to the other parent, then the likelihood of them abusing their children is highly likely. When a child witnesses abuse, it should be considered child abuse. So many survivors, not only in my state or country but worldwide, have horrific stories dealing with the court system, so familiar that I feel lucky I didn't have to go through custody. Through recent social media posts, I learned a new term, DARVO, an acronym for "deny, attack, and reverse victim and offender." Researchers have identified this as a common manipulation strategy with abusers. It can be used during a relationship to project behavior, escape exposure and accountability, and as a strategy in court. I can relate to both! The organizations I joined were heavily involved with the bill rewritten in part by our state's Bar Association Family Law section, and we were hopeful of getting it passed during the 2023 legislative session. I could not go to the Capital to speak like many others, but I wrote several letters to the House and Senate supporting the bill. I am thrilled to say it unanimously passed during the 2023 session, signed by our Governor on 5/24/2023, and went into effect on July 1, 2023. Laws have been passed or filed in Connecticut, Pennsylvania, New York, Colorado, Maryland, Montana, Illinois, Florida, and California, named after children and victims murdered by their abusers. Besides Kayden's Law, some of the names I am familiar with are Jennifer's Law, Kyra's Law, Greyson's Law, and Piqui's Law. The passion of many groups and organizations involved in ensuring these laws are passed in all 50 States is overwhelmingly honorable. The United Nations Human Rights Council recognizes domestic abuse as a pattern of controlling behavior. Many other countries, including Scotland and Australia, have passed laws to protect victims, survivors, and children from coercive control types of abuse.

> "These are not "custody battles." This is a human rights crisis that includes ongoing, premeditated violent attacks, and a daily fight to survive under the most horrific, unimaginable circumstances."
>
> Custody Peace

For a long time, only a handful of movies had focused on domestic violence (The Burning Bed and Sleeping With The Enemy come to mind). I appreciate that over the last few years, Hollywood has been getting more involved by producing movies and shows, bringing awareness (some are listed at the end of this book), and they are steering away from producing shows and movies that normalize intimate partner and family violence. I remember being desensitized to the abuse and violence in movies and shows from many years ago, and when I watch them now, I'm horrified. Besides the Dirty John series, I have watched Maid, which highlights nonviolent abuse. They could have done better with the story, but anytime nonviolent types of abuse are brought to light, it brings much more awareness and understanding. When it first came out, I saw the movie Alice, Darling. This movie also highlights nonviolent abuse and its emotional and mental toll on victims. Again, they could have done better, but it shows more of what nonviolent abuse looks like behind closed doors. Ms. Magazine has written a couple of articles highlighting coercive control in relationships. They are valuable enough to include the links to each of the articles: https://msmagazine. com/2023/02/28/domestic-violence-coercive-control-massachusetts/ and https://msmagazine.com/2023/08/31/california-court-coercive-control-restraining-order-domestic-violence/

Thank you Ms. Magazine for bringing awareness.

One of my group members asked me to be a guest on her 2-hour podcast/live radio show – The Never Give Up Show – thenevergiveupshow. com. I, of course, said yes and was a guest. It was my first podcast experience, and it was fulfilling to share some of my stories and help spread awareness. She described mine as highly similar to hers; however, her abuser was physically violent. I feel this is an experience that could eventually lead to my own podcast. We have become friends and even met in person when I traveled to visit another friend for her birthday. She also wrote a book and asked if I would contribute material on coercive control and post-separation abuse. The information I gave her is included in her book. Her title is Married to an Illusion: A Survivor's Guide to Recognizing and Escaping Narcissistic Abuse by Bailey Smith and is available on Amazon.

"The weight of the world often lands on broken shoulders, but that deeper wound becomes the root of the strongest wings."

A.Shea

As much as I thought I was past the worst experiences after leaving Dennis, in January 2023, I discovered one of the bank credit cards filed a civil suit against me for the money I owe them. Then, at the end of July 2023, the other credit card filed a civil suit. My bankruptcy attorney hadn't negotiated yet, so I must now deal with this permanent blemish on my financial and legal records. It was extremely stressful and took a year to settle the first civil suit and my wages were almost garnished. Towards the garnishment deadline and having nothing to lose, I emailed the opposing counsel and the partners of her firm a very detailed email explaining the reason why I was in this situation. I was not pleased with the settlement amount, but at least I got her to stop the garnishment and take a lump sum. I hope if that firm ever deals with another case like mine, they remember my story. Oddly, I haven't been served by the second credit card civil suit, so I don't know that outcome. So, like everything else, I'll use it to try and bring awareness to United States financial institutions regarding financial abuse. I learned that 95% to 99% of reported domestic violence cases include financial abuse. This is only for the reported cases. Nonviolent, coercive control case statistics aren't even tracked yet. Dennis knew precisely what he was doing throughout the marriage to make sure I was penniless and then worked hard to ruin me financially through the divorce. I'm still working through the aftermath of his destruction. Through my research, I discovered that HSBC Bank in the United Kingdom has a program to educate its staff members, customers, and the public. I applaud them and will use their program as an example to other banks.

I most recently met a woman with a daughter through another friend who's in a similar relationship. What she is experiencing and how he is treating her is heartbreaking. I have personally heard just a minute of a verbal attack toward both of them and can't imagine what else he is saying and what's happening. The abuse will only continue to escalate. I believe they are in danger and that he's capable of anything. Hopefully, I will be able to meet with her soon and see what I can do to help. Her daughter is only 12, and I would hate for her to wait until she's 18 before leaving. I can see and feel the trauma the mother is experiencing, and it's like I'm looking at my previous self. I want to tell her I understand what she's going through and know she's afraid. I want her daughter to know that how her father treats her and her mother has to do with how he feels about himself and not them. With the resources that are now available, I'm hoping we can figure out a way for her to leave safely and prevent as much post-separation abuse as possible, especially with the custody of their daughter. Update: In November 2023, I was able to help the mother and daughter by offering my guestroom while they found a place for them both to stay, after the abuse escalated to physical violence. I am still helping her navigate through the flawed legal system, giving her as much information as I can, as well as providing her with emotional support and understanding.

Every time a door opens, it is another step forward, and one thing leads to another that leads to another. This is only the beginning of what I would like to accomplish. I'm just one person with one relationship experience. There are millions of us out there. I hope victims and survivors continue to come forward and tell their stories. We need to talk about what happened and is happening if there will ever be change. We can win this war with the numbers if victims and survivors speak out and tell their truth and stories. For each one, it is taking back power and control.

"Each time a woman stands up for herself, without knowing it possibly, without claiming it, she stands up for all women."

Maya Angelou

9

HARLOW'S COLLEGE GRADUATION

My story comes full circle

FOR THE FIRST TWO YEARS I'D BEEN WRITING MY STORY, I DIDN'T REALIZE the book ending until right before Harlow's college graduation. This was the point of my story that goes all the way back to my pregnancy when Dennis first verbally attacked me. I knew I wanted Harlow always to have a way out, and her education was very important from that day on. This was the moment and the event I'd been looking forward to, and she finally reached my hope for her. I am thankful and grateful she had a fantastic education and graduated with honors at the top of her class. I was incredibly proud of her for her achievements, intelligence, talents, heart, and beauty.

Harlow's college graduation was taking place on June 16, 2022. While preparing for the trip outside the country, I picked up my passport from my safety deposit box after work on Friday, May 20th. My heart dropped when I took it out because it had expired in April! I was traveling on June 11th, three weeks later. In shock, I told the bank manager, a friend, about the expiration. She told me about her own experience and suggested I ask for help from my legislators. I immediately drove to my Representative's office and spoke with someone I know on her staff, and then, Monday morning, I expedited my paperwork at the post office. When I called the passport agency a week later to follow up, they told me the only way I would get it in time was if I flew to Puerto Rico for an appointment on the 10th, and I broke down and cried. I was so upset that there was a chance that I was not getting my passport in time or would have to go to great lengths and a lot of extra money to get it. I had to be at the graduation, and nothing would stop me, even my passport. I desperately contacted the staff member, and she contacted my U.S. Congresswoman. Within one day, her staff member received confirmation that my passport was on its way, and I received it on June 4th. Initially, I was going to wait and stop at my safety deposit box on the way to pick up Harlow's necklace from my jeweler, which was a week later. If I had done that, I really would not have received it on time, and I knew there was a reason I decided to go early. About an hour after I found out the good news, I attended a House Party for my Representative and shared the amazing story about her staff and the US Congresswoman's staff. I was proud to have two outstanding legislators who support their constituents. Who knows, maybe one day I'll run for office.

I was extremely grateful that Sarah offered to accompany me to the graduation, especially when I found out Dennis was bringing Kip. I now consider her 'my ride or die,' and I am so happy she is in my life. We were perfect travel partners and had a fabulous time when Harlow was seeing them. I really needed her support, and it was priceless. It was a wonderful week, and my time with Harlow was amazing. The first day Sarah and I were there, Harlow was our tour guide and took us to all the historic and notable sites in town. We all cooked together that night, one of our favorite things to do. During the week, I met many of Harlow's friends, her roommate, and her roommate's family and saw the coffee shop where she's worked for the last three years. The night before graduation, we went out to a nice dinner, and I gave Harlow the diamond necklace she designed and a single post earring created from the other diamonds in my wedding ring for her gift. They both came out beautifully, and she loved them. At her university, graduation ceremonies and garden parties took place each day during that week, depending on the student's major. Each graduate only receives two tickets to the graduation and garden party, but when available, I purchased an additional ticket for Sarah to attend the party with me. When I picked up the tickets for Harlow, I noticed Kip didn't have a ticket for the party. After thinking about it for a minute, I actually asked if I could purchase a ticket for her. As I write this now, I'm still shaking my head in disbelief, and I guess I'm not an asshole.

Harlow really appreciated my checking, even though the party was sold out, and mentioned it to Dennis and Kip.

The graduation was meaningful in multiple ways. The university is one of the oldest and most prestigious colleges, and the ceremony was filled with history while also intimate and beautiful. I was so happy for Harlow, finally reaching this milestone, and when her name was called and she walked across the stage, tears of joy and pride streamed down my face. It was amazing that in the quad after the ceremony, friends and families gathered to take pictures and congratulate one another. I am thrilled she has such caring friends; watching them was heartwarming. Before the garden party, I took Harlow to a celebratory lunch with Sarah and one of her close friends. Later, at the party, Harlow told me she could get a ticket for Kip, and I saw when she and Dennis walked in. A few minutes later, they walked up to Harlow, Sarah, and me, and Dennis asked me to take a picture. Specifically, he confrontationally asked, *"Is it allowed if we take a picture together?"* I said yes, and as I handed my cell phone to Kip, I hugged her (yes, I actually did and still can't believe it!). After the pictures, they stayed with us for the rest of the party, and Kip, Sarah, and I spoke most of that time. What I noticed about her was that she didn't seem like the Kip I knew. There definitely was something different, almost like she was a little scattered in her conversation (I remember those days), and it concerned me. I hugged her goodbye at the end and wondered what was going on behind closed doors that she may not even be aware of. I believe he is somewhat abusing her, although not in every way, because he will never have her as helpless as I was. She has her own residence and job and will never have his child. She also has two grown sons, so I'm sure he's very careful. Her demeanor leads me to believe it's at the very least emotional and mental, and most likely as subtly as possible. I actually kept my composure and didn't feel triggered or stressed, which was huge, but it was undoubtedly a bittersweet situation. I will always consider Dennis my abuser and a monster, and besides saying yes to the picture, I did not directly communicate with or touch him in any way. I wondered what he was thinking about that day and week and what made him want a 'family' picture. He even nostalgically brought up some stories of Harlow when she was a little girl, which felt weird. At one point, he told Sarah about her and Mike's divorce and let Mike know he disagreed with what he was trying to do to her. REALLY? I wonder if anyone said that to him during our divorce??? In my thoughts then, besides my happiness for Harlow, was the sadness about the family we never were, all the hurt Dennis caused but would never acknowledge or take responsibility for, and in his twisted mind, blamed me for everything. It was definitely a strange situation, being there with my abuser, and I cried that night and many nights afterward. What gives me peace is that it was one of the most important days of Harlow's life, and she didn't need anxiety of any kind that day. She thanked me a few times afterward, which made it absolutely worthwhile.

So, that day, everything from my pregnancy onward had come full circle. She is the woman I dreamed my daughter would become. However, this was not the ending of my story as I hoped. I still have to deal with the aftermath of my debt issues, among a couple of other things.

"Some days she's a warrior.

Some days she's a broken mess.

Most days, she's a bit of both.

But every day she's there.

Standing. Fighting. Trying."

Thinkology

10

SUMMING UP MY STORY

A new beginning

Still healing, but will continue moving forward

REFLECTION IS A FITTING WORD FOR THIS LAST SECTION OF MY BOOK. As I continued to process everything that has happened from 1998 until the present, I thought about things a lot and continued putting the puzzle pieces together. There was a piece of art in the master bedroom of the house. Dennis and I purchased it at an art festival many years ago. At first sight, Dennis loved this picture and had to have it. It is a silhouette of a naked man and woman lying beside each other in bed. The man is fully intact, but the woman doesn't have a head or arms and only has partial legs. At first, it just seemed like an artistic picture for our bedroom. Now, I can see it holds incredible symbolism. He wanted that picture for a specific purpose because he was whole and wanted me broken. I think about that picture now, and it breaks my heart.

I wonder if part of spiritual abuse is that abusers want to control how we think and feel about God. They are jealous and controlling with most relationships in our lives to isolate us from whom we care about and who cares about us, so I wonder if they are also jealous about how we feel about God, and by spiritually abusing, they isolate us from and maintain control and more power than Him. They feel like they are and should be our God, and He threatens them. Maybe it's why some people turn away from God because they were spiritually abused. I also wonder if Dennis didn't want to tithe because he believed he was above it. I think it's an interesting theory. I believe churches and houses of worship need to be aware of the different types of abuse, including spiritual abuse. In my experience, they aren't educated in this area. During the early years of my marriage, my pastor and the two ladies who helped me had no idea what was happening to me was abuse, and the same with our Christian Counselor, Mary. And even after my marriage was over, the church I attended didn't know either. Most abusers considering themselves Christians will use the Bible and twist the wording to validate their abusiveness and can manipulate unsuspecting Christians, who are vulnerable, forgiving, and least suspecting. They wear the mask of a good Christian so well that pure evil can hide in plain sight. Abusers have no problem using God's name and scripture in their lies and manipulation. Every church should be educated because more information given to them will help them identify when someone is being abused. Instead of telling the victim or survivor they should automatically forgive their abuser, church leaders and attendees should be supportive. Not doing so just makes everything much worse for the victim, blaming and shaming, retraumatizing, and revictimizing, while it supports the abuser and abuse. I have personally been judged for not immediately forgiving Dennis. Still, they couldn't even begin to comprehend what took place behind closed doors and to me and immediately forgave his abuse. I can say with ease that God does not support any abusive relationship, whether an intimate partner, parent, child, or in any other situation, and he also understands our pain and the evils of abuse. God forgives those who ask for forgiveness, but most abusers will never genuinely ask God or their victim(s). It takes a lot of healing and strength to reach the point of forgiveness, and it could take years, if ever. Forgiveness should never be forced, guilted, or shamed upon a victim or survivor by anyone. They need support, understanding, and grace, just as God gives, and it's between them and God to decide when and how. This applies to any religion or house of worship.

Little things come to me, and I wonder if they have a meaning for his control and abuse. When Dennis and I started dating, and actually for years before that, my parents would have an annual New Year's Day party and celebrate with black-eyed peas, rice, greens, and other traditional foods. I now wonder if he decided we should have a New Year's Day party to take away us going to my parents' party as a part of his isolation and control. During our entire relationship, I was only able to wear one perfume. He said he was allergic to scents and would get a headache, but miraculously, he wasn't allergic to the perfume I wore when we first dated, so that's what I stuck with for 20 years. At least I liked it. It was nice shopping for a new perfume. I went through the perfume section, and it seemed like I smelled around a hundred scents, which was therapeutic and freeing. I fell in love with Valentino Donna Born In Roma Eau de Parfum, which I now wear. When I think about it, he was only allergic to women's scents, not men's. Stevie habitually wore heavy cologne; although Dennis would mention it, he never pretended to have a headache. When Harlow wore perfume around him, he made her wash some of it off or would open the car window and breathe out for dramatics. I also think about my favorite foods and restaurants. The foods I liked the most, he didn't like. He also eventually would frown upon my favorite restaurants. He had an entire shelf in the pantry with snacks, but if I had something aside for Harlow or me, he would be upset and want it. He also hated the music I liked. He pretended he liked it when we were dating, but as soon as we were married, he hated it and would call it 'shit.' His music wasn't my favorite, but I would never say that. I've always liked dance music, especially Electronic Dance Music (EDM), because it makes me feel free. I can close my eyes and dance while everything in the world stops. I can forget what's happening in my life and feel the music.

With all of the times Dennis gaslighted me by saying he told me something when he really hadn't, I thought there could be something wrong with my hearing and actually went to the Ear, Nose, and Throat doctor! They didn't find anything wrong, which added to my confusion. Remember when I said Dennis would take longer than me to get ready to go out? I recently read that a narcissistic abuser wants to stall and prevent their victim from having a good time and take a long time to get ready to go somewhere as a strategy and on purpose. He wanted me to wait for him to stall our plans and sabotage and take away some of my enjoyment. I JUST LEARNED THIS!!! He also didn't want me to be dressed nicely or in good physical shape, which is why he complained so that I would be less desirable to other men. His calculating strategies were truly disturbing but, unfortunately, very common. My friend

Janice dated someone who made her stop working out, didn't want her to dress nice, and wasn't allowed to wear makeup for the same reason. In the early part of my relationship with Dennis, he told me that when I walked into a room filled with people, all heads turned to look at me. He said he liked that, and the reason why was that it brought attention to him and made him look good. At some point, that changed. As his abuse progressed and escalated, he became jealous and resentful that the focus was on me and not him. I believe that's why he also started ensuring I was in a bad mood when we were going somewhere, so I no longer lit up a room. He had to extinguish my shining light. The enemy wants to do that, and he chose to be mine.

Janice and I reconciled our friendship over four years after I left Dennis. For all of the years since she and Blake broke up, I still believed the story Dennis told me, which I should have realized sooner was sensationalized and embellished to make her look like a horrible person so I'd stop being friends with her. He completely villainized her and victimized Blake. I feel horrible that I abandoned my friendship with her and judged her for things she didn't even do, which was why she never understood how I wouldn't be her friend. Not knowing the truth fuels the lies, reminding me of how many lies exist about me that others still believe. Janice told me precisely what happened, which made sense, although it was sad that their marriage was destined to fail. Janice remembers how Dennis had no respect for women, and she didn't like going out with us because of that (like so many other females). She told me I usually seemed tense and uptight, and even though I had a fake smile, I guess my demeanor was noticeable to more people than I thought. She remembered that when Dennis and I went to their house, I would be so paranoid if they had scented candles lit and would blow them out because of his allergies. I remember how nervous and tense I was about going anywhere with a scent because he would get annoyed. Like with women's perfume, I bet he had no allergies and just liked to control his environment and victimize himself. Like many women, myself included, who have had breast surgery because of breastfeeding and sagging, Dennis would make false, chauvinistic accusations. He told Blake that after Janice had her surgery, he gave her 3-5 years (he said that about all women and would change his numbers with that as well) before she started cheating. She even remembered Dennis joking for her to show everyone, which was incredibly inappropriate and demeaning. She also told me that one of her daughters was afraid of Dennis. I remember the occasion when we were taking Harlow and her daughter Tina to a theme park, and he was in a huge rush to get there before the crowds, so we stopped at a fast food restaurant to get breakfast. Harlow and Tina didn't like anything on the menu, which infuriated him. I was so afraid of Harlow and I getting in trouble later that I tried so hard to convince them to get it anyway, and they were upset about being forced to get it and with me as well. I also remembered that Tina told her mom that Dennis sped away angrily. The rest of that day, I was secretly a wreck and felt sad for them but helpless. My heart hurt for them back then and when Janice recounted the story. Those occasions happened so often that it was more common than not, which is heartbreaking. The weekend Janice and I reconciled, Tina told her mom when she was on speaker call, and I had some conversation with her that I seemed like a completely different person and happy. I am thankful Janice and I are friends again.

I learned through Sarah that years ago, when we would go out as couples with her and Mike, one night, I excused myself to use the ladies' room, and Dennis turned to them and said I was going to the bathroom to throw up! When she told me it hurt, he would make that up and calculatingly try to make me look bad to our friends, and even though it's been many years since it happened, I cried that night. She told me she noticed and didn't like how Dennis treated, spoke to, and spoke about me. Apparently, it was enough of a regular occurrence that Sarah told Mike she wouldn't go out with us unless there was another couple as a buffer. I suppose Dennis made up for Sarah not liking me because Mike obviously said something to him. Whenever I learn something he did to hurt me purposefully, my wounds open up. When I told someone else about it, he said I should ask my friends not to tell me, but I told him I wanted to know everything, even if it hurt. I want to know every horrible thing he has said about me and lied about me to others, and I have the right and deserve to know all of it. He created false narratives about me to most people in our lives, but I vow to correct as many as I can.

In my journey of educating myself, I also realized that in his abuse and with all abusers, it escalated over time. I'm almost positive that if I hadn't been in a relationship with Dennis as long as I had, his abuse might not have gotten bad enough for me ever to realize it was abuse, and all the gaslighting, projecting, and blame-shifting may have led me to believe it was all my fault and he was a good and decent person (like with Dennis's first wife – I believe she thought he was a good person due to them not being together long enough – I wonder if she blamed herself – I wish I could sit down and have a conversation with her if she were alive). The same goes if I hadn't gotten the proper counseling after I left to heal and recognize the truth of what he did. I'm sure that is very common. As I have said and will always remind everyone, abuse is about power, control, dominance, and breaking down boundaries. As I also said, his abuse escalated to violence when he shoved me on the airplane. As soon as he did, I looked him in the eyes and told him if he ever touched me again, I would leave him in a second; he knew I meant it because my first husband was physically abusive, and I left him because of that. So, that was HIS boundary. He knew he could get away with all the other things, escalating year after year (maybe even worse since he couldn't be violent), since I didn't realize it was abuse, and he knew not to cross that line again. He absolutely wanted to when he would get right in my face and bait me to hit him. He wanted me to hit him so he could hit me back. That would have been enough for him to validate his violence because he could blame me. This premeditative and calculating motive is nothing short of sinister with his evil mastermind. I'm so thankful I could contain my reactions when he did that, and he was never physically violent again. The normal human response to trauma is fight, flight, or freeze. I couldn't defend myself or dare argue back, which took away my fight response. I wasn't allowed to walk away from him (he threatened if I walked away that our marriage was over), which took away my flight response. So, what I was left with was to freeze. I also learned about the fawn response. I used that quite a bit when telling him I loved him during verbal attacks or would do or say anything to him to get him to stop. I also used fawn when he was 'saying something' to Harlow when I'd try to change the subject or said she needed to do something.

For all of the times Dennis judged people with tattoos, as of now, I have three, and for the record, none of them hurt, even for a second. I have a cross on my right calf as a symbol of God walking with me every step during my divorce, healing, and new life. I only realized afterward that it was on Good Friday 2019, the day Jesus died on the cross. I have the North Star on the other calf, symbolizing change, hope, and moving in a purposeful direction. I got that one before the North Star was visible near Christmas 2020. I originally planned for two sets of wings on my right shoulder to symbolize freedom for Harlow and me, but she may never be free from him. It ended up as a silhouette of a female angel centered under the back of my neck in the color blue of my eyes because I want to be a human angel, which symbolizes my advocacy and activism. The angel was done in October 2021 during domestic abuse awareness month. Not long after, I had a nightmare that the tattoo flaked off, and what appeared was an angel but with an evil spirit trying to take over. I woke up terrified, like it represented the evil I was fighting against. I had previously considered selling my wedding ring and told my jeweler that it symbolized hate, but he said I would regret it. I'm glad he said that because I decided to keep it. I used to consider the main diamond pear-shaped, but now I see it as a teardrop. I made it into a pendant to symbolize what I went through to fuel my passion for helping others, and it is close to my heart. Interestingly, Dennis never asked what kind of ring I wanted and chose the pear shape. How ironic and destined it now represents the abuse I endured from him. It's also ironic because the one piece of jewelry I asked for several times was a diamond pendant (which he made sure never to get for me), and now I have it. The baguette diamonds and the rest of the ring made the necklace given to Harlow for the graduation gift she designed.

My wish and prayer would be to help victims of these types of abuse and help abusers identify what they are doing. Not only are they hurting their loved ones, but they're actually hurting themselves as well. They are destroying their lives just as much as others because their life is a lie, and what life can be happy, productive, or sustainable if it's a fabrication?

Their legacy is destruction. Interestingly and tragically, abusers use coercion, threats, and abuse of their partners to exert power, control, and dominance and to reduce them from a whole person to a broken shell so they do not leave. But the reality is that all of the things they are doing are what make them want to leave. I believe any human being who abuses any other human being or living creature should be exposed and held accountable and be mandated to receive extensive therapy. We must protect and prevent abuse rather than react to it once it happens.

"Exposing predators is not immature or petty.

It can help to save future victims from harm and bring justice to victims of perpetrators who have never been held accountable.

While it cannot always be done and safety should come first, it can be a public service."

Shahida Arabi, MA

Did Dennis really believe his actions and threats would make me want to stay, or was he okay with having my fear of leaving him? Did he think I loved him through his abusiveness? What were his feelings toward me? I wish I could get into his head and figure it out, but he mostly wanted my obedience, attention, affection, admiration, and adoration. Dennis painted our life together as an elaborate stage, almost like the set of a movie. It reminded me of the movie with Jim Carrey when he was part of a massive TV set, and all of the people he knew were actors, but the exact opposite. Dennis was the actor, as well as Harlow and me, and our lives were part of his massive TV set, and it was all for show. The tone of a household starts at the top. A household can be a place of positivity or negativity. Dennis represented that he was a Christian, but our household was not run with Christian values. It was run on judgment, lies, schemes, and abuse. When he told me that he avoids the appearance of evil, it was to fool me because he knew he was evil. And, when he said emotions and feelings don't matter, he just wanted to invalidate my emotions and feelings during his abuse. In a quote from Brene Brown, "There's nothing more human than emotions." It was so painful and is still painful that I hoped so much to be a happy family and loved, but I knew it would never be. It would have been so nice to all be ourselves. Every person on the face of the earth is imperfect. We should be able to make mistakes, cry, and genuinely help each other with love and understanding. How you handle things says so much about your character. Dennis always judged our character and treated us like we were his possessions, defective, and not human beings. We were just his shiny objects to use, control, and impress the outside world. It was tragic that not only could Dennis not be himself because he was so afraid of what others thought of him, but we also couldn't be ourselves because we were afraid of him. I have told my previous therapist, Ross, and my current therapist, Nora, that I feel like I failed as a mom and made many mistakes I wish I could fix. Still, both have told me I was in a constant state of survival because of how he treated us, and it prevented me from being the mother I wanted to be or could have been. I felt double the pain and trauma because I was experiencing and living through it as both his victim and as a mother. The one thing I wanted to give her, I couldn't. I felt such powerlessness, so I tried to make her happy by overcompensating other ways and with things while counting down the years. As I was being controlled, I felt out of control. That's exactly what being controlled is like, not being in control of yourself. I still have a hard time forgiving myself for not being able to give her the life she deserved. I wish I knew what I know now because maybe I could have done something to help or protect us. Maybe the only way I can forgive myself, take my power back since I couldn't prevent and can't change what happened, and release my shame and inadequacy as a mother is to help others. I hope the world will become a better and safer place.

Dennis was and still is a master at taking a shred of the truth and building lies around it. He was a liar all the time (pathological), but then would say, "You know what they say? The lie takes the elevator, and the truth takes the stairs, and at some point, they meet at the top." If someone is telling the truth, they don't have to say they're speaking or telling it continually. It goes without saying. But, if they have something to hide, are lying, or are trying to deflect, they must tell people that they only speak the truth. He tried to catch me in lies, to project and hide his. Sure, I lied to him, but mine were either to protect both Harlow and myself or were due to his severe judgment. I stand behind my lies, and the sad part is that I felt the need to in the first place. We weren't allowed to be upset, angry, or annoyed. Those were emotions that he did not accept. If we can never address how we feel, the hurt never goes away, the sadness never goes away, and the pain never goes away. The pain had to be hidden, which is probably one of the greatest tragedies in our family life besides the abuse that was going on behind closed doors.

So many times, Dennis tried to present himself confidently to impress others but wasn't at all. He would always tell me that people told him they wanted to be him and have his life, everyone liked him, people would come to him for advice because they thought he was such an intelligent person, and even say his I.Q. was at a genius level. His reputation was important, and he valued how strangers thought of him rather than his family. I wonder if he treated us like he did because he wanted to keep us down beneath him because he knew we were better, genuine, and authentic. In my opinion, I think he felt such an incredible amount of shame, lack of self-esteem, and self-loathing, and he couldn't put his feelings about himself in perspective. He also had to continually remind us of what we were ashamed of in ourselves, even if he twisted everyday things or made them up because of his self-shame. He told others so many things about us, false narratives and lies to hide behind them, and projected who he was. I also believe that he couldn't allow us to be happy because he wasn't happy. When I told him things from my past that hurt me, he had to use them against me. He reminded me, put down my feelings, belittled me, and accused me of being a victim. Like I've said before, though, we did have some good times. There were some good days. He could 'act' loving, affectionate, and generous, but none of it was genuine, and he only did them for his agenda and as part of the cycle of abuse. When he treated us with love, it wasn't authentic, and the abusiveness made all those times completely worthless. As I've also said, abusers are not seeking love from you but your obedience.

They aren't capable of returning it or appreciating it. The time Dennis videotaped me reminds me of something I read online about the dark truth. His abuse was fuel. He wanted me to get irritated and annoyed, raise my voice, and see tears in my eyes. When he saw this, it made him feel powerful. He provoked me to use my reactions against me so I'd be confused in a way that I didn't trust reality through cognitive dissonance. What he also did was project his character defects on me by accusing me of what he was doing. He still tells people I'm ill, was cruel to him, have daddy issues, needs therapy, and most likely much more. He is talking about himself. However, I still need therapy because I was in the hands of a monster for so many years. Dennis truly is the Boogeyman.

Dennis had to smear and blame me for many things, so he looked like the victim. It was so strategic and calculating. He had to hide what was going on behind closed doors. This way, it would be dismissed if the real truth got out. People wouldn't believe me. It would hurt so much when I felt comfortable enough with someone to be honest about what was going on, and they didn't believe me. I often heard that Dennis was such a good guy and couldn't be doing the things I said. Throughout the years since I left Dennis, I also hear many of his friends don't even like him that much; he's just there. I now know why Dennis took down all of the pictures in the house with me in them, even when he thought I was reconciling. I was told he was bringing twenty-something girls home from the downtown bars at night to hook up and was bragging to his friends about it (while he was trying to ensure I wasn't seeing anyone else). I think it was when Sam was living with him. His friends have even acknowledged that Dennis treated and spoke about me horribly throughout our marriage, especially when he bragged about how he hid money and wanted to purposefully destroy me financially during the divorce and even that he would ruin my relationship with Harlow. It hurts as much today getting validation and confirmation about what he was doing to me as it did while he was doing it. I wish someone would have spoken up and told Dennis to stop or called him out that his actions were wrong. I still wish someone would. So, remember how often you see domestic violence on the news, and family, friends, and neighbors ignored it, looked the other way, or said they had no idea and never saw it coming? There's a whole other world behind the scenes, behind the painted picture, behind the white picket fence. Domestic abuse and violence are not a private matter; it's societal and affects all communities somehow. If someone trusts you enough to share this information, don't dismiss it. Yes, there are liars; I was married to one. There will be subtle hints if you pay close attention. Remember the saying, "If you see something, say something." Educate yourself. If someone or something seems too good to be true, you know the saying........ salt and sugar looks the same. Think about what we went through during the pandemic wearing masks and how they cover our faces. Abusers wear invisible masks to protect themselves so their true identity isn't known, and their victims wear fake smiles to hide their pain. I could not even imagine if I was still with Dennis during the pandemic, and I hate to think how much abuse has escalated during quarantining and isolation. As much as Covid was a global pandemic, the hidden evils of domestic abuse are just as much a global crisis.

"The world will not be destroyed by those who do evil, but by those who watch them without doing anything."

Albert Einstein

In the years since I left Dennis, my vision and memory are much clearer, which I read is called Fog Lifting. I remembered so much like it happened yesterday, but I'm so thankful to have taken notes for years along with writing my story on paper because, over time, the memories fade. This is also a common occurrence named Abuse Amnesia due to the gaslighting, cognitive dissonance, complex trauma, the brain blocking specific traumatic experiences and becoming overwhelmed, and as a protection mechanism. My story may lead other victims and survivors to remember things that had been previously blocked. As much as I don't want them to reconnect with the pain of their abuse, I hope it will bring more of our stories into the light to validate further what is happening hidden behind closed doors to help others. We can't change the past, but we have the power to change the future because not knowing or recognizing the truth fuels lies and abuse.

"If a survivor tells you what happened to them and it doesn't 'make sense' to you then the problem is not with the survivor's story or how they're explaining it the problem is with your understanding of how abusers abuse."

Paula Goodwin

I had so much built up inside me for so long that it led to so much 'trauma dumping,' trying to get everything out. I felt compelled to tell anyone and everyone my story and experiences. I finally had a voice and the education to tell people what I'd been through and to teach everyone what I learned to save the world from monsters and the evils hidden behind closed doors. It took a long time for me to recognize it was a lot for someone to take in all at once. Initially, my mind was still in a giant traumatic state, and I rambled almost like I was crazy (I wonder how many people thought I was crazy). I was, in a way, but as I slowly healed, my mind and words became more focused and organized, as well as my mental and emotional well-being. It took over four years to be healed enough to stop dumping, only tell bits and pieces, or wait until I'm asked. I also try not to talk about it now if I'm out having fun, and it feels good just to set it aside, enjoy myself, and feel normal. I was talking to my friend Shana and explained about a recent "meltdown" and how I was "bawling my eyes out." She told me crying is part of the brain processing pain and memories. Instead of a meltdown, she calls it processing and says it's healthy to process. I am so thankful she said that, and that validation was vital for my piece of mind. She also validated that I've been through so much trauma and compared what she has heard about my relationship with Dennis to Sleeping With The Enemy, which gave me the chills since it was after I wrote what I did for the marketing pitch of my story. For the first couple of years after my escape, I had welts on my back from the trauma leaving my body, and when I scratched them, they would bleed. For about two years after that, I had welts on my scalp, and my hair is still thin and growing from the damage I caused by scraping little bald spots all over my head. Other than that, my body, mind, and heart feel healed, and I weaned myself off medication.

Through therapy and minor dating experiences, I recognized that I was still terrified and named it 'date panic.' It's a significant breakthrough, 4 ½ years post-separation. I feared having someone or something I care about or pieces of me taken away to hurt me. I'd also been self-sabotaging as a defense mechanism, telling too much of my story right away so they'd think I was too broken and wouldn't want me because not wanting me was better than wanting me because then I was safe. I can control who I am and what I do, but I can't control someone else, which scared me, and when I looked at them, I thought, "What would you do to me, say to me, or TAKE AWAY from me? This major breakthrough made me more conscious, and I felt like my armor fell right off my heart. I am forever grateful to the person who helped me realize what led to this important step forward in restoring trust. I spent years healing, practicing, and learning, and now I'm applying. It's been empowering, especially my confidence in myself and knowing exactly what I want and don't want. I have courage, vulnerability, self-worth, and self-love. I have learned to look for positive and negative behavior patterns, emotional intelligence and safety, and meaningful communication. I want a relationship where we feel and understand each other's soul. I want my soulmate and have the faith and belief that he's coming as soon as I'm ready. Another breakthrough came just after Tina Turner died. I read some posts online about when she left her abuser and what she went through. What particularly resonated with me is that she gave him everything just to be away from him. Dennis can have what he has; I wouldn't want any of it, just as much as not wanting to spend one more day with him. I have my spirit, joy, amazing friendships, health, and future. He has money and possessions. For the miniscule amount I am receiving in alimony, one day, I will tell him I don't need or want it. I told Shana I realized why my alimony was so low because I would happily give it up when the timing was right. Then I'll be even more free from him.

I still have bad days. I have gone through the healing and grieving process several times. Healing is messy, takes a long time, has breakthroughs and setbacks, and is different for everyone. Throughout my healing, every part has happened exactly when and how it was supposed to. Indirectly as it may be, I have received restoration and restitution. I realized I didn't need any of it from Dennis, I received it on my own and through the abundant blessings I have received. I have also had the rare opportunity to build back my spirit and who I am from almost scratch, which I consider a gift. Although I'll never be perfect, I will try to be the best version of myself possible. Interestingly, since I've left, people I don't know and know well have told me I light up a room, am high-spirited, have a bright aura, and am like a magnet to other people. One person said that when I walk, it's like the world is my runway. Another said that when I walk into a room full of people, everyone turns to look my way. My close friend and neighbor Summer has often told me that I'm so friendly and that I bring people together and should start a business or jokingly become Mayor. The group of fabulous girlfriends I hang out with regularly call ourselves a squad; Sarah, of course, is a part of it. My dear friend Shana sweetly said I was the squad leader. Comments like that have played a role in my returning spirit and having many incredible male and female friends. I love every one of my friends and enjoy bringing people together. Because I know what it's like to have friendships taken away from me, my friendships are my treasure. In honor of that, in 2023, I began handing out 'treasures' to my friends, bartenders, servers, hostesses, and strangers because I like making people feel special. For my birthday this year, I gave out small crystal hearts, symbolic of my healed heart. I also feel it's really important to compliment people every chance I get. It feeds my spirit and soul to make others happy, and when I look at people, I see past the surface and look to their hearts. I feel blessed to have more friends than I've ever had. I am happier and have more fun than ever, and my spirit has never been higher. I feel love, joy, peace, patience, goodness, kindness, gentleness, faithfulness, and self-control.

"When we embrace the cracks inside of us, it allows the light to shine in, and then shine out."

Jeanelle Maraid

I know the real Dennis more than anyone else on Earth and realize he can't feel any of those things, so I actually feel pity for him. His life and self are lies, and all of his abuse was because of his shame and judgment. Dennis was so afraid of others judging him, while he judged others, especially the two people he was supposed to love the most. Instead of his love, we received his judgment and abuse. Our family was ruined before it even began. When I see couples, families, and children, I think to myself, I hope they are happy, love each other, and treat each other like they deserve. I recently went to a funeral for a law partner I worked with. He was such a kind-hearted and good man who was well respected. His adult daughters got up to speak at the service and had meaningful stories about their father. His love for them and theirs for him was so incredibly strong that it brought tears to my eyes. I was so happy they had such a great dad and sad they lost him. It puts the legacy he leaves behind to his children in perspective, and he will be remembered and spoken about for generations. Then I thought about Dennis and teared up even more. He will die one day, and what will be said at his funeral?

I'll repeat: The enemy is out to kill, steal, and destroy. Dennis was the enemy; he killed our spirits, stole the happy family we could have been, and left a huge trail of destruction behind him. This is the legacy he leaves behind for eternity. Even worse, the abuse we endured by him was not illegal. He can get away with all of it because nothing could have been done to make him stop. He has no recourse, punishment, accountability, or fear of getting in trouble for his actions. He can deny it, and that's that. There's no accountability, no truth, justice, or fairness. However, I get to write the ending to this story, so I'm writing now that Dennis will be exposed and held accountable for his actions. There will be truth and justice for everything he has done to me, taken from me, that I had to give up, and that he said to and about me. Because I now know most of what he said were lies, and he's still doing it, it's incredibly important that the real truth is out there. His lies took the elevator, and the truth took the stairs. We are now at the top, and the two are together.

"Take no part in the unfruitful works of darkness but instead expose them."

Ephesians 5:11

As previously stated, I wrote a 22-page letter to Dennis. I felt it was necessary to tell him some of the specific things he said and did to us that made me not love him and want to leave him, especially since I wasn't allowed to ever defend myself during his verbal attacks and any time I tried telling him what he was doing, he would twist it around or dismiss it completely. I had the power to speak, even though I knew he would never admit to any of it. I recognized in rereading it recently that there was so much more I could have added, but at the time, writing those things was traumatic. I'm not publishing it because it has very specific things about Harlow. I also think he started treating her better after I sent him the letter because he had to prove me wrong. However, I believe he still wants financial control over her to ensure, at least in part, her survival depends on him so she doesn't abandon him.

I've learned so much through my now five-year journey from November 10, 2018, through November 10, 2023. Not only has it given me so much clarity about my past and future, but it has made me so much stronger and more focused. It's given me the opportunity and time to educate myself and become involved in bringing awareness and understanding, which will lead to changes not only in my county and state but maybe even the country and the world. So many doors have opened for me, and I will continue walking through each one. I decided it was important for me to forgive Dennis. It's not for him at all but for myself. I learned and realized that Dennis will likely never acknowledge or admit he did anything wrong or apologize for any of it to me, Harlow, anyone else, or even himself. Also, my forgiveness doesn't validate or condone his abuse; I don't believe he deserves it. But my forgiveness sets me free to live a better life. Although his abuse hurts sometimes, it takes away his power and control over my heart for love and my future happiness. It will never help Dennis, but it is priceless for me. So, I forgive him. It has given me a new sense of calm and peace.

"When you live with resentment, you close your hands tightly around your heart, hoping that no one will penetrate this strong-fisted protection. When you forgive you open those hands, let your heart out to love again, freely and confidently.

Why? Because evil cannot defeat you; evil cannot destroy your heart's capacity to love."

Dr. Robert Enright

Dennis chose to become a monster because of his inner demons, and he knew he was the boogeyman all along. His actions were evil, and I never stood a chance against him. He had too much power, control, and dominance and broke down as many boundaries as possible.

"She's different now. She has peace in her heart instead of chaos. That's how she saved herself. She became the peace and she doesn't accept anything less. It's beautiful."

"Forgive yourself for loving the person you loved before you knew that person was a monster."

Both quotes by Stephanie Bennett-Henry

There is a lot more that he did and said that's so much worse than what's in this book, but I am leaving it out to respect my daughter. I'm still in therapy and have nightmares most nights. It feels like I'm being haunted by him or almost like he's still lying beside me, which is horrifying. I plan on looking into EMDR for this type of PTSD to see if it would help alleviate them. I still feel pain sometimes and have a hard time understanding the level of evil Dennis was capable of to destroy my spirit, friendships, my relationship with Harlow, threats, verbal attacks, all of the other abuse, and anything else to purposefully hurt me so I wouldn't or couldn't leave him, and when I did, his motive changed to punish and gain revenge. It messes with me knowing he chose to do all of these cruel and horrific things. I will always hurt for Harlow, but I need to find a way to forgive myself for how I feel as a parent. I still have feelings of inadequacy, guilt, and shame. Even so, I don't feel sorry for myself or want anyone else, and I choose to accept everything that has happened to me. I have had experiences that I can only hope will help other people and could be considered a foundation to spread awareness, education, and understanding of what abuse looks and feels like, hidden carefully and unknowingly behind closed doors.

"Some hearts grow softer by breaking. The more sorrow they're given, the more tender they become. Those are the beautiful ones."

J. Lynn – The MindsJournal

I have continued reading, learning, editing, and adding things as they happened, and in my reflection and thoughts came wisdom and healing. Instead of stumbling blocks, my experiences have been stepping stones and a voice for others who don't have one. My testimony is being told to shed light on those currently in the dark, and my scars are there to heal the wounds of others. I can't change what happened or even prevented it. As much as I wished to have had that happy family and the monstrous acts never happened, I can't control the past, but I can control the future. The only thing I can do now is to try and prevent it from happening to others. When society says domestic abuse and violence should be considered a private or family matter, that is incredibly incorrect and a tragedy. Domestic Abuse and Violence affect every community on the planet. The Pastor who baptized me when Harlow was a little girl once said that to make a change, your desire for the change needs to be stronger than to stay the same. That always stuck in the back of my mind and is so incredibly accurate. My goal is to change how the world recognizes and acknowledges all types of abuse. Obviously, my being a mother is a priceless treasure, but changing the world to bring a better future for all people brings an incredible amount of meaning. I know now that to beat these hidden evils is to take back power, control, dominance, and boundaries from the monsters.

My story is my power, faith is my control, determination is my dominance, and bringing exposure and accountability to those choosing to become monsters is breaking down their boundaries. All of this will win in the fight against evil. I am no longer a victim. I'm a survivor. I am a warrior.

"Though you may hold your sword in a shaky hand, I see the demons you are slaying.

Carry on, Warrior, you are stronger than you realize."

Sarah Beth McClure

Now, the evil will no longer be hidden, which brings me to my friend Ashley's famous line:

"NOT TODAY, SATAN!"

My purpose in telling my story, writing this book, and the passion of my advocacy and activism is to hope that no other human being will ever have to lie in bed next to a monster and no child will ever need to know monsters exist. My fight against these monsters and their evil is the battle I will claim victory. This is the legacy I wish to leave behind. And with that, the last piece of my spirit is in place. This is the real ending to my book.

"I want to leave my mark, but I want to make it with my heart."

A Shea

So now that you know my entire story, do you believe in monsters?

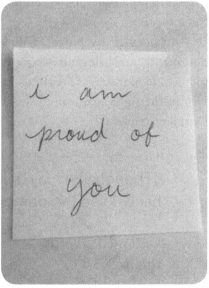

One picture with many post it notes and the other with one post it note

GRATITUDE AND ACKNOWLEDGMENTS

I feel very blessed

I would like to thank the following people for helping me, as well as for their love and care:

<u>My daughter</u> – I love you so much! Thank you for keeping me strong, encouraging me, and supporting me. You are amazing, strong, smart, talented, beautiful inside and out, and inspiring. You are such a thoughtful friend and daughter. I wish things were so much better for you growing up, but you are an incredible person and woman. Our relationship and love for each other are significant to me, and I am grateful and thankful. I wish you blessings, happiness, good health, and all the love in the world for you and your future! I'm very proud of who you are.

<u>My mother, stepdad, sisters, and the rest of my family</u> – Thank you for all you have done for me. Thank you for listening when I needed you to, thank you for helping me move, thank you for lending and giving me money, thank you for feeding me and giving me food, thank you for the kind and generous things you have done for me, thank you for caring, and thank you for your love. You all have been so supportive and loving.

<u>My sweet kitties</u> – Thank you for your love, the cuddles, and the company. I didn't realize it, but you really are my emotional support pets. You kept me from feeling alone when I needed it, and you both are there to love me every day. I love my sweet kitty kids.

<u>My friends</u> – I am incredibly blessed with so many amazing friends. I'm amazed at how important every one of you has greatly impacted my spirit and the love in my heart. Thank you so much for my friends who

have stuck by me no matter what came my way; I couldn't have come through the other side without you. Thank you so much for the friends who cared enough to come back into my life and all the new friends who have come into my life. Thank you to my 'squad.' You know who you are – I love you all very much. My friendships are my treasure.

Both counselors – Thank you for your encouragement, validation, and help in my healing process. It has been priceless.

My church – Thank you for your prayers, support, and friendship. Thank you to the pastors who baptized me – it helped me keep faith and hope.

In addition, thank you for all of the podcasts, websites, social media posts/support groups, and courageous women/survivors who tell their stories that helped educate me and continue to fuel my passion.

RESOURCES
- And warriors from around the world

- The United States Government in the reauthorization of The Violence Against Women's Act (VAWA), along with Kayden's Law
- The United Nations for their report on the travesty regarding parental alienation and the injustices worldwide to domestic abuse and violence victims and children
- Ms. Magazine
- Elizabeth Shaw - Overcoming Narcissistic Abuse and @ coachelizabethshaw
- Narcissistic_abuse_is_real
- Rise From The Ashes and Ashley's Closet
- Raising Awareness of Hidden Evils
- Narc Wise
- The Court Said
- No More Domestic Violence And Child Abuse - Belgium
- Family Court Hurts – Canada
- The War At Home If Only Someone Knew – South Africa
- Connecticut Protective Moms
- Florida Protective Parents Association
- Justice For Greyson!
- Justice for Cassie Carli
- Justice for Ashley – Stop Domestic Violence
- Justice For Gabby Petito
- One Mom's Battle
- Custody Peace
- National Safe Parents
- Stand Up Survivor
- Rise Up Against Domestic Violence – The Truth

- Children without Mothers – MOTHER'S without their BABIES (prayer chain)
- Sarah Speaks Up
- Dusted in Gold
- Bonshea Making Light of the Dark
- A. Shea – With These Wings
- Poetry Broken Into Thoughts
- Art by Kalen
- Author Lundy Bancroft
- Podcast – The Never Give Up Show – Bailey Smith
- Bailey Smith's book – Married to An Illusion: A Survivor's Guide to Recognizing and Escaping Narcissistic Abuse
- Podcast - Understanding Today's Narcissist by Christine Hammond, MS, LMHC, a licensed psychotherapist, speaker, and author
- Podcast - Married to a sociopathic narcissist My Story by Karla Diane
- Podcast – Something Was Wrong by Tiffany Reese
- Dr. Joshua Coleman's book - The Rules of Estrangement
- Barbra Drizin and Author Joyce Maynard for their education on estrangement and separation of adult children
- Many other posts on Pinterest, Facebook, and Instagram
- Quotes by Maria Consiglio, along with various other articles and quotes on Pinterest, Facebook, and the internet
- Brene Brown. I listened to her podcasts – Dare to Lead and Unlocking Us. I appreciate her reminding me how important emotions and vulnerability are in my life. I highly recommend her books and podcasts to everyone.
- Psychologytoday.com
- Psychcentral.com
- Insider.com
- Diagnostic and Statistical Manual of Mental Disorders, 5th Edition: DSM-5
- Movies and shows bringing awareness:
- Movies – just a small handful, but if you google movies with domestic abuse, many more will come up:

- Gaslight
- The Burning Bed
- Sleeping with the Enemy
- Enough
- The Invisible Man
- Alice, Darling
- A Vigilante
- Some shows to look into:
- Maid
- Dirty John
- Big Little Lies
- Ginny and Georgia
- Virgin River

Printed in the United States
by Baker & Taylor Publisher Services